D1382087

Language Disorders in Children and Adults
New Issues in Research and Practice

Language Disorders in Children and Adults

New Issues in Research and Practice

Edited by

Victoria Joffe
Madeline Cruice

and

Shula Chiat

WILEY-BLACKWELL

A John Wiley & Sons, Ltd., Publication

Library of Congress Cataloging-in-Publication Data is available

A catalogue record for this book is available from the British Library.

ISBN 978-0-470-51839-7

Set in 10/12.5pt Garamond by SNP Best-set Typesetter Ltd., Hong Kong
Printed in Singapore by Markono Print Media Pte Ltd

1 2008

Contents

Preface

ABIGAIL BEVERLY (1983–)

Abigail has a speech and language disorder and experiences difficulties with the understanding and expression of language and communication. She has problems understanding complex language and also in using language to organize and express her ideas, particularly in written form. Her difficulties have affected many aspects of her life and meant that she has to find different ways to convey her thoughts, feelings and ideas to others. Problems with 'words' have changed how she looks at the world and make sense of it. This has influenced and informed her artwork.

In December 2005, Abigail was granted the Sir Sigmund Sternberg Award from the charity Afasic to mount an exhibition of work inspired by her experience of growing up with a speech and language disorder. The exhibition, **Making Sense of the Puzzle**, was the outcome of that award. Abigail has also obtained a distinction for her thesis **'How Do We Understand Words?'** produced for her degree in Textile Design at the Central Saint Martin's College of Art and Design.

The following is an account of the difficulties she experiences, in her own words:

> Words 'get everywhere'. When doing simple, everyday things like shopping, using the Internet, asking directions, we are required to assimilate and respond to words all the time. For those without difficulties it is probably hard to imagine what it is like if you cannot understand the words.
>
> Until I was coming up to five years old, words went over my head. Then, it was suggested to my parents that they make a little book of photographs for me, showing my daily routine, actions I was very familiar with. As we read the sentences describing the pictures day after day, I came to understand the words by linking them to the actions shown in the pictures. I started to become familiar with related words and sounds for each routine.
>
> I still have problems understanding complex language and also in using language to express my ideas. This has affected many aspects of my life and

meant that I have had to find different ways to convey my thoughts, feelings and ideas. Problems with 'words' have changed the way I look at and interpret the world and I have used my artwork to express these feelings.

In my artwork I try to convey the range of feelings I get when faced with a page of words. *'Help! I'm sinking in words'* for example, shows how, when you try to understand the meaning of a sentence, the words seemed to be swirling away from you – literally going down the plughole – and you are left desperately trying to grab at them and makes sense of them before they disappear. This piece was part of a series of sculptures made from a collage of commonly misspelled words.

Instead of the lexicon in my brain processing words and syllables automatically, I have to almost manually organise each set of words as I come across them. This led me to design the compositions, *'Jigsaw, Puzzle (21)'* and *'The missing word'*, where I show how, instead of the words being in friendly patterns that make sense; I see a puzzle, a jigsaw, a jumble. These puzzles represent the pieces I am trying to put together to get the whole picture and make sense of the text. In **Jigsaw, Puzzle (21)**, I tried to show what it was like when you are faced by lots of words that have to be de-coded to make sense. A competent reader sees no problems with the words – they are all in friendly, recognizable patterns – but I am busy trying to unscramble the patterns and make sense of it. **The missing word** shows how, when you use words as if they were jigsaw pieces to construct a sentence, there may be one piece of the puzzle that you just can't get – and this turns out to be vital in making sense of the whole thing. Without it, you just can't work out what it means. In **String of words**, I tried to convey how words

Jigsaw, Puzzle (21)

The missing word

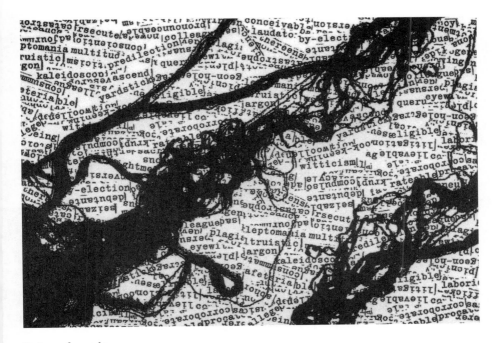

String of words

can become 'tangled' and you are left trying to unravel the sentences – often getting yourself in a knot!

I hope the artwork will bring the issues of speech and language difficulties out into the open and create images that will have a positive influence on future understanding of the problems.

Abigail Beverly
Abigailrbeverly@aol.com

Language disorders in children and adults: current themes, issues and connections

VICTORIA JOFFE, MADELINE CRUICE and SHULA CHIAT

City University

This edited book brings together a series of papers which formed the basis of the *Making New Connections 2* conference hosted by the Department of Language and Communication Science at City University in September 2006. The conference marked the tenth anniversary of the first *Making New Connections* conference held in 1996 by City University, together with Afasic and Action for Dysphasic Adults (now Speakability). At this first conference, presentations addressed the traditional divide between developmental and acquired language impairments and attempted to bridge this gap, bringing together researchers and therapists from the 'child' and 'adult' worlds. The impetus for this first conference was the growth of psycholinguistic approaches to language processing and psycholinguistically motivated therapies, which were typically evaluated within single-case study designs. These new ways of thinking were as relevant to developmental language disorders as they were to acquired language disorders, and hence, they interested therapists from both worlds. The conference produced a wealth of papers across a range of topics in language processing in both developmental and acquired fields, spanning phonological processing, lexical processing, sentence processing and pragmatics. These formed the basis for *Language Disorders in Children and Adults* (Chiat et al., 1997), which continues to attract interest today.

Speech and language therapy has progressed in several new directions in the last 10 years. There have been changes in awareness and attitudes to disability and intervention, increasing demands for evidence-based prac-

Language Disorders in Children and Adults: New Issues in Research and Practice. Victoria Joffe, Madeline Cruice, Shula Chiat.

tice, and changes in service provisions in both health and education. Corresponding changes in areas of research and research methodologies have occurred – for example, holistic consideration of clients and efforts towards using shared terminology amongst health professionals, emphasis on user involvement and user perspectives in services, increased recognition of the importance of environmental facilitators and barriers in living with consequences of diseases, and increased recognition of self-report and patient-reported outcomes in health care. However, the traditional divide between developmental and acquired language disorders seems to persist. Advances with one client group have not always been paralleled in the other. For example, the personal and social consequences of language difficulties and the quality of life for individuals with language impairments have, for some time, been an important focus in adult research (Cruice et al., 2003; Hilari et al., 2003), but not to the same degree and emphasis in paediatric research. Adolescents, who bridge the gap between children and adults, seem to be a forgotten client group (Larson et al., 1993; Leahy and Dodd, 2002), as do adults with developmental language disorders (Sievers, 2005). Both groups illustrate how problems do not disappear, and this is evidenced by numerous longitudinal research studies (Stothard et al., 1998; Johnson et al., 1999; Snowling et al., 2001; Clegg et al., 2005); and yet, services for these age groups continue to be scarce.

The second *Making New Connections* conference was held to reflect some of the changes that have occurred in the speech and language therapy profession over the past decade and debate the new and different issues of today, and to set out some of the challenges for the next 10 years. It attracted an audience of around 100 researchers and practitioners in the fields of speech and language therapy, education, linguistics and psychology, and addressed a range of subjects including psychosocial issues, evidence-based practice, language processing and cognition, with reference to children, adolescents and adults (Joffe and Dodd, 2006). The conference illustrated many commonalities across paediatric and adult client groups, and identified both existing and new connections between the two groups. Children and adults share the same mechanisms for recognizing and producing language, so that research on impairments in one group inevitably provides insights for the other, with regard to both processing mechanisms and research on intervention for specific processing difficulties. Language impairment will result in some degree of exclusion and social disadvantage, no matter where on the developmental pathway these difficulties occur. The impact of language impairment on quality of life and psychosocial and emotional functioning was a new focus for the conference, and a topic highly applicable for both child and adult client groups. The conference also highlighted the key differences and distinctions between developmental and acquired disorders. The consequences of impairment to a developing language system compared with impairment to an established system that breaks down are clearly different considering issues such as plasticity, modularity and language experience

(Lenneberg, 1967; Pinker, 1994). Likewise, the consequences or the impact of the language impairment on everyday life will differ at different points in the developmental trajectory and beyond.

This edited volume reflects some of the main themes and debates in speech and language therapy at the beginning of the twenty-first century. It presents some of the main commonalities and differences in the paediatric and adult domains and provides insights for researchers and practitioners on research and clinical practice, encompassing identification, diagnosis, assessment and intervention. The works presented here reflect language development, language impairment and functioning across the lifespan, starting at the very earliest stages of development, with Roy and Chiat looking at a clinically referred group of 2- to 3-year-olds with developmental language delays; working up to chapters by Joffe, and Lindsay and Dockrell, of primary- and secondary-school-age children with developmental language impairments; including adults with acquired language disorders in chapters by Varley, Marshall and Cruice et al.; with Rutter presenting data from a longitudinal study of individuals with autism and specific language impairment (SLI) spanning approximately 25 years. It also incorporates some innovative artwork from Abigail Beverly, a young artist with long-term language impairment, representing her perspective of living with developmental language impairment. This introduction serves to review the different chapters within the volume for their contribution to making *newer* and *different* connections. The text concludes with a final chapter by Law, who sets the agenda for the next decade in addressing differences and disorders of language in individuals across the lifespan.

The volume makes many connections between and across areas such as language, cognition and social functioning, practice and research, assessment and intervention, medicine and speech and language therapy, humans and animals, autism and SLI, and, obviously, childhood and adulthood. Readers may note that a potential disadvantage of making connections across the lifespan is the inappropriate application of terminology, usually from the adult to child field. Authors have endeavoured to explain terminology and highlight instances where such inappropriate transfers have occurred. The volume is also thought provoking, with authors encouraging us to reflect on how we use language for thought, language for maths, language for everyday living and language for reflecting on quality of life. It encourages us to think about, but not assume, relationships. For example, research, unsurprisingly, indicates that social functioning is altered with acquired aphasia; however, there is no direct prediction between the severity of someone's linguistic impairment and the degree of restriction on their life participation (Cruice et al., 2003). It cautions us to consider not only the commonalities and relationships, but also the distinctions and differences across the child-adult divide. It reminds us to consider heterogeneity amongst our clients, in both their language impairments and also their life situations. And finally, one of the greatest challenges of all, it serves as a wake-up call to consider when and where our

clients and their families live or have lived. That is, when we interpret research from years gone by, we need to remember that services,
opportunities and life situations were different to the current climate in
which we all live now. We need to be mindful that the predictions and
implications made then may need modification when applied to today's
children and adults with language difficulties. Of the themes that have
emerged, this introductory chapter will focus on the following: (1) dimensions, profiling and continuum, as alternatives to diagnostic categories in
isolation; (2) dimensions and profiling of life experience; (3) longitudinal
perspective, with attention to development and the dynamic; (4) the wider
context; (5) updating how we use psycholinguistic theory; (6) challenges
in researching intervention; and (7) perspectives in assessment and intervention. The chapter will conclude with some brief pointers for future
research and practice for the next decade.

Dimensions, profiling and continuum

Many contributors address the nature of language impairment, and other
processing abilities, at different ages and stages of development. Differences in the presenting linguistic impairment, depending on the stages
and ages of investigation, are crucial factors in diagnosis, assessment and
management. Rutter, for example, in his chapter on a series of longitudinal studies of individuals with autism and SLI, clearly shows how the
profiles of impairment in both disorders change across time and become
more similar and dissimilar depending on the *age* of investigation, as well
as the *area* chosen for investigation. Thus, the discrete diagnostic categories of autism and SLI, whilst apparent earlier on in development, were
much less distinct in adulthood, with individuals with SLI and individuals
with autism sharing similar profiles in language and social functioning in
adulthood. The similarities and differences across and within the disorders
lead Rutter to reflect on the potential benefits of viewing developmental
disorders on a *continuum* and from a *dimensional*, rather than a *diagnostic*, perspective. This is a proposal that has been explored previously
by others, for example, Bishop and Norbury (2002), in considering the
relationship between SLI and autism, and Bishop and Snowling (2004),
who propose a two-dimensional model to characterize the relationship
between SLI and developmental dyslexia. Profiling encourages the exploration of an individual's relative strengths and areas of needs (i.e. different
dimensions of language), and attempts to identify processes that underlie
the language impairment and may be shared across diagnostic categories.
Therapists working with adults with aphasia will recognize the profiling
approach behind identifying relative strengths in fluency versus relative
strengths in auditory comprehension. Profiling is focused on the individual, and as such is an attractive approach to practitioners who can use
diagnostic categories as a starting point in the process of identification of

an impairment – as an aid to justify specific types of service provision and facilitate inter-professional communication – and then explore profiles that underlie these diagnoses, drawing on dimensional perspectives. The importance of such psycholinguistic profiling is illustrated in Roy and Chiat's chapter, wherein the different early profiles demonstrated by the children are shown to have important implications for their developmental trajectories, guiding different intervention approaches. It can be argued that dimensional approaches to classification and diagnosis are also relevant to profiling language processing in the acquired language disorders field. For example, profiles of individual strengths and areas of difficulty and cognitive neuropsychological approaches to assessment and intervention allow for innovative, individualistic, effective and functional therapies, as described by Marshall and proposed by Varley.

As pointed out above, the use of diagnostic categories can serve a purpose and is necessary in some contexts and for some specific purposes – for example, in multidisciplinary team discussions where a common understanding of terms is essential, as well as, sometimes, for an appropriate school placement or access to a specialist support service. However, we need to challenge the integrity and durability of such categories across time. Research has shown how children fitting one diagnostic category at one point in time change and meet criteria for a different category at another point in development. Conti-Ramsden and Botting (1999), for example, report on a 2-year longitudinal study examining the stability of subgroups of children with SLI. Their results suggest that whilst there is stability over time in the patterns of difficulties manifested by the children, there is poorer stability in the classification of the children, with 45% of them moving across subgroups. Several chapters in this volume discuss SLI and raise the issue of identification and definition of this diagnostic category. The traditional definition of SLI is one that emphasizes the difficulties in learning language in the absence of any other primary coexisting physical, emotional, neurological or intellectual impairment (Leonard, 1998). The specificity of the language impairment in children with SLI has more recently, however, been contested with findings of associated cognitive and/or sensory impairments with this disorder (Johnston, 1999; Norbury et al., 2002; Botting, 2005). Certainly, the group of individuals with SLI studied by Rutter, and described in this volume, presented with impairments that were not restricted to language, showing significant social impairment in adulthood. This convergence of diagnostic categories should provide much food for thought to practising clinicians working in specialist units with specific entry criteria.

Dimensions and profiling of life experience

On a completely different level, a dimensional approach can be used to profile an individual's life. For some years now, researchers and practitioners have used the World Health Organization's International Classification of Functioning, Disability and Health (ICF; World Health Organization, 2001) to conceptualize their understanding of aphasia, traumatic brain injury, dementia and hearing impairment to name a few clinical groups. The application of the ICF to children is more recent, as illustrated by the development of the Speech Participation and Activity-Children for use with children who have speech disorders. This asks questions about the children's daily lives and the impact of having a speech impairment (McLeod, 2004, 2006). Profiling abilities and deficits in an individual's personal and environmental life context, and identifying facilitators of and barriers to their functioning, activity and participation, are enabled through the use of the ICF conceptual framework. The use of such a framework furthermore helps professionals to see commonalities between client groups and make connections at levels *other than* the impairment. For example, three adults may have completely different impairments (e.g. dysarthric speech output, moderate hearing impairment, fluent aphasia with impaired comprehension) but may experience similar limitations in their daily and life activities (e.g. difficulties conversing with others on the telephone). Garcia and colleagues (2002) clearly demonstrated that barriers that prevent people from returning to work (such as noise, tasks requiring speed, attitudes of others) are *shared* across persons with a range of communication disabilities, namely, dysfluency, dysarthria, laryngectomy, hearing loss, voice disorder and aphasia. In their study of communication between service users and primary care practitioners, Law and colleagues (2005) found that teenagers with developmental language disorders, adults with communication difficulty associated with learning disability and adults with aphasia from stroke *shared* common difficulties in communicating with their General Practitioner during consultations. A similar joint approach to addressing the activity and participation needs of children and teenagers with language difficulties in schools, home, and social or civic life could be pursued in research and practice in the coming years. Restrictions on employment potential and work opportunities are important for young adults with developmental language difficulties, as well as those with acquired problems, and also beg for the attention and imagination of researchers and clinicians.

Taking a life perspective encourages us to focus on more than just the language impairment, and in doing so, we begin to see the impact of language on everyday functioning and social life. Abigail Beverly's artwork very clearly reflects the frustrations and difficulties experienced as a result of a language impairment on a range of everyday activities including shopping, using the Internet and asking directions. It encourages us to look at words and language in ways different to how we typically conceptualize them, and to consider the centrality of language to life. When we broaden our professional gaze or remit to include such life areas, we are forced to change our thinking because the concept of *diagnostic categories* for daily and social life is inappropriate. Profiling of abilities and impairments will be just one dimension in profiling life experience. The importance of profiling, rather than categorization, is illustrated more acutely when we take a longitudinal perspective, which is the focus of the next section.

Longitudinal approach, development and the dynamic

The second significant connection this volume makes is between profiling, development and long-term perspective. The importance of longitudinal studies, such as the one detailed by Rutter, becomes clear from the different profiles he presents of autism and SLI across the lifespan, yet such studies are currently woefully lacking (most likely because of the significant challenges in financing and managing such studies). Karmiloff-Smith (1998) argues convincingly about the importance of *development* in investigating developmental disorders, a call repeated in the chapter by Roy and Chiat. Karmiloff-Smith (1998) uses the example of SLI to show how consideration of developmental timings can impact on causal theories of SLI. For example, auditory processing impairments may be evident in very young children with SLI, which could lead to grammatical impairments later on in the developmental trajectory. At adolescence, however, these processing deficits may be undetectable (due perhaps to compensation), but their impact on other areas of language may still manifest. She stresses the importance of developmental timing in research into developmental disorders and argues strongly for a *neuroconstructivist approach* to developmental disorders. This emphasizes the importance of studying at-risk populations at the early stages of development (see Roy and Chiat for such an approach) and employing longitudinal studies to chart developmental progression (as evident in Rutter's chapter).

This call for putting *development* back into the research arena in developmental disorders is not always as obvious as it may look on the surface, nor is it necessarily adopted by all researchers working in the developmental disorders field. It seems logical that an injury to a mature and established language system, for example, in acquired aphasia, will have repercussions different to an injury of a developing system, for example, in a child with developmental language impairment. Thus, one anticipates that a different thinking and terminology would be used. However, terms used to describe selective impairments in adult neuropsychological patients, like 'spared modules' or 'impaired modules' and 'double dissociations' (see chapter by Varley), have also been used in an attempt to describe the language and cognitive abilities in developmental genetic disorders such as SLI and Williams Syndrome (WS) (see, e.g. Pinker, 1999). SLI and WS have been used to further the debates around modularity and the independence of language and cognition, as well as the independence of modules within the language system itself (Fodor, 1983; Pinker, 1994, 1999). Modularity in both adults and children is an area that attracts a great deal of attention. Readers are directed, for example, to Varley's chapter for a discussion on the interplay of language and cognition and modularity debates in relation to adult language disorders. Pinker (1999) discusses the issue of modularity in children presenting with SLI and WS as an example of developmental double dissociation, that is, impaired language and age-appropriate cognition in the former, and the opposite profile in the latter. Other research, however, has contested this traditional picture of SLI and WS (Karmiloff-Smith et al., 1997, 2003; Johnston, 1999). The idea of modularity and viewing modularity as a product of development is an intriguing one. It is not the case that a developmental theory is necessarily unable to encompass the idea of modularity and the concept of the human mind at a later point having independent modules. Karmiloff-Smith (1992) acknowledges the process of modularization which occurs in the course of development. Some researchers argue that studies looking at cross-syndromic disorders at static points in time ignore the dynamic nature of development and cannot accurately reflect the developing brain and its interactions, both genetic and behavioural (see Thomas and Karmiloff-Smith, 2005 and Karmiloff-Smith et al., 2006 for further discussion). As Thomas and Karmiloff-Smith (2005) assert, 'the key difference between adult-acquired aphasia and language deficits in developmental disorders is the process of development' (p. 76).

It is this dynamic process of development which we cannot ignore when working with children and adults with developmental disorders. Furthermore, an understanding of the role of development in developmental language impairments provides insights into normal language development as well as acquired adult disorders. For example, we need a greater understanding of the stages and timings of the developmental sequence and interactions between verbal and non-verbal processing, interactions between different components of language (e.g. impact of phonological complexity on grammatical acquisition) as well as between language and other abilities (e.g. speed of processing, memory), timings of specific vulnerabilities in different components of language, the role of genetic and environmental interactions on language performance, and the potential for compensatory strategies to facilitate language abilities. Using the term 'dynamic' in a much wider life context, it is also important in both child and adult fields to consider the dynamic relationship that exists between the person and their environment, to understand how language, ability, activity, participation and life context work together. A consideration of *dynamic* encourages a focus on interrelationships and interactions.

The wider context

At a completely different level of analysis, the impact of the different interactions of the key elements of the therapeutic process – the client, clinician, task and context – on overall performance should be charted: for example, the interactions of client variables (including mood, personal views, motivation), clinician variables (such as philosophy, years of training), task variables (oral versus written, response mode) and contextual variables (school versus home, for example). Chapters by Dodd and Joffe focus, to some degree, on all four of these variables. They explore the challenges of conducting intervention studies that are rigorous and replicable, whilst at the same time staying realistic and within the reach of clinicians working in typical clinic settings with heavy caseloads. The expertise of the clinician in the intervention process is highlighted in both chapters, with Dodd giving consideration to the relationship between clinician variables such as length of work experience and clinical intuition in choice of intervention. Joffe explores the range of task and contextual variables that can be used to assess changes in performance and discusses ways of enhancing the functional nature of therapy by targeting skills (vocabulary and narrative) required in the National Curriculum, as well as incorporating outcome measures that reflect educational performance, for example, the use of the standard assessment tests that all children in the United Kingdom take at 10 and 14 years of age. Marshall, in her chapter on aphasia therapy and cognitive neuropsychology, describes a functional approach to therapy with a single-case study of a gentleman with aphasia by focusing on a life goal of the client, whose preference was to work on his note-writing skills, which was relevant for his role as a political counsellor. However, there is little research evidence, as Dodd notes, in the field of speech and language therapy, on the involvement of clients' preferences in the management of therapy. It is probably true to say that the involvement of clients in choosing a therapy approach and in exploring their perspectives on their disorder is more commonly associated with adult than developmental disorders. The focus on the client's perspective is clearly evident in the chapter by Cruice et al., who investigated the views of adults with aphasia and their family (and friends) through structured interviews about the aphasic person's quality of life. Similar kinds of qualitative research with parents of language-impaired children and professionals working with those children needs to be undertaken in the future (see Markham and Dean, 2006 for a start), as does specific research with children and teenagers who have language impairments about *their own experiences* of quality of life. Beverly, through her artwork showcased in this book, gives a unique perspective on the impact of language impairment on the quality of her life. Qualitative research exploring the views and perspectives of clients need not only rely on language through the more traditional questionnaires and/or interviews, but can, for example, incorporate the use of other modalities such as drawings. There is, for example, a strong move in the area of learning disability, with the use of photoelicitation to invoke discussion and explore the perceptions and views of adults with learning disabilities (Banks, 2001).

The chapter in this edition by Lindsay and Dockrell gives the perspectives of the individual with the language impairment, the professional and the parent: a triangulation of views that is one of the first of its kind in the field of developmental disorders. Whilst some research has explored the views of the children directly (see, for example, McLeod, 2006 and Owen et al., 2004), this work is still in its infancy relative to the work undertaken in the acquired language field. Conducting research interviews with individuals with impaired language skills does raise questions about people's capacity to participate in this kind of self-evaluation. Individuals will, by the very nature of their problems, experience problems in understanding the oral and written language used in interviews and questionnaires. A combination of visual and verbal techniques has been used to help overcome these difficulties (Owen et al., 2004). Further work needs to be done both in research and clinical practice to develop communicatively accessible tools and procedures to support adults (and children) with impaired language to be able to comment and give opinions about their life quality.

Conducting quality-of-life research exemplifies the interaction between the child or person and their environment, which was raised earlier in this chapter, and highlights the importance of context. For example, who you share life with, where you live and whether you are engaged in satisfying activities mattered greatly in life quality to older women with chronic aphasia (Cruice et al., 2006). Older age and worse physical condition (hemiplegia) restrict aphasic adults' social activities (Code, 2003), whereas having a partner or spouse (especially for driving) facilitates maintaining social activities after stroke and aphasia (Code, 2003). We know that speaking partners can be 'good' or 'poor' depending on the communication strategies they use, which reveal or mask the competence of someone with aphasia (Simmons-Mackie and Kagan, 1999). Similar issues are worthy of investigation in children and teenagers, for example, the influence of family versus friends versus teachers, and the influence of home versus school versus work on everyday communication, confidence and sense of self. It is worthwhile, for example, to obtain the views of students, their teachers and parents, as exemplified by Lindsay and Dockrell in their chapter. The influence of friendships and leisure time are also important areas for investigation. Recent work, for example, by Davies-Jones et al. (2007), has shown how young people with language and communication impairments value attending an after-school youth club. We need to know what opportunities and possibilities different life contexts provide to individuals with language impairments, and consider how speech and language therapy can address barriers in these contexts and facilitate opportunities for personal growth and development despite language difficulties. The impact of context on outcomes can be seen by comparing the results from the Rutter longitudinal study and that reported by Lindsay and Dockrell. More positive longitudinal outcomes are reported by Lindsay and Dockrell, who acknowledge that a variety of contextual differences in the two studies (including schooling, time frame of study) could account for some of these differences.

Updating how we use psycholinguistic theory

The adoption of cognitive neuropsychological models emerged in the 1970s more strongly in the field of acquired adult disorders than developmental disorders, and has been successfully used, as outlined by Marshall, in producing targeted assessments and interventions. In her chapter, Marshall explores the current role of psycholinguistic theory in acquired aphasia, and shows through a number of studies that despite some problems (potentially exhaustive assessments, for example), it provides a useful framework for the identification of functional and individualized assessment and therapy targets. She ends her chapter by throwing down the gauntlet to therapists working with developmental disorders, urging them to follow suit and adopt a more cognitive neuropsychological approach to intervention. More recent research in developmental language disorders has explored the use of psycholinguistic profiling in describing language and literacy disorders (e.g. Stackhouse and Wells, 1997; Chiat, 2001) and in devising focused treatment approaches targeting specific levels of breakdown identified within a psycholinguistic profile (Stackhouse and Wells, 1997, 2001; Pascoe et al., 2006). Roy and Chiat, in their chapter, argue for the role of psycholinguistic processing in the field of developmental language disorders, for drawing on strengths in processing, as well as targeting difficulties, and discuss ways of adopting such an approach whilst taking account of the developmental nature of the disorder. As Marshall argues, cognitive neuropsychology can be employed as a useful tool to plan specific, individualized and targeted interventions that may lay the foundations for a meaningful evaluation of efficacy, as outlined by Dodd. However, the true challenge is to find a sufficiently thorough assessment of key skills that provide diagnostic and prognostic information together with indicators for intervention that can be implemented within a realistic time frame. This is a theme explored by Marshall in her chapter, where she talks about the need for time efficiency and economical assessments.

Challenges of researching intervention

The difficulty inherent in conducting intervention research is a theme taken up in the chapters by Dodd and Joffe. Both suggest the adoption of a combination of single-case studies, case-series studies and randomized control trials in speech and language therapy intervention research. The example presented by Marshall of a single-case study within a cognitive neuropsychological framework provides an interesting way forward for developmental intervention research that can be both functional and individualized and can be realistically conducted by a practitioner in a school or clinic environment. There appears to be an over-dependence on single-case studies in adult research, and on larger group studies in developmental work, and the need for an adoption of both methodologies across age groups is highlighted by Dodd and Joffe. The importance of clinicians getting involved in research and researchers getting involved in clinical practice is emphasized in the chapter by Joffe. The implications of the need for increased evidence-based research in the everyday practice of clinicians with regard to training, financial resources, ethics and time constraints are explored by Dodd and Joffe.

Many chapters in the volume highlight interactions, for example, between precursor skills and language development, between language and psychosocial development, between cognition and language, between autism/SLI and social functioning, between assessment and intervention, and between researcher and practitioner. Each of these variables and their interactions raise challenges for both research and practice. Furthermore, the impact of impairment-related practice on functional tasks remains a challenge for outcome measurement (see chapter by Marshall). In Cruice et al.'s chapter, the findings suggest that daily and social activities, social networks and conversation may be possible targets for outcome measurement in quality-of-life intervention. As we widen our gaze from language processing and impairment, through to social functioning and quality of life, the need for more and varied outcome measures increases. Future research needs to develop and pilot ways of capturing change and go beyond simply conducting isolated language assessments in the classroom. We need to be assessing change through the various contexts in which the children are educated, for example, using the child's performance in geography to monitor performance or the teacher's report of classroom performance. Therapists need to boldly go where few have gone before. Schools, social clubs, leisure centres and homes are all potentially ideal contexts in which functional outcome measures can be generated.

Perspectives on assessment and intervention

Many of the issues explored in this volume pose significant challenges for clinical assessment. Joffe discusses the role of standardized and non-standardized assessments and emphasizes how performance changes depending on what assessment is chosen. The true challenge for clinicians is choosing the most appropriate and sensitive assessment measure/s that provide a reflection of the client's current performance, and perhaps even an idea of future learning potential within a dynamic assessment type of framework (see Hasson and Joffe, 2007 for a discussion of the role of dynamic assessment in speech and language therapy), spanning specific language skills and broader social and functional abilities within a realistic time frame. The dynamic nature of language development and breakdown is a recurring theme across the chapters, and this is again evident in assessment, with performance varying across a multitude of levels, including the purpose of assessment, the type of assessment used, the context in which the assessment takes place, the person conducting the assessment, the persons being assessed including the person with the impairment and family members and/or school/hospital staff as communication partners, and so on. It is important to acknowledge that the performance we observe is not static and will change. This variability, of course, produces its own challenges with regard to building a solid evidence base. Whilst contributors to this volume explore possible assessment choices and provide interesting and innovative ways of assessing or profiling someone's language and communication, it is fair to say that a task such as this one will continue to challenge researchers and practitioners in the field of speech and language therapy for the decades to come.

Whilst most of us are clear about the importance of obtaining the clients' perspective of language impairment and of the impact it has on their lives, very little has been generated in this respect, particularly with developmental language disorders. However, Lindsay and Dockrell, in their chapter, discuss innovative work they have carried out exploring the views of young people, and those of their parents and teachers. They report that parents' ratings of psychosocial functioning were different to those of teachers, with parents consistently producing higher rates of significant conduct problems and emotional symptoms than teachers (Lindsay et al., 2007). These discrepancies are interesting and suggest the need for further investigation. Cruice et al., in their chapter, describe work that explores aphasic adults' views about their quality of life – whilst 'verbal communication' (ability, as well as difficulties with it) is a strong factor in quality of life with aphasia after stroke, other factors are equally important in life quality, such as having others in one's life and engaging in activities. Furthermore, they collect the views of family members (two friends included in the sample), which allows for interesting comparisons between the two groups. Emphasis on the subjective experience and interest in quality of life has a much longer tradition in acquired disorders (as discussed by Cruice et al.) than in developmental disorders, although recent steps have been taken in the developmental sphere to rectify this (see chapters by Joffe, and Lindsay and Dockrell; Markham and Dean, 2006). It could be argued that a more in-depth knowledge of how clients and caregivers view their language difficulties, and the impact on their daily living, would help make intervention more functional and effective and ultimately satisfying for clients and their families. Even though one of the obvious challenges that immediately presents itself is how we go about eliciting views from language-impaired individuals, speech and language therapists are the most skilled of all educational and health professionals in facilitating understanding and expression in order to obtain reliable and meaningful responses from individuals. We see from the chapters by Dodd and Joffe that the speech and language therapy profession has still some way to go to develop a solid evidence base for its intervention, and ensuring that it is grounded in relevance for persons with language impairments and their families would be a wise move. The different priorities of researchers and practitioners involved in intervention work are discussed. Without argument, researchers and clinicians would concur that intervention at its most effective should be functional and meet the needs of the client. This is a recurring theme across the chapters in the book, but specifically exemplified by Marshall, illustrating how cognitive neuropsychology can be used to implement a functional therapy approach by addressing the life goals of the client.

The potential for focused linguistic and cognitive therapy, as outlined by Marshall and Varley, to impact on broader psychosocial functioning is an exciting possibility that needs further exploration in both client groups. The importance of the generalization of specific linguistic interventions to more functional aspects is a crucial commonality across adult and child client groups and a remaining challenge for us all. There is a small but significant body of research in aphasia that attests to the strong relationship between language functioning and functional communication abilities (Cruice et al., 2003; Marshall, 2005), and there are increasing numbers of studies that provide intervention at both impairment and conversational levels (sometimes simultaneous, but more often sequentially delivered therapies; see Marshall, 2005 and Nickels, 2005 for discussion). What this research does highlight is that whilst there is a link between the two, specific training and intervention is needed to facilitate the carry-over of learnt words or sentences from impairment intervention. What may challenge clinicians and researchers even further in the future is taking a completely reversed stance, such as that of Ylvisaker and Feeney (2000) in traumatic brain injury. That is, instead of starting with the impairment and then working towards functional communication and then social participation, we could begin with the person's life context and their participation, and then move back to how speech and language therapy can be of use to support and maximize the person's communication and language skills. Ultimately, what it reminds us is that in order to be able to sufficiently meet the needs of clients, it is essential to adopt the approaches discussed by Cruice et al., exploring the clients' perspective of their life experiences (either their quality of life or their language impairment or both) and probing what is meaningful to the person and their family in order to derive relevance in our therapy services provision.

In conclusion, the papers in this volume highlight the shifts in thinking over the last decade and the current themes in research and practice in the fields of developmental and acquired language disorders. Whilst Law's final chapter in this volume will draw together the present and the future of child and adult language impairment and therapy, we highlight here some goals and challenges of our profession over the next 10 years:

1. a consideration of the interplay between language and other processing skills, compensatory strategies and contexts, and how these may inform assessment and intervention;
2. the conduct of longitudinal studies similar to that described by Rutter and commencing at the very earliest stages of development, as well as longitudinal studies starting immediately post-stroke;
3. an acknowledgment of the dynamic nature of language development and impairment, and of the dynamic relationship between language and life;
4. a consideration of the impact of environmental context on an individual's language and lifelong development and the implications for measurement (multiple context profiling of ability and difficulty);
5. the building of a robust evidence base for speech and language therapy;
6. the development of strong collaborative working amongst clinicians, researchers, clients and family members; and
7. the incorporation into routine clinical practice of assessments and interventions that take into account client preferences, focus on the life goals and functional skills that are important to them and will assist them in achieving their life aims and fulfilling their own individual destinies.

References

Banks M (2001) Visual Methods in Social Research. London: Sage Publications.

Bishop DVM, Norbury CF (2002) Exploring the borderlands of autistic disorder and specific language impairment: a study using standardised diagnostic instruments. Journal of Child Psychology and Psychiatry 43: 917–29.

Bishop DVM, Snowling MJ (2004) Developmental dyslexia and specific language impairment: same or different? Psychological Bulletin 130: 858–86.

Botting N (2005) Non-verbal cognitive development and language impairment. Journal of Child Psychology and Psychiatry 46(3): 317–26.

Chiat, S. (2001) Mapping theories of developmental language impairment: Premises, predictions and evidence. Language and Cognitive Processes 16: 113–42.

Chiat S, Law J, Marshall J (eds) (1997) Language Disorders in Children and Adults. London: Whurr.

Clegg J, Hollis C, Mawhood L et al. (2005) Developmental language disorders – a follow-up in later adult life. Cognitive, language and psychosocial outcomes. Journal of Child Psychology and Psychiatry 46(2): 128–49.

Code C (2003) The quantity of life for people with chronic aphasia. Neuropsychological Rehabilitation 13(3): 379–90.

Conti Ramsden G, Botting N (1999) Classification of children with specific language impairment. Longitudinal considerations. Journal of Speech, Language, and Hearing Research 42: 1195–204.

Cruice M, Worrall L, Hickson L et al. (2003) Finding a focus for quality of life with aphasia: social and emotional health, and psychological well-being. Aphasiology 17(4): 333–53.

Cruice M, Worrall L, Hickson L (2006) Perspectives of quality of life by people with aphasia and their family: suggestions for successful living. Topics in Stroke Rehabilitation 13(1): 14–24.

Davies-Jones C, Myers L, Botting N et al. (2007) Teenagers deserve to have fun! Afasic News Autumn: 10–12.

Fodor J (1983) The Modularity of Mind. Cambridge, MA: MIT Press.

Garcia L, Laroche C, Barrette J (2002) Work integration issues go beyond the nature of the communication disorder. Journal of Communication Disorders 35: 187–211.

Hasson N, Joffe VL (2007) The case of dynamic assessment in speech and language therapy. Child Language Teaching and Therapy 23(1): 9–25.

Hilari K, Wiggins RD, Roy P et al. (2003) Predictors of health-related quality of life (HRQL) in people with chronic aphasia. Aphasiology 17(4): 365–81.

Joffe VL, Dodd B (2006) Making New Connections at City University. RCSLT Bulletin 656: 12.

Johnson CJ, Beitchman JH, Young A et al. (1999) Fourteen year follow-up of children with and without speech/language impairments: speech/language stability and outcomes. Journal of Speech, Language, and Hearing Research,42: 744–61.

Johnston J (1999) Cognitive deficits in specific language impairments: decisions in spite of uncertainty. Journal of Speech-Language Pathology and Audiology 23: 165–72.

Karmiloff-Smith A (1992) Beyond Modularity. A Developmental Perspective on Cognitive Science. Cambridge, MA: MIT Press.

Karmiloff-Smith A (1998) Development itself is the key to understanding developmental disorders. Trends in Cognitive Science 2(10): 389–98.

Karmiloff-Smith A, Grant J, Berthoud I et al. (1997) Language and Williams syndrome: how intact is 'intact'? Child Development 68: 274–90.

Karmiloff-Smith A, Brown JH, Grice S et al. (2003) Dethroning the myth: cognitive dissociations and innate modularity in Williams syndrome. Developmental Neuropsychology 23: 227–42.

Karmiloff-Smith A, Ansari D, Campbell L et al. (2006) Theoretical implications of studying cognitive development in genetic disorders: the case of Williams-Beuren syndrome. In: C Morris, H Lenhoff, P Wang (eds), Williams-Beuren Syndrome: Research and Clinical Perspectives. Baltimore, MD: John Hopkins University Press, pp. 254–73.

Larson V, McKinely N, Boley D (1993) Clinical forum: adolescent language. Service delivery models for adolescents with language disorders. Language Speech and Hearing Services in Schools 24: 36–42.

Law J, Bunning K, Byng S et al. (2005) Making sense in primary care: levelling the playing field for people with communication difficulties. Disability & Society 20(2): 169–84.

Leahy M, Dodd B (2002) Why should secondary schools come second? RCSLT Bulletin 60: 11–13.

Lenneberg EH (1967) Biological Foundations of Language. New York: John Wiley & Sons, Inc.

Leonard L (1998) Children with Specific Language Impairment. Cambridge, MA: MIT Press.

Lindsay G, Band S, Cullen MA et al. (2007) The Parent Support Adviser Pilot: The First Interim Report from the Evaluation DCSF-RR020. Nottingham: Department for Children, Schools and Families.

Markham C, Dean T (2006) Parents' and professionals' perceptions of quality of life in children with speech and language difficulty. International Journal of Language and Communication Disorders 41(2): 189–212.

Marshall J (2005) Can speech and language therapy with aphasic people affect activity and participation levels? A review of the literature. In: P Halligan, D Wade (eds), The Effectiveness of Rehabilitation for Cognitive Deficits. Oxford: Oxford University Press, pp. 195–210.

McLeod S (2004) Speech pathologists' application of the ICF to children with speech impairment. Advances in Speech-Language Pathology 6: 75–81.

McLeod S (2006) An holistic view of a child with unintelligible speech: insights from the ICF and ICF-CY. Advances in Speech-Language Pathology 8(3): 293–315.

Nickels L (2005) Tried, tested, and trusted? Language assessment for rehabilitation. In: P Halligan, D Wade (eds), The Effectiveness of Rehabilitation for Cognitive Deficits. Oxford: Oxford University Press, pp. 169–84.

Norbury CF, Bishop DVM, Briscoe J (2002) Does impaired grammatical comprehension provide evidence for an innate grammar module? Applied Psycholinguistics 23(2): 247–68.

Owen R, Hayett L, Roulstone S (2004) Children's views of speech and language therapy in school: consulting children with communication difficulties. Journal of Child Language Teaching and Therapy 20(1): 55–73.

Pascoe M, Stackhouse J, Wells B (2006) Persisting Speech Difficulties in Children: Children's Speech and Literacy Difficulties 3. Chichester: Whurr.

Pinker S (1994) The Language Instinct. New York: William Morrow and Co.

Pinker S (1999) Words and Rules. London: Weidenfeld and Nicholson.

Sievers R (2005) Time to plug a shocking gap in service provision. RCSLT Bulletin 643: 22.

Simmons-Mackie N, Kagan A (1999) Communication strategies used by 'good' versus 'poor' speaking partners of individuals with aphasia. Aphasiology 13(9): 807–20.

Snowling M, Adams JW, Bishop DVM et al. (2001) Educational attainment of school leavers with a preschool history of speech-language impairment. International Journal of Language and Communication Disorders 36: 173–83.

Stackhouse J, Wells B (1997) Children's Speech and Literacy Difficulties: A Psycholinguistic Framework. London: Whurr.

Stackhouse J, Wells B (2001) Children's Speech and Literacy Difficulties 2: Identification and Intervention. London: Whurr.

Stothard S, Snowling M, Bishop DVM et al. (1998) Language impaired preschoolers: a follow-up into adolescence. Journal of Speech, Language, and Hearing Research 41: 407–18.

Thomas M, Karmiloff-Smith A (2005) Can developmental disorders reveal the component parts of the human language faculty? Language Learning and Development 1(1): 65–92.

World Health Organization (2001) ICF: International Classification of Functioning, Disability and Health. Geneva: World Health Organization.

Ylvisaker M, Feeney F (2000) Reflections on Dobermanns, poodles, and social rehabilitation for difficult-to-serve individuals with traumatic brain injury. Aphasiology 14(4): 407–31.

CHAPTER 1

Beyond outcomes: the importance of developmental pathways

PENNY ROY and SHULA CHIAT

City University

Introduction

In the field of acquired aphasia, the advent of psycholinguistic theories and models in the 1970s was a springboard for research on the nature of language processing impairments. In the field of developmental disorders, it caused much less of a stir, and its impact has been largely confined to disorders of speech. This difference between the 'child' and 'adult' worlds was already evident at the first Making New Connections (MNC) conference 10 years ago, when psycholinguistics was at the height of its influence and at the heart of the conference, which aimed to make connections between psycholinguistically motivated interventions for adults and children. In the introductory chapter of the conference volume, Chiat observed:

> Psycholinguistic questions about the point of breakdown in input/output processing are as pertinent to developmental as acquired disorders. However, they have appeared to be impossibly complicated by what we might term the 'developmental dimension'.
>
> Chiat, 1997, p. 3

So what has happened over the following decade? In the 'adult' world, as Marshall's chapter points out, the excitement has waned somewhat as it has become apparent that results and implications of psycholinguistically motivated therapy are by no means straightforward. In the 'child' world, on the other hand, theories have begun to address the missing 'developmental dimension', shifting the focus from the nature of complex

Language Disorders in Children and Adults: New Issues in Research and Practice.   Victoria Joffe,
Madeline Cruice, Shula Chiat.
© 2008 John Wiley & Sons, Ltd. ISBN 978-0-470-51839-7

cognitive outcomes to the nature of processes that give rise to these. In this paper, we outline and exemplify this shift in perspective, present an extensive investigation into early precursors of language disorders in children and argue that this new attention to the developmental dimension opens new doors to psycholinguistic research and insights into the nature of developmental language disorders.

The developmental dimension

It is hardly controversial that breakdown in a fully established language system will have different effects from breakdown in the acquisition of that system, and that language impairment will have different effects on a developing child from a previously fully functioning adult. These differences were implicit in the traditionally separate treatment of language impairment in children and adults in clinical research and practice. Arguably, it was only the emergence of linguistics and psycholinguistics that drew attention to the commonalities. Since all language processors are dealing with the same cognitive system, it was assumed that theories of language and models of language processing should be able to account for findings on any individual's language processing, intact or impaired, developing or acquired. The very aims and themes of the first MNC conference illustrate this assumption.

In practice, however, the developmental and acquired fields have drawn on linguistics and psycholinguistics in rather different ways. The take-off of Chomskyan linguistics in the 1960s and 1970s generated huge excitement about the syntax of human language, which inspired a new interest in developmental language disorder and directly shaped that interest. The spotlight fell on syntactic deficits and the development of syntactic tools to describe those deficits. Crystal et al. (1976) led the way in the United Kingdom with their Language Assessment, Remediation and Screening Procedure (LARSP), a framework for analysing grammatical structures in language samples produced by children with language impairment, and comparing these with grammatical structures characterizing stages of normal language development. In the United States, Bloom and Lahey (1978) – influenced by the emerging analyses of semantic relations and their application to the early language of typically developing children – supplemented the analysis of 'form' with analyses of 'content' and 'use'. Back in the United Kingdom, the syntactic profile of LARSP was in turn supplemented by profiles of lexical and grammatical semantics, phonology and prosody (Crystal, 1982). Since those early days, research on the nature of syntactic – and occasionally semantic – deficits has proliferated (see Leonard, 1998). A key drive behind this research has been the quest for evidence to support competing claims about language acquisition and its impairment. These have largely polarized between 'modular' accounts postulating deficits in specific language capacities and 'processing' accounts postulating deficits in peripheral skills, such as auditory process-ing and speech perception, or general deficits in processing capacity (see Bishop, 1992, 1997).

We note a number of features of research over these years:

- a focus on children's language production and particularly on language samples, with more limited investigation of comprehension;
- a focus on syntax, with secondary attention to semantics, and almost no attention to phonology beyond the single-word level; and
- limited attention to the relation between deficits observed in language and in other processing abilities.

The missing psycholinguistic pieces in developmental research become evident when we compare developments in the acquired world. Here, the psycholinguistic microscope was turned on the complex processes of understanding and producing language. Emerging models of input and output processing begged questions about the locus of impairment in individuals with aphasia, and new methods for tapping different stages of processing (including a host of judgement tasks such as lexical decision, grammaticality judgement and judgement of semantic anomaly) enabled these to be addressed. Evidence from research on aphasia was in turn used to evaluate and motivate the detailed architecture of processing models.

Clinical studies of adults occasionally inspired similar studies of chil-dren's lexical difficulties (Chiat and Hunt, 1993; Constable et al., 1997) and difficulties with verb–argument structure (Bryan, 1997; Ebbels et al., 2007). But it is only at the periphery of language processing, in the study of developmental speech disorders, that psycholinguistics has loomed large. Here, we find detailed models of input and output processing, theorization about the nature of processing deficits, development of child-appropriate techniques to investigate different stages of processing, exten-sive investigation of these in single-case and group studies, and evaluation of therapies (see Dodd, 2005; Pascoe et al., 2006).

What lies behind this skewed impact of psycholinguistics on the devel-opmental field? As we pointed out 10 years ago, psycholinguistic approaches are just as relevant to developmental as acquired language disorders; what differentiates these is the 'developmental dimension'. If the child's input phonology, lexical semantics and sentence-level processing are intact, and only output phonology is impaired, potential sources of impairment are limited to representations of lexical phonology and the accessing, plan-ning and execution of these. Difficulties with output phonology, free of potentially complicating influences from deficits in earlier levels of process-ing that occurred at previous stages in the child's development, are more likely to be characterized by systematic patterns. These can in turn be systematically explored in investigations of phonological representation and production, with relatively clear implications for the locus of deficit. In contrast, when a child's difficulties go beyond lexical phonology, the psycholinguistic floodgates open. As with adults, observed difficulties in lexical and sentence output may be due to difficulties at one or more stages of input, representation or output. In the case of children, however, they may also be a product of deficits that occurred earlier in the child's development and disrupted the developmental trajectory. The possible developmental pathways to deficits in lexical and sentence-level processing are therefore many and complex. Not surprisingly, observed outcomes are rarely characterized by systematic patterns, are open to description at different levels of language (phonology, semantics and syntax), and hence compatible with multiple psycholinguistic interpretations. Even the best-designed psycholinguistic investigations are dogged by psycholinguistic ambiguity between a variety of concurrent and developmental sources of observed performance.

Until recently, these complications have remained in the background. For the most part, studies of developmental disorders have been cross-sectional, investigating patterns of intact and impaired performance at one point in time. If they have drawn on models of language processing, these have been adult models characterizing the language processing system which is the end point of language acquisition. It is true that some studies address the possible contribution of developmental processes retrospectively. In some cases, contributory processes are considered in the interpretation of patterns observed in language outcome. For example, extensive evidence of patterns of difficulty with grammatical morphology spanning a wide range of languages led Leonard to put forward the 'surface hypothesis'. According to this hypothesis, difficulties with grammatical morphology arise from difficulties in processing of perceptually non-salient forms (see Leonard, 1998; Bortolini et al., 2006). In other cases, studies start from a hypothesized impairment in a prerequisite processing capacity. Examples of such prerequisite capacities are perception of rapid auditory transitions (Tallal and Piercy, 1974) and phonological short-term memory (Gathercole and Baddeley, 1990). Typically, the hypothesized capacities are investigated *at the same point in time* as the language deficit itself, limiting evidence for paths of development and implications for causal relations.

Only recently has development itself been identified as a key issue for developmental theories. Constructivism, in particular, has asserted the importance of understanding the role of development for understanding children's achievement of complex cognitive and linguistic outcomes (Karmiloff-Smith, 1998; Tomasello, 2003; Thomas and Karmiloff-Smith, 2005). Taking a constructivist position, adult modular structures are not assumed to be present in infants, but emerge as a product of development from relatively less differentiated information processing systems. As Thomas and Karmiloff-Smith (2005) point out, 'Inferences drawn from developmental behavioural deficits to affected underlying structures are *entirely contingent on a precise specification of the developmental process*' (pp. 85–6, their emphasis). The precise specification of the developmental process is particularly challenging for complex language and communication outcomes.

As we have argued, children's problems in input and output processing may be the product of different underlying problems and their ramifications. To exemplify the point, limitations in vocabulary and lexical semantic errors could be a repercussion of problems with storing or retrieving the phonological forms of words, which could in turn be due to problems with early speech processing and memory. However, the same lexical problems could be due to difficulties with semantic processing, which could in turn be due to earlier deficits in the conceptual processing that underpins semantic development. On the other hand, all these phonological and semantic processes could be intact, with problems arising only in making or recalling the links between semantics and phonology. Differentiation of these possibilities requires a constructivist approach.

As is evident from the discussion in Thomas (2005), this approach has a number of implications:

- It requires us to construct task-specific trajectories, with hypothesized pathways from early processing systems to complex outcomes.
- These hypothesized trajectories should allow us to trace developmental deficits back to precursors in infancy.
- Hypothesized trajectories – typical and atypical – require longitudinal studies to test predicted relations between early deficits and later outcomes.
- Predicted relations can also be tested using developmental computational models to simulate behavioural data.

This agenda puts the developmental dimension at the centre of research and neatly captures our approach to the developmental dimension of developmental language deficits.

Pathways to typical and atypical language: some hypotheses

In a paper entitled 'Mapping theories of developmental language impairment', Chiat (2001) argued that precursors of language are the first place to look for possible sources of language deficits, and put the case for three key precursors: phonological skills, mapping skills and sociocognitive skills.

Phonological and mapping skills

The acquisition of words hinges on children's ability to segment word forms from the stream of speech, store these forms and recognize them when they crop up again. A raft of studies over the last two decades has revealed sophisticated phonological processing skills in the first year of life (for collections and reviews of findings, see Morgan and Demuth, 1996; Jusczyk, 1997; Weissenborn and Höhle, 2001). These have demonstrated that infants are rapidly able to separate out rhythmic units of their language and the stress patterns within these units. By 8 months, they are able to recognize sequences of sounds within rhythmic units: amazingly, after brief exposure to novel streams of syllables, infants distinguish sequences that always occur consecutively from those that only do so by chance (Saffran et al., 1996). These skills are vital for picking out and remembering word forms. Not long after – by 14 months – infants reach the turning point that leads to meaningful language: not only are they able to distinguish subtly different word forms, they are also adept at mapping these onto distinct meanings (Werker and Yeung, 2005).

These findings on infant speech processing provide ample evidence of a set of basic yet complex processing skills that are necessary precursors of language. If these phonological and mapping skills are slow to emerge, or limited, we would expect disruptions in the child's journey to words. And we would expect these disruptions to escalate further down the road, as the phonological challenges of target forms increases. Even salient forms of language – those that naturally carry stress in sentences – will be affected, but we would expect less salient forms – unstressed function words and inflections – to be more so. We would also expect difficulties with recalling and recognizing longer stretches of phonology, a prerequisite for identifying syntactic relations between words.

This construction of the developmental trajectory for words and morphosyntax yields the hypothesis that deficits in words and morphosyntax may be the outcome of early deficits in phonological and mapping skills. Is there any evidence to support this? As we have pointed out, most research on language impairment in children focuses on language outcomes, which provide limited and ambiguous evidence for origins. We can certainly point to evidence in our favour. After years of research focusing on syntax in specific language impairment (SLI), dramatic findings on children's difficulties with the simple task of repeating nonsense words, which is used to tap phonological processing and memory skills, have drawn attention to possible deficits in these skills. Investigations of children's non-word repetition using different tasks, with different age groups, have come up with the same finding: performance of children with SLI is significantly poorer than performance of typically developing children, and significantly related to performance on other assessments of language (see Gathercole, 2006 for a review). The findings are so robust that non-word repetition has been proposed as a marker for SLI (Bishop et al., 1996). Equally robust is the finding that children with SLI have difficulties with grammatical morphology, and that the relative difficulty of grammatical morphemes both within and across languages depends on the relative demands of their phonology. This was evident from the earliest studies of children's language production (Leonard, 1998) and from more recent experimental investigations of tense and agreement marking (Bortolini et al., 2006). Even more recently, attention has turned to children's difficulties with repeating sentences and how this relates to their performance on other language assessments. Sentence repetition has also been proposed as a possible marker for SLI (Conti-Ramsden et al., 2001). Interestingly, analysis of children's sentence repetition reveals particular difficulties with function words and inflections, which are phonologically weak (Seeff-Gabriel et al., 2005).

So, we have evidence of difficulties with phonology, evidence of difficulties with phonologically challenging aspects of morphosyntax and evidence that these are related to deficits on general measures of language. On our own argument, however, this evidence is no more than circumstantial: correlations are not causal. To demonstrate that deficits in phonology are *precursors* of morphosyntactic and wider language deficits, we need to identify children with early deficits in phonology, and demonstrate relations to later deficits in morphosyntax. Ideally, we would track the developmental trajectory right back to early infancy. Some studies are beginning to do this by testing infants whose family history puts them at risk of language disorders (Kemp et al., 2006; Weissenborn et al., 2006). The research we describe below starts somewhat later in the developmental trajectory, at the point when first concerns about a child's language development have been voiced. This research investigates these children's early phonological skills, together with another precursor of language development and deficits to which we now turn.

Sociocognitive skills

Many studies have demonstrated the emergence and importance of sociocognitive skills in the first year of life. From their first months, infants are responsive to others' expression of emotion (Trevarthen and Aitken, 2001). Between about 8 and 13 months, they show increasing engagement with others, demonstrated by following the direction of others' finger-pointing and gaze to find out what they are looking at, finger-pointing themselves to direct others' attention, and alternating gaze between people and objects to check that others are looking at what they are looking at (Carpenter et al., 1998). By about 18 months, they tune into the intentions behind other people's utterances (Baldwin, 1995; Tomasello, 1995), which is crucial if they are to discover the meaning of other people's words.

These evolving sociocognitive skills, we suggest, constitute further precursors for language. They underpin children's understanding of intentions behind utterances and their discovery of utterance meanings, and these in turn underpin their own use of semantically and contextually appropriate language. If these sociocognitive precursors are slow to emerge, or limited, we would expect disruptions in the child's journey to words and the use of words.

This construction of a developmental pathway from sociocognitive skills to meaningful and appropriate communication yields the hypothesis that deficits in meaningful communication may be the outcome of early sociocognitive deficits. In this case, we do have some longitudinal evidence for hypothesized relations between early joint attention and later language and communication in typically developing children (Carpenter et al., 1998), and between deficits in joint attention and later language and communication in children with autism (Charman et al., 2005). Our prediction is that these relations may extend beyond children with autism, occurring in children who present with deficits in social communication, which may be identified as pragmatic language impairment (PLI). Research studies indicate that differential diagnosis of PLI (as opposed to 'typical' SLI) is problematic and subject to change over time (Botting and Conti-Ramsden, 1999; Bishop and Norbury, 2002; see Rutter, Chapter 7 this volume). The changing picture of outcome deficits and relations to earlier deficits may be understood better, we suggest, if we carry out longitudinal studies tapping early sociocognitive skills and later language and social communication. This was the second goal of our research.

The very early processing skills (VEPS) project: an investigation of VEPS as predictors of later language disorders

We have identified VEPS which

- develop in early infancy;
- play a key role in language development; and
- are impaired in children with deficits in language and social communication.

We hypothesized that deficits in these skills will affect the route a child takes to language and produce different – though potentially overlapping – outcomes. More specifically, we hypothesized that

- early phonological processing deficits and early sociocognitive deficits would predict later difficulties with language, but
- early phonological processing deficits would predict later difficulties with morphosyntax, whilst
- early sociocognitive deficits would predict later difficulties with social communication.

Participants in the VEPS project were 209 children who were referred to clinical services at 2–3 years due to concerns about language, not just speech, with no report of other problems and no diagnosis of autism or hearing loss. Of these children, 187 were seen again 18 months later, aged

4–5. Of these 187 children seen at both phases of the study, 163 met our non-verbal criterion for participation, scoring at least 70 on the British Ability Scales II (Elliott, 1996) at both phases of assessment, or at least 80 at one phase.

At Phase 1, we administered the following measures to assess 'predictor' skills:

Phase 1 skills and measures

Receptive and expressive language
Preschool Language Scales-3 (United Kingdom) (PLS; Boucher and Lewis, 1997).

Phonology
The Preschool Repetition Test (PSRep), a novel word–non-word repetition task. This comprises 18 words and 18 phonologically matched non-words varying from one to three syllables and controlled for prosodic structure, for example, *lamb–lomm*, *machine–shameen*, *dinosaur–sinodaur*.

Sociocognition
A combination of three novel tasks:

- Social responsiveness, assessing whether children looked at the face of an adult expressing a feeling. The therapist acts out a script that includes six emotionally charged events, and reacts to these with appropriate expressions of feelings such as surprise and hurt.
- Joint attention, assessing whether children alternate gaze between a novel object and the researcher's face, and whether they follow the researcher's gaze or finger-point at another object. This takes the form of a game centred on a box of six plastic eggs containing small objects, each of which corresponds to a larger object placed strategically around the room. The therapist brings out one egg at a time, shakes the egg to one side and opens it to reveal the object inside. She then looks at and comments on the corresponding object in the room to see if the child follows her gaze, and if not, repeats the comment and points to the object.
- Symbolic understanding, assessing whether children can find an object corresponding to a gesture, miniature or pretend use of a different object. In each of these three conditions, the child is presented with a choice of six objects and must select the one matching the gesture, miniature or pretend object and roll it down a chute.

More details of the phonological task can be found in Roy and Chiat (2004) and Chiat and Roy (2007), and both phonological and sociocognitive tasks are currently being prepared for publication (Chiat and Roy, forthcoming; Roy and Chiat, in preparation).

At Phase 2, when children were aged 4–5 years, we administered the following key outcome measures:

Phase 2 skills and measures

Receptive and expressive language
Again, the PLS.

Morphosyntax
A novel sentence imitation test (SIT-16, adapted from Seeff-Gabriel, 2005), with score for repetition of function words serving as the key measure.

Social communication
A combination of two parental questionnaires:
- Children's Communication Checklist-2 (Bishop, 2003)
- Strengths and Difficulties Questionnaire (SDQ; Goodman, 1997).

Since we were making predictions about *clinically significant* impairments in skills, we classified children's scores on all measures categorically, distinguishing scores that fell in a clearly normal range (at or above the 16th percentile) from those that fell in a clearly low range (at or below the 7th percentile). Scores between these two clear-cut ranges were classified as borderline. According to our hypotheses, we would expect our sample to include children scoring in the low range on our measures of phonological and sociocognitive skills at Phase 1. And so they did – in interestingly different proportions and combinations.

Overall performance on the PSRep was exceedingly poor. As illustrated in Figure 1.1, just under a quarter of scores were in the normal range, and over half in the low range. Strikingly, half of the children scored more than two standard deviations below the mean for their age. Although our criteria for participation in the project excluded children with just speech problems, it is not always possible to differentiate these children based on information at referral, and a proportion of the sample were subsequently identified as having only speech difficulties. Since our hypothesis was that difficulties with phonological processing and memory – not just speech – would predict later morphosyntactic skills, this group of children was considered separately in our profiling of the sample (see below).

In contrast to our findings on the PSRep, only a minority of children performed poorly on our sociocognitive composite measure. As shown in

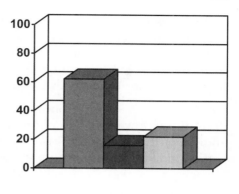

Figure 1.1 Distribution of performance on phonological measure.

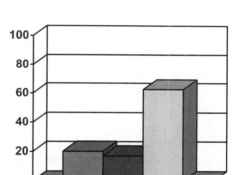

Figure 1.2 Distribution of performance on sociocognitive measure.

Figure 1.2, the distribution of scores on this measure was a mirror image of the distribution on PSRep. Nearly two-thirds were in the normal range, with just under a quarter in the low range. Furthermore, the vast majority of children with low sociocognitive scores also had low scores on PSRep: only three of these children (8.3%) attained PSRep scores in the normal range.

In contrast, 55 children who had low scores on PSRep (54.5%) had sociocognitive scores in the normal range. Since these children had a significantly higher mean PSRep score than the children who had low scores on both, it is possible the children with low sociocognition were simply more severely impaired. However, their low sociocognition points to qualitatively different difficulties, and it is possible that these difficulties, rather than difficulties with phonology *per se*, are responsible for their poor scores on the repetition test. This possibility is supported by our finding that the lower mean score in this group of children was due to the higher rate of total refusal on the test: once the 13 'refusers' were excluded, repetition performance did not differ between children with and without sociocognitive difficulties.

The possible associations and dissociations between phonology and sociocognition led us to identify four clear-cut VEPS groups, defined by scores that were in the clearly demarcated low or normal ranges:

Low: low scores on both phonology and sociocognition

Phonology: low scores on phonology, normal on sociocognition

Sociocognitive: low scores on sociocognition, normal on phonology (as mentioned above, the number of children with this dissociation was negligible; it was too small for this group to be included in subsequent analyses)

Normal: normal scores on both phonology and sociocognition

In addition, we separated out a **Speech** group (as explained above), and identified two borderline groups:

Borderline hybrid: borderline scores on phonology and/or sociocognition

Borderline speech: scores between the phonology and speech groups

According to our hypotheses, these groups should have different outcomes on our measures of morphosyntax and social communication. Children who had poor phonology at Phase 1 – those in the 'low' and 'phonology' groups – should present with poor morphosyntax at Phase 2. Figure 1.3 shows that they did: the error bars in this figure indicate that the scores of these two groups were significantly lower than the scores of the 'normal', 'speech' and 'borderline speech' groups. Whilst there is an

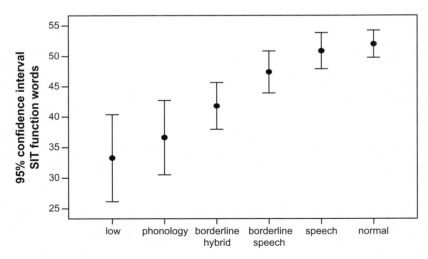

Figure 1.3 Error bars showing performance of Phase 1 very early processing skills groups on Phase 2 morphosyntactic task (SIT-16 function word score).

apparent trend towards improvement across the remaining groups, only the 'borderline hybrid' differed significantly from the 'normal' group, with the difference between the 'borderline hybrid' and the 'speech' groups approaching significance ($p = 0.06$). In line with our argument that the difference between the 'low' and 'phonology' groups is not one of severity, they did not differ from each other on this measure of morphosyntax.

However, only the 'low' group, who had low sociocognition as well as low phonology at Phase 1, should present with poor social communication at Phase 2. As predicted, the social communication outcome of this group was differentiated from the rest. Looking at the error bars in Figure 1.4, we find the 'low' group out on a limb: there is no overlap with any of the other groups. In contrast, the 'phonology' group, with normal sociocognition at Phase 1, show full overlap with the rest, including the normal group. The differential social communication outcome for the low and phonology groups again suggests that these groups differ in the nature rather than severity of their difficulties.

These group comparisons indicate that early processing skills are significantly related to later language and social communication outcomes. In order to investigate the predictive value of all our early measures individually for all our outcome measures, we ran a series of simple regressions. These showed that:

- early PLS predicted all outcome measures – outcome on PLS, morpho-syntax as measured by function word score in sentence imitation

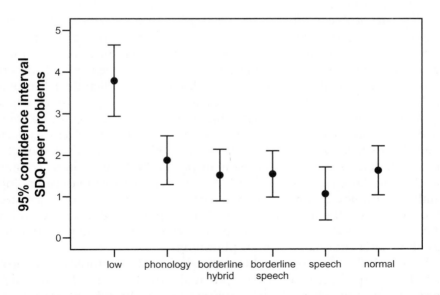

Figure 1.4 Error bars showing performance of Phase 1 very early processing skills groups on a Phase 2 social communication measure (Strengths and Difficulties Questionnaire peer problems).

and social communication as measured by the two parental
questionnaires;
• early PSRep predicted outcome on morphosyntax and expressive PLS;
  and
• early sociocognition predicted all outcome measures.

Thus, all early measures are significantly predictive of some – and in
most cases all – outcome measures.

In order to investigate the *unique* contribution of each of our early
measures to each outcome, we ran a series of multiple regressions, entering all our predictors simultaneously. This allows us to look at the predictive value of each measure, with the contribution of other measures
partialled out. Combined entry revealed that

• early PLS was the best predictor of later PLS, but
• early PSRep was the best predictor of later morphosyntax and
• early sociocognition was the best predictor of later social communication.

These results are in keeping with our predictions. Performance on
all Phase 1 measures was related to later performance on PLS, with
PLS itself, unsurprisingly, being most predictive when other predictors
were taken into account. However, morphosyntactic difficulties at
Phase 2 were best predicted by PSRep once other predictors were partialled out. Nevertheless, in the absence of sociocognitive difficulties,
children with poor phonology were no more likely to have social communication problems than children with normal VEPS performance.
Children with early deficits in sociocognitive skills, on the other hand,
were more likely to have later deficits in social communication. Unexpect-
edly, almost all children with early sociocognitive deficits also had early
phonological difficulties (and later morphosyntactic difficulties). This may
be due to the nature of our sample: it may be that 2- to 3-year-olds whose
phonology is intact and who have fluent speech are not seen as a cause
for concern about language at this age, and are therefore less liable to
referral for speech and language therapy. Another possibility is that children with deficits in social engagement pay limited attention to communication and language, and that this delays their processing of phonology
– unless phonological processing is a particular strength and even a source
of pleasure for them. Longer-term follow-up is needed to determine
whether some of the children with poor sociocognition and poor phonology show later 'normalization' of phonology.

We conclude from our findings that longitudinal studies can throw
new light on sources of developmental language deficits and how
these evolve. But what are the implications for clinical assessment and
intervention?

Factoring in the developmental dimension: clinical implications

Having established the key role of developmental pathways as integral to our understanding of language and communication outcomes, we are now in a position to re-address the role of psycholinguistic investigation with children and adults, with the developmental dimension taken into account. In considering the implications of our approach and findings, we find echoes of the points Marshall made in her discussion of current and new directions in the acquired world.

First, the identification of underlying processing deficits shifts the psycholinguistic focus. In assessing children's language difficulties, our findings indicate the importance of exploring underlying processing skills – amongst which we have highlighted phonological and sociocognitive skills – rather than focusing exclusively on syntactic and semantic outcomes. This leads to a similar shift in intervention. We are not arguing that a child's current language skills – syntactic and semantic – are uninformative and can be ignored. Assessment of these skills is still necessary to establish the developmental stage the child has reached, which is a key factor in selecting therapy targets. Our argument is that intervention approaches to selected linguistic targets will be more effective if they take into account the processing deficits that are responsible for the limitations in the child's language.

In the case of children thought to have difficulties with phonological processing and memory, but not with sociocognition, achievement of targets might be facilitated by

- selection of minimal chunks of phonology that are sufficient to exemplify target morphosyntactic structures;
- seeking to place linguistic targets in prosodically salient positions;
- slower delivery of models, using exaggerated intonation;
- support with cuing from other modalities, for example, visual;
- careful timing of models to ensure the child is attending to the speech and to the relevant referential context; and
- frequent exposure to individual exemplars, combined with some variety to provide foundations for generalization.

Whilst these manipulations of linguistic input are designed to facilitate phonological processing and memory, it would still be important to facilitate accessing of semantics by ensuring that linguistic targets are introduced in contexts that focus their meaning.

Where children are thought to have exclusive or primary difficulties with sociocognition, a different balance of techniques is called for. Where the goal is to facilitate access to linguistic targets, we can ensure joint attention by following the child's focus of interest, timing linguistic models to coincide with the child's attention to the relevant referential context. However, if the child always relies on the interlocutor sharing the child's attention, access to the meanings and intentions behind linguistic forms will be limited. How can we overcome this limitation? Intervention cannot enable the child to understand others' affective or cognitive states, which is key to spontaneous interest in and attention to others' intentions and communication. However, we can use techniques to draw the child's attention to others' expression of emotion and attention, which will facilitate access to at least some aspects of the meaning behind their words. Techniques for achieving this might be non-verbal or verbal, depending on the child's responsiveness to linguistic input. If interest in – or at least attention to – others' focus can be achieved, this will increase the child's access to the linguistic forms used by others, and the meanings and intentions they are used to express.

By now, experienced therapists may be feeling somewhat sceptical. The manipulations we have suggested for different underlying difficulties differ in emphasis but not necessarily in specific content (recalling Marshall's comment (Chapter 3 this volume) on identification of psycholinguistically different impairments not necessarily resulting in different intervention methods with adults). Furthermore, our proposals are hardly revolutionary. Indeed, the suggestions we have made for adjusting input are likely to strike most therapists as just the sort of things they do, and have always done, in working with children. They are also built into programmes for parents to promote early language development. So what is new? We would argue that a theoretical rationale for interventions provides a useful framework, helping to clarify who might or might not benefit from these interventions and serving as a springboard for further investigation. In the case of the manipulations we have proposed, we suggest that our theoretical rationale makes psycholinguistic sense of therapeutic modifications that are more usually seen as extralinguistic, based on 'clinical instincts', and marginal to linguistically targeted intervention. These modifications, motivated by analysis of the developmental dimension, are geared towards reducing demands on impaired processing skills in order to promote the child's progress along the developmental trajectory to linguistic targets. Construed in this way, the nature of these modifications becomes a key factor in the development and evaluation of psycholinguistically based therapy (see Dodd, Chapter 4 this volume; Joffe, Chapter 5 this volume). So, timing of linguistic models, length and prosodic structure of linguistic targets, intonation and tempo of target input are all factors that merit systematic investigation in language-focused interventions.

We have argued for the importance of studying developmental trajectories. Equally important – and integral to a developmental approach – are longitudinal investigations of children who have received theoretically driven interventions at an early age. Such research might eventually enable us to develop therapy packages that target particular structures using particular balances of techniques, and specify the profiles of children for whom these packages are appropriate – along the lines that Marshall (Chapter 3 this volume) has proposed for adults. Putting the developmental dimension back into development, we suggest, strengthens the case for taking a psycholinguistic approach to developmental disorders and for continuing to make psycholinguistic connections across the child-adult divide.

References

Baldwin DA (1995) Understanding the link between joint attention and language. In: C. Moore, PJ Dunham (eds), Joint Attention: Its Origins and Role in Development. Hillsdale, NJ: Lawrence Erlbaum Associates, pp. 131–58.

Bishop DVM (1992) The underlying nature of specific language impairment. Journal of Child Psychology and Psychiatry 33: 1–64.

Bishop DVM (1997) Uncommon Understanding: Development and Disorders of Language Comprehension in Children. Hove, East Sussex: Psychology Press.

Bishop DVM (2003) The Children's Communication Checklist, Version 2 (CCC-2). London: Psychological Corporation.

Bishop DVM, Norbury CF (2002) Exploring the borderlands of autistic disorder and specific language impairment: a study using standardised diagnostic instruments. Journal of Child Psychology and Psychiatry 43: 917–29.

Bishop DVM, North T, Donlan C (1996) Nonword repetition as a behavioural marker for inherited language impairment: evidence from a twin study. Journal of Child Psychology and Psychiatry 37: 391–403.

Bloom L, Lahey M (1978) Language Development and Language Disorders. New York: John Wiley & Sons, Inc.

Bortolini U, Arfe B, Caselli MC et al. (2006) Clinical markers for specific language impairment in Italian: the contribution of clitics and non-word repetition. International Journal of Language & Communication Disorders 41: 695–712.

Botting N, Conti-Ramsden G (1999) Pragmatic language impairment without autism: the children in question. Autism 3: 371–96.

Boucher J, Lewis V (1997) Pre-school Language Scale-3 (UK adaptation). London: Harcourt Brace & Company Books.

Bryan A (1997) Colourful semantics. In: S Chiat, J Law, J Marshall (eds), Language Disorders in Children and Adults: Psycholinguistic Approaches to Therapy. London: Whurr, pp. 143–61.

Carpenter M, Nagell K, Tomasello M (1998) Social cognition, joint attention, and communicative competence from 9 to 15 months of age. Monographs of the Society for Research in Child Development 63 (Serial No. 255).

Charman T, Taylor E, Drew A et al. (2005) Outcome at 7 years of children diagnosed with autism at age 2: predictive validity of assessments conducted at 2 and 3 years of age and pattern of symptom change over time. Journal of Child Psychology and Psychiatry 46: 500–13.

Chiat S (1997) Making new connections: in whose interests? In: S Chiat, J Law, J Marshall (eds), Language Disorders in Children and Adults. London: Whurr Publishers Ltd, pp. 1–8.

Chiat S (2001) Mapping theories of developmental language impairment: Premises, predictions and evidence. Language and Cognitive Processes 16: 113–42.

Chiat S, Hunt J (1993) Connections between phonology and semantics: an exploration of lexical processing in a language-impaired child. Child Language Teaching and Therapy 9: 200–13.

Chiat S, Roy P (2007) The Preschool Repetition Test: an evaluation of performance in typically developing and clinically referred children. Journal of Speech, Language, and Hearing Research 50: 429–43.

Chiat S, Roy P (forthcoming) The Preschool Repetition Test. In: B Seeff-Gabriel, S Chiat, P Roy (eds), Early Repetition Battery. London: Pearson, Inc.

Constable A, Stackhouse J, Wells B (1997) Developmental-word finding difficulties and phonological processing: the case of the missing handcuffs. Applied Psycholinguistics 18: 507–36.

Conti-Ramsden G, Botting N, Faragher B (2001) Psycholinguistic markers fo specific language impairment (SLI). Journal of Child Psychology and Psychiatry 42: 741–8.

Crystal D (1982) Profiling Linguistic Disability. London: Edward Arnold.

Crystal D, Fletcher P, Garman M (1976) The Grammatical Analysis of Language Disability. London: Edward Arnold.

Dodd B (2005) Differential Diagnosis and Treatment of Children with Speech Disorders, 2nd edn. London: Whurr Publishers.

Ebbels SH, van der Lely HKJ, Dockrell JE (in press) Intervention for verb argument structure in children with persistent SLI: a randomized control trial. Journal of Speech, Language, and Hearing Research 50: 1330–49.

Elliot CD (1996) BAS II: British Ability Scales, 2nd edn. Windsor, Berkshire: NFER-Nelson.

Gathercole SE (2006) Nonword repetition and word learning: the nature of the relationship. Applied Psycholinguistics 27: 513–43.

Gathercole SE, Baddeley AD (1990) Phonological memory deficits in language disordered children: is there a causal connection? Journal of Memory and Language 29: 336–60.

Goodman R (1997) Strengths and Difficulties Questionnaire, http://www.sdqinfo.com (accessed 05.11.06).

Jusczyk PW (1997) The Discovery of Spoken Language. Cambridge, MA: MIT Press/Bradford Books.

Karmiloff-Smith A (1998) Development itself is the key to understanding developmental disorders. Trends in Cognitive Sciences 2: 389–98.

Kemp N, Werker J, Bernhardt B et al. (2006) Early word-object associations and language skills in children at-risk for language delay. Paper presented at the X International Congress for the Study of Child Language, Berlin, Germany, 25–29 July 2005.

Leonard LB (1998) Children with Specific Language Impairment. Cambridge, MA: MIT Press.

Morgan JL, Demuth K (eds) (1996) Signal to Syntax: Bootstrapping from Speech to Grammar in Early Acquisition. Mahwah, NJ: Lawrence Erlbaum Associates.

Pascoe M, Stackhouse J, Wells B (2006) Persisting Speech Difficulties in Children: Children's Speech and Literacy Difficulties, Book 3. Chichester, West Sussex: John Wiley & Sons, Ltd.

Roy P, Chiat S (2004) A prosodically controlled word and nonword repetition task for 2- to 4-year-olds: evidence from typically developing children. Journal of Speech, Language, and Hearing Research 47: 223–34.

Roy P, Chiat S (in preparation) Tests of Early Social Cognition.

Saffran JR, Aslin RN, Newport EL (1996) Statistical learning by 8-month-olds. Science 274: 1926–8.

Seeff-Gabriel B (2005) An investigation into the relationship between the overt speech patterns of different sub-groups of speech disordered children and their production of syntax. Thesis (PhD), University of London.

Seeff-Gabriel B, Chiat S, Dodd B (2005) The relationship between speech disorders and language. In: B Dodd (ed.), Differential Diagnosis and Treatment of Children with Speech Disorder. London: Whurr, pp. 100–116.

Tallal P, Piercy M (1974) Developmental aphasia: rate of auditory processing and selective impairment of consonant perception. Neuropsychologia: 12: 83–93.

Thomas MSC (2005) Constraints on language development: insights from developmental disorders. In: P Fletcher, J Miller (eds), Language Disorders and Developmental Theory. Amsterdam: John Benjamins, pp. 11–34.

Thomas MSC, Karmiloff-Smith A (2005) Can developmental disorders reveal the component parts of the human language faculty? Language Learning and Development 1: 65–92.

Tomasello M (1995) Joint attention as social cognition. In: C Moore, PJ Dunham (eds), Joint Attention: Its Origins and Role in Development. Hillsdale, NJ: Lawrence Erlbaum Associates, pp. 103–30.

Tomasello M (2003) Constructing a Language: A Usage-Based Theory of Language Acquisition. Cambridge, MA: Harvard University Press.

Trevarthen C, Aitken KJ (2001) Infant intersubjectivity: research, theory, and clinical applications. Journal of Child Psychology and Psychiatry 42: 3–48.

Weissenborn J, Höhle B (eds) (2001) Approaches to Bootstrapping: Phonological, Lexical, Syntactic and Neurophysiological Aspects of Early Language Acquisition, Volume 1. Amsterdam: John Benjamins.

Weissenborn J, Wermke K, Suhl U et al. (2006) Early precursors of delayed language development: results from a longitudinal study from age zero to age four with German learning children. Paper presented at the X International Congress for the Study of Child Language, Berlin, Germany, 25–29 July 2005.

Werker JF, Yeung HH (2005) Infant speech perception bootstraps word learning. Trends in Cognitive Sciences 9: 519–27.

CHAPTER 2

Substance or scaffold? The role of language in thought

ROSEMARY VARLEY

Human Communication Sciences, University of Sheffield

Introduction

People with severe language impairments are faced with the constant challenge of expressing their thoughts to others, and interpreting the beliefs and ideas of the people around them when these are couched in linguistic form. Regular interlocutors of individuals with severe language impairment are often convinced that beneath the linguistic difficulty, there is a rich mental world. However, this impression runs counter to some theories on the relation between language and thought. For some scientists, the ability to think certain thoughts is intimately related to language. Without certain linguistic forms, some thoughts should become unthinkable. In this chapter, I will consider how the evidence from language impairment can illuminate long-standing debates on the relationship between language and thought.

The role of language in creating distinctively human cognition is an important topic in the cognitive sciences. The human species appears to be uniquely endowed with the capacity for sophisticated cognition. Human cultures are marked by achievements such as science and technology, art, religion and large social networks bound together by an intricate web of relationships. These achievements are universal in human culture, and even hunter-gatherer communities have sophisticated technologies linked to hunting and elaborate cultural practices. The question then arises as to the source of these unique achievements and what within the human profile has allowed for the emergence of this sophisticated cognitive and behavioural repertoire. Such questions lead to comparisons

Language Disorders in Children and Adults: New Issues in Research and Practice. Victoria Joffe, Madeline Cruice, Shula Chiat.
© 2008 John Wiley & Sons, Ltd. ISBN 978-0-470-51839-7

with other species, particularly primates but even birds and fish. Research with animals sometimes reveals startling evidence of smart cognition in non-human species. For example, monkeys, when tested in ecologically valid situations such as food theft, have insight into the knowledge states of others (Santos et al., 2006). Western scrub jays are able to plan for the future and can store up food on the basis of the prediction that there might be no breakfast in a particular location the next morning (Raby et al., 2007). Some dogs are capable of instant learning (or 'fast mapping') of the link between a spoken word and its referent. Kaminski et al. (2004) report the fascinating study of Rico, a Border collie, who understood over 200 spoken words. Rico was able to select a novel object from seven familiar items (for which he already knew the names) when he was presented with a novel spoken name. Furthermore, Rico was able to retain the association between the novel word and object when re-tested 4 weeks later, despite no further training on the novel pairs.

Although it is possible to identify precursors of human cognition in other species, it remains the case that humans appear unique in the range and depth of their cognitive abilities and the resulting cultural achievements. This might be because the human brain is large relative to body size and so there is more capacity for storing information and more computing resource. Linked to larger brain size, the human brain contains large amounts of polymodal cortex. These are brain regions that are not dedicated to processing inputs from single sensory modalities, such as sound and vision. Instead, these regions respond to both sound and vision, or other combinations of input signals and outputs. This capacity to intermingle inputs might be crucial to human cognition, and certainly is important in learning to read and write where linkage between spoken and visual forms is crucial.

Brain size and the extent of polymodal cortex are two examples of biologically based accounts of the uniqueness of human cognition. Other scientists have sought to explain the cleverness of humans through examination of their cognitive repertoire. The most obvious competence that distinguishes humans from other species is the possession of language. We know that other species have naturally occurring primitive communication systems. For example, vervet monkeys have a basic lexicon consisting of predator calls. Hence, the call for 'leopard' is distinct from that for 'snake' (Seyfarth and Cheney, 1990). The dancing behaviour of bees by which they communicate the location of food sources to their hive-mates is well established (von Frisch, 1954). But these communication systems are of limited capacity and differ in fundamental ways from the linguistic abilities of humans. Vervet monkeys generate calls in the presence of a predator and therefore under conditions of strong autonomic nervous system drive. Their calls are more akin to 'shrieks' than 'names'. The communications of bees (to the best knowledge of human observers) is limited to messages about actual food sources. Bees do not perform courtship dances or dance to warn their fellows of predator threats. They do not appear to chat about future events or possible events ('wouldn't it be wonderful if she planted another honeysuckle' is an unlikely bee communication). By contrast, human communications are generally volitional and can be withheld if we are feeling unhelpful, or can describe events in ways that do not match the realities of the world – we can lie and also talk about things that do not exist ('fairies' and 'unicorns') and abstractions such as 'honesty' or 'serenity'.

The study of naturally occurring animal communication systems indicates that although there are limitations, non-human species might have precursors of full-blown language capacity. The factor that might limit the development of a system that might truly be described as language might be that the culture/environment of a species has not facilitated the emergence of language. Based on this possibility, there have been attempts to enrich the linguistic culture of animals and teach them language, usually in the form of visual symbolic systems such as signs or pictograms. Experiments with chimpanzees, gorillas and orangutans have shown some capacity for vocabulary learning. However, the size of chimp vocabularies is insignificant when compared with that of humans. For example, Washoe, a chimpanzee studied by the Gardners, achieved a vocabulary of around 200 signs (Gardner and Gardner, 1969). The ability to learn grammar appears limited in non-human primates, with little evidence of generative use of symbols or consistency of structure that would provide convincing evidence for a grammar (Terrace et al., 1979). The limitation or absence of a structured use of symbols in animal language systems leads to the claim that the capacity for grammar is unique to humans, and the ability to amalgamate previously isolated chunks of information into coherent propositions is the source of many human cultural achievements. However, even in the domain of grammar, more recent research is beginning to show that some non-human species do show capacities that equate, at least, to subcomponents of syntax (Hauser et al., 2002b; Gentner et al., 2006).

In a subsequent section, I will describe why some scientists claim that language has enhanced developments in other cognitive domains such as reasoning about the causes of events and the thoughts of others, and in abilities such as mathematics and navigation. The philosopher Peter Carruthers characterizes this as a *cognitive conception* of language (Carruthers, 1996). Those that adopt this view claim that, in addition to the obvious use of language for interpersonal communication, language has significant intrapersonal uses in terms of acquiring and sustaining certain forms of thinking. Before detailing some of the claims of the cognitive view, it is worth considering why this chapter appears in a volume dedicated to the discussion of children and adults with language impairments. What is the relevance of the information and ideas in this chapter to language pathology?

Language pathology and the language and thought debate

Impairments of interpersonal communication have interactional and emotional consequences for both the person with a language disorder and their usual interlocutors. But following from the cognitive conception of language, if language is necessary for certain forms of thinking and reasoning to develop, then a developmental language impairment should result in cognitive limitations beyond the specific domain of language. The label of *specific* language impairment (SLI) appears to indicate that the developmental delay is restricted to language and that progress in other areas follows a normal trajectory. However, definitions of SLI are sometimes cagey in that it is described as a *relatively* pure delay in the development of language, or that the delay in language is disproportionate to that in other cognitive domains. Such caveats suggest that SLI might represent something more than a pure language disorder. A reasonable response to the observation might be that a substantial amount of human learning is mediated via explicit instruction through language. A child with SLI who shows delayed learning in a domain such as mathematics might simply not have been able to access the explanations delivered in verbal or written format from his or her teachers. A cognitive view of language might propose an alternative account of a delay in mathematical learning. Some scientists suggest that the grammatical mechanisms underpinning language are also involved in other domains of cognition (Hauser et al., 2002a). For example, a subtraction problem in maths has syntax inherent within it. In just the same way as subjects and objects play different roles in sentences, the numbers 7 and 3 play different roles in the subtraction problem $7 - 3$ versus $3 - 7$. By this cognitive account, delay in mathematical acquisition might stem not only from the effect of degraded instruction, but directly from impaired grammatical procedures resulting in computations being performed inefficiently on symbol strings, whether words or numbers.

With regard to acquired language impairment, aphasia is also viewed as a specific disorder language, although again, there is recognition that the individual with aphasia might have impairments in other cognitive domains. These linked impairments are often viewed as a consequence of the anatomical proximity of various neural systems. Hence, the co-occurrence of aphasia with hemiplegia is a result of the juxtaposition of the primary motor cortex and the neural systems involved in processing language in the frontal lobe. However, when aphasia co-occurs with calculation difficulties (Delazer et al., 1999) or difficulty in completing non-verbal reasoning tests such as Raven's Matrices (Kertesz, 1988; Raven et al., 1998), is this necessarily a result of incidental anatomy, or does it reflect a true functional interrelationship between these processes? Just as in the case of SLI, the situation in aphasia is complicated by issues of understanding linguistic instructions. Many apparently non-verbal tests of reasoning and problem solving such as the Wisconsin Card Sorting Test (Heaton et al., 1993; Baldo et al., 2005) or 'performance' tests found within the Wechsler Adult Intelligence Scale (Wechsler, 1981) require the understanding of linguistic instructions and, sometimes, a capability for speeded bimanual action in order to achieve scores within a normal range.

There is a further reason, independent of understanding task instructions, why impairments in apparently non-linguistic domains may be observed in the performances of people with developmental or acquired language disorders. When engaged in a piece of complex problem solving, many people use either overt self-directed speech or silent 'inner speech' to structure their attempt and work through to a solution (Vygotsky 1962). This self-directed speech is apparent in both children and adults, and appears to be an effective resource in learning. For example, Berk (1994) reported that children who used higher levels of self-directed speech were quicker to solve non-verbal problems (Winsler and Naglieri, 2003). Evidence as to the status of inner speech in developmental and acquired language disorder is sparse and the methods are necessarily indirect. Typical experiments involve determining whether there is phonological mediation of performance on an apparently non-linguistic task such as memorizing a string of pictures. If memory performance declines when the items to be remembered are labelled by long versus short words, or rhyming versus non-rhyming words, this is an indication that internal phonological mediation of performance is taking place (Conrad, 1971; Baddeley, 1986). Alternatively, if memory performance improves when items are nameable rather than non-nameable, this again might provide indirect evidence of phonological mediation. The experiments that have been conducted on people with impaired language suggest that inner speech is disrupted (Goodglass et al., 1974; Whitehouse et al., 2006). If these findings are robust across people with language disorders, it would indicate that language impairment results in a reduction of a valuable cognitive resource. It might be the case that alternative mechanisms to scaffold reasoning and problem solving might be utilized, such as visuospatial imagery. However, placing language impairment within a broader cognitive perspective allows a recognition that language impairment may never be 'pure' or 'specific', and may result in diminished performance in other cognitive domains due to impoverished learning opportunities, difficulties in understanding task instructions and reduction in language-linked problem-solving strategies.

Language therefore has an important role in scaffolding learning and reasoning. However, this is a relatively weak claim regarding the role of language in human cognition, and there are much stronger proposals within cognitive science that language is necessary for certain forms of thinking in that it represents the substance or the code in which the thought is represented. Following from the latter view, there should be some forms of cognition that would not be possible for an individual with a severe language disorder. Such suggestions are often surprising to clinicians and to other people who frequently interact with people with language impairment. For example, you meet individuals who despite aphasia are capable of managing their finances, play chess, drive cars and are immensely resourceful in finding ways of communicating with you. However, the strong form of the cognitive conception of language makes more subtle claims than the global proposal that all thought is linguistically mediated. There is no suggestion that all forms of reasoning are mediated by language. For example, visuospatial reasoning of the type required to complete a task such as Raven's Matrices is not likely to require language. Therefore, performance within the normal range on this test would not be seen as counterevidence to the cognitive hypothesis. In addition, not all impairments of language processing would necessarily result in consequences for non-language cognition. Individuals with difficulties in surface levels of language processing, such as perceptual difficulties influencing word discrimination and recognition or in accessing surface forms in output lexicons, are unlikely to have impairments in other cognitive domains, particularly in the case of acquired language disorders, where previously established grammatical and semantic-conceptual knowledge would still be in place. Similarly, impairment of inflectional morphology or difficulty restricted to processing more complex grammatical structures would not impact upon other domains. However, severe impairment of the deep mechanisms of language, either grammatical or lexical-semantic, might, under the cognitive stance, result in a corresponding inability to sustain certain forms of reasoning. A person with severe agrammatic aphasia who is unable to comprehend or produce language propositions in any modality of use (spoken or written) would be predicted to display impairments in some forms of thinking and reasoning in which the grammatical mechanisms of language are implicated.

The clinical context provides an important opportunity to test the claims of the cognitive view of language. It is possible to identify individuals with severe impairment of particular language mechanisms and determine if they retain behaviours such as calculation or reasoning about others' thoughts (theory of mind). Evidence from developmental and acquired language impairment can contribute to the debate in different ways. Developmental evidence can show whether language is necessary to acquire certain forms of thought. If a cognitive process can develop in the absence of language mediation, then this is powerful evidence of autonomy from language. However, SLI rarely results in radical impairments of language processing that would satisfy the criterion that a particular component of language was not available. For example, van der Lely et al. (1998) report the case of AZ, a boy with a marked and persisting grammatical deficit, who displayed impairment particularly at the level of morphology. Despite these linguistic difficulties, AZ showed a normal profile of scores on non-linguistic cognitive tasks. However, it is clear that

AZ was able to construct sentences (e.g. 'My dad go to work'), albeit simplified ones, which indicated that basic grammatical mechanisms were available.

Aphasia is a condition that can result in radical impairments of components of the language system. Severe agrammatic aphasia provides an opportunity to test claims regarding the role of grammar in high-order cognition and in capacities such as social and causal reasoning, navigation and mathematics. Similarly, global aphasia, where there is extensive disruption of lexical-semantic processes, permits exploration of the role of the lexicon in sustaining particular forms of thought. However, the evidence from aphasia does have a serious limitation. People with aphasia generally experience a brain lesion in adult life and their minds and cognitive mechanisms have been established with the ready support of language. If a cognitive system requires language in order to configure it in a way that enables new forms of sophisticated cognition, this configuration work would have taken place and language could subsequently be withdrawn without the entire cognitive edifice tumbling down. Aphasia represents a means to determine whether language is necessary for ongoing or current cognition, but it can tell us little about whether language was necessary to acquire a process in the first place.

Considerations of SLI and aphasia appear to have reached an impasse – SLI does not result in severe or selective enough impairment, and aphasia provides no insight into the developmental role played by language in configuring sophisticated cognition. However, *savant* syndromes provide an additional source of evidence. Savant abilities are found in rare cases of individuals with severe autism or other serious developmental disability. In the face of global developmental delay, often including language, the individual has quite extraordinary capabilities in isolated cognitive domains, for example, in music, drawing or calculation (e.g. Hermelin and O'Connor, 1990; Cromer, 1991; O'Connor et al., 2000). Similarly, investigations with profoundly deaf individuals raised in non-signing environments may also provide an important test ground for hypotheses regarding developmental claims for the role of language in configuring the human mind (Schaller, 1995; Goldin-Meadow and Zheng, 1998). The abilities of these people, combined with evidence from other forms of language disability, provide important insights and opportunities for testing claims regarding the role of language in creating distinctively human cognition.

Lexicon and grammar: the role in thinking

Debates regarding the role of language in thought usually make reference to the work of Benjamin Whorf and controversies as to how many words Eskimo languages have for snow (Pinker, 1994). In its strongest form, the Whorfian hypothesis suggests that language determines thought and in the Eskimo example, Inuit people can conceptualize the difference between various forms of snowflake only because they have a large snow lexicon. Steven Pinker (1994), in his book *The Language Instinct*, provides a colourful alternative perspective on Whorf's claims – that the number of snow words in Eskimo was wildly inflated, that English also has a number of words for snow (e.g. snow, sleet, slush, hail) and that the observation is trivial. Inuit people have lots of snow in their environment and so it should come as no great surprise that this is reflected in their language. Rather than words determining conceptualization, it is the case that the environment in which you live determines what you talk about. Dairy farmers have lots of cow terminology, and only those inducted into the mysteries of cricket can distinguish a googly from a full toss, and silly mid-off from third slip.

More recent work with members of the Pirahã tribe (who live in the Lowland Amazonia region of Brazil) provides some support for Whorf's hypothesis (Gordon, 2004). The Pirahã have a limited set of number words in their language, consisting of 'one', 'two' and 'many'. Gordon gave members of the tribe a set of numerical tasks and their performance suggested that the small number system resulted in restricted numerical cognition. For example, one test involved participants observing nuts being placed into a can. Nuts were then removed from the can one at a time and after each removal the participant was asked to predict if the can still contained any nuts. The accuracy of responses fell markedly when the trial involved more than three nuts, presumably reflecting a difficulty in conceptualizing (or perhaps easily encoding) quantities beyond the limits of the number lexicon. However, an anthropological study undertaken with speakers of Mundurukú, another language spoken in Brazil, suggests that people could make judgements about the approximate addition of large numbers, even though the language has number words only up to five (Pica et al., 2004). Speakers of Mundurukú observed animations of large numbers of dots being pooled into a can. They then had to judge whether the number of dots in the can was larger than a further set. The results were not significantly different from those of control French speakers, even though the quantities involved were considerably outside the range of numbers within the Mundurukú lexicon.

The evidence for and against the Whorfian hypothesis is not clear-cut. Vocabulary – or 'having a word for it' – is likely to be important for the performance of a range of cognitive tasks. If there is an easily available lexical item that matches incoming information, then the input can be rapidly encoded into a word. The complex input then becomes encapuslated into a tight package of information that is easy to store and to retrieve. For example, at the back of our offices in the middle of urban Sheffield, a colleague and I watched with some surprise as a bird of prey killed a pigeon. Neither of us were expert bird spotters, but we noted the size of the bird, the shape of its beak and wings and the colouring of its feathers. We relayed the information back to an expert, who promptly delivered the classification of a peregrine falcon. Now we have an exact word for the bird – our increasingly fuzzy memory for the various perceptual characteristics can fade, but we can still reconstruct our memory for its appearance through checking out pictures of peregrine falcons. Words provide powerful tools for encoding and retaining our experiences. But this does not entail that I would not be able to mentally represent my observations of the falcon without the word, merely that my representations would be less exact.

We can therefore acknowledge the role of the lexicon in supporting cognition. However, this does not lead to a commitment to a strong form of the Whorfian hypothesis or a cognitive conception of language. But what of the role of grammar – the apparently unique human endowment? Could this be the cognitive mechanism that makes human thinking so flexible and sophisticated? Interest in grammar as the enabler of cognition has a shorter history than that of the lexicon. However, the failure of primate language training studies to show much success in grammatical acquisition fuelled interest in the possibility that the mechanisms that allow combination of isolated pieces of information into language propositions might be crucial in the success of humans. One reason for the interest in grammar stems from the significance of Jerry Fodor's book *The Modularity of Mind* (1983). Fodor suggested that the human mind is composed of a suite of specialized processing systems or modules. Fodor would describe language as an example of a modular system, and the cognitive neuropsychological models of language which represent language processing as a series of independent modules are an example of the modular approach. Fodor proposed a set of features that characterize the operation of modular systems. These allow processing to be fast and to function autonomously from other cognitive systems. For example, processing is mandatory (you cannot choose whether or not to understand a word once you have heard it, the processing just happens automatically). The operations of modules are described as 'informationally encapsulated' and 'cognitively impenetrable'. In essence, these mean that the modules operate with their own codes and specialist knowledge stores (e.g. a phonological input lexicon), and that other cognitive systems cannot influence the stages in processing or the final product. For example, if I walk into a field and in good lighting conditions, see a large grey creature with a trunk, tusks and big floppy ears, my visual processing system will yield up the percept 'elephant' even though I am not expecting to see an elephant and despite it being a rare occurrence to find an elephant in a British field. My mandatory processing system is not penetrated by my expectations, or knowledge of British mammals. I see what is there and not what I expect to be there.

The notion of modularity has been enormously influential, particularly in neuropsychology where evidence for the autonomy of modules and sub-modules has been sought in evidence of dissociations between intact and impaired cognitive processes. However, the cognitive architecture suggested by modularity is inherently rigid. The focus on mandatory processing, encapsulation and autonomy suggest a mind that is inflexible. But a fundamental characteristic of human intelligence and problem solving is its fluidity and flexibility. Steven Mithen (1996), in his book *The Prehistory of the Mind*, suggests that the capacity for intermixing of different cognitive domains resulted in human cognitive and cultural advancement. When knowledge of natural history (knowledge of the environment and the plants and animals found within it) can be combined with toolmaking ability, then the products of animals, such as bone and antlers, could be used to develop a whole new technology of tools. If the human mind was modular in structure, then there has to be a mechanism that allows a breakout from the inherent inflexibility. Many cognitive scientists viewed language as just such a mechanism, particularly within the combinatorial power of the grammar that permits isolated chunks of information to be interwoven into coherent propositions. Some cognitive scientists saw the sentences of natural languages ('natural language' here means languages such as English, German or Mundurukú) as acting as cognitive intermediaries between encapsulated modules, whilst others saw a more abstract, underlying propositional code playing this role. Pinker (1994) discusses the notion of *Mentalese* or a language of thought, a universal human cognitive language with a lexicon consisting of abstract concepts and a grammar equivalent to that of universal grammar – the structural regularities found across all the languages of the world. Pinker (1994) suggests that people with severe aphasia would still be able to entertain complex thoughts as despite impairment of natural language, the underlying Mentalese code would still enable them to maintain high-order intellectual abilities. By contrast, those suggesting natural language as the cognitive intermediary would suggest that severe aphasia would result in a corresponding loss of some high-order ability.

The case of navigation

Navigation is a cognitive domain for which claims of language mediation of performance have been made. This is perhaps surprising, given that it is a visuospatial function that is not obviously language-involving. In addition, the advanced navigational abilities of various non-human species suggest that it is an unlikely candidate for a function that is mediated by language. However, in a series of experiments, Spelke and colleagues (e.g. Hermer-Vasquez et al., 1999) showed that after being disorientated through being spun about, healthy children and adults appeared to require language in order to reorientate themselves. In the experiments, participants observed an object being hidden in one of the corners of a rectangular room, and they were then asked to find the object after they have been disorientated. In one condition, the room had four blank walls, and participants used the cues inherent in the room's geometry to search at the two geometrically appropriate but opposite locations (e.g. right of the long wall). However, when some local, landmark information was also provided – one of the short walls of the rectangle was coloured blue – adults and older children were able to combine the geometric and the landmark cues (e.g. at the intersection of the long wall and the blue wall) to find the hidden object. Spelke and colleagues demonstrated that pre-school children who had not yet mastered spatial language were unable to combine the geometric and the landmark information to locate the object. Even more surprising, adults' ability was disrupted when they were asked to do a verbal shadowing task whilst the object was hidden. The verbal shadowing task involved repeating a heard story and was presumed to engage the resources of the language system so that language was not available to conjoin the landmark and geometric information. As a result, healthy adults reverted to searching at the two geometrically plausible opposite locations. In another experimental condition, healthy adults were able to locate the object whilst at the same time tapping out a rhythm. This suggests that divided attention or competing demands of performing two tasks was not the source of the disruption of reorienta-tion in the verbal shadowing condition. Instead, it would appear that language is important in integrating two sources of visual information (landmark and geometric) that otherwise would be encapsulated and independent.

It is not clear whether lexical resources (understanding and using spatial expressions such as 'left') or whether the ability to understand and form spatial propositions (such as 'the object is to the right of the blue wall'), or both, are important in performance. The evidence from people with language impairments might provide valuable evidence in teasing apart lexical from grammatical influences. Some people with aphasia have impairments in understanding and forming spatial propositions ('put the penny to the left of stamp'), whilst retaining the ability to comprehend the spatial terms ('show me your left thumb'). Others display impairments in the comprehension of spatial terms, hence they make errors on the 'show me your left thumb' test. In this way, experiments with people with aphasia might provide a unique window on the contributions of lexicon and grammar to thinking and reasoning.

Other researchers have failed to replicate the results of Spelke's exper-iments, and small changes in the experimental set-up can alter the results. For example, Learmonth et al., (2001) found no language mediation effect when the dimensions of the experimental room were altered and the participant had to search in a larger space. There is evidence from experiments with non-human species that other creatures such as fish can combine landmarks and geometry in order to reorientate (Sovrano et al., 2003). Therefore, the role of language in reorientation is yet to be determined. Spelke's work provides an example of how language might provide a mechanism that allows for fluidity in cognition by permitting the combination of information from two encapsulated visual mechanisms (object and location). In addition, it shows how evidence from people with impairments of language might be important in contributing to debates on the role of language and its sub-component systems in higher-order cognition.

Evidence from aphasia

In a series of experiments, we have examined whether people with severe agrammatic aphasia can sustain forms of thinking that some scientists propose necessarily involve language and, in particular, a capacity for grammar. Our first studies investigated theory of mind reasoning. Theory of mind is a component of social cognition and involves making inferences about what other people are thinking. A classic test is the false belief task. In the Smarties (or changed container) task, a participant is presented with a familiar container such as a tube of Smarties, but the contents are revealed to be unusual. For example, the tube contains pencils. The participant is then asked what a third person, who has not seen the strange contents, would think was in the container. In order to respond correctly, it is necessary to inhibit one's own knowledge of the real state of affairs and make an inference as to the state of another's knowledge and the content of his or her belief and, in this instance, a belief that is false. Children begin to pass false belief tests between 4–5 years and some researchers have pointed to the parallel emergence of more complex sentence structures between these same ages (Astington and Jenkins, 1999; De Villiers and Pyers, 2002). For example, children begin to use sentences containing subordinate clauses (e.g. 'Richard thinks that there are Smarties in the tube'). Astington and Jenkins (1999) suggested that there is a direct relation between grammatical development and theory of mind, and that natural language sentences with subordinate structures are the substance in which theory of mind inferences take place.

An important element of scientific training is to understand that correlations or associations do not necessarily reveal causal relationships between two observations. The ability to pass false belief tests and the appearance of more complex grammatical structures might occur at the same time because the two depend on some shared but hidden factor that regulates both. The evidence from people with severe language impairments allows exploration as to whether there is a true causal relationship between theory of mind and subordination within language. If complex syntactic structures are necessary for theory of mind, then individuals with grammatical impairment should fail false belief tests.

In our investigations, we work with people who have severe aphasia. These individuals generally have large left hemisphere lesions, with profound impairments of language comprehension and production. For example, SA is a 62-year-old man who had a bacterial infection of the brain 15 years ago. This caused extensive damage to the left hemisphere and the resulting aphasia was characterized by severe grammatical impairment. SA performed at chance level on tests of spoken and written comprehension of reversible sentences. Similarly, performance was at chance level on a written grammaticality judgement test. For SA, 'sentences' with no verbs or with misplaced verb phrases were acceptable, and at the same time, he classified many acceptable sentences as ungrammatical. SA's understanding of spoken and written words was less impaired, although he still scored markedly below normal levels on more complex lexical comprehension tests such as synonym judgement. His speech output was severely restricted and he generally communicated via writing single words, complex drawings and gestures. His writing usually consisted of nouns and adjectives, and when encouraged to produce sentences, the output consisted of bizarrely structured pseudo-sentences (e.g. 'women a age the red a scissor'). However, despite this profile of severe grammatical impairment that meant he could neither understand nor produce simple subject–verb–object sentences, let alone more complex structures involving subordination, SA could complete false belief, changed container tasks (Varley and Siegal, 2000; Siegal and Varley, 2002). A similar result was found with another man with severe aphasia, MR (Varley et al., 2001). On the basis of these findings, it would appear that natural language sentences are not necessary to support theory of mind reasoning in the adult cognitive system.

A second set of experiments investigated whether the ability to link sentences together with connectives such as 'because', 'if . . . then' might be necessary for reasoning about the causes of events, for example, he broke his leg *because* the ladder slipped (Varley, 2002). Again, SA and MR participated in the study. Both men had to generate causes of both realistic and hypothetical events and complete a practical causal reasoning task. In the latter, SA and MR were presented with a machine that raised and lowered a small basket. The design of the machine was outlandishly complex in relation to its function. It had multiple parts consisting of various cogs, and drive shafts, and a number of decoy systems whose operation was immaterial to the raising and lowering of the basket. The participant observed the functioning of the machine and then he was blindfolded. The machine was then sabotaged and the participant was asked to identify the source of the failure. The sabotage could result in very visible faults, such as disconnection of a power lead, or could be subtler, such as disconnecting a cog from a drive shaft. Both participants could identify the location of the damage, and SA, not content to complete the task he had been set, also spontaneously introduced improvements into the original design. Both participants showed an ability to generate causes of both possible and improbable events. For example, faced with the improbable event of a baby knocking over a wall, using a sophisticated combination of drawing, gesture and writing of single words, SA systematically speculated on the properties of the wall (could it be made of Lego), the properties of the atmosphere (could the event occur on the moon where the atmosphere was thinner) and the baby (superhuman, kryptonite strength?).

In a third set of experiments, we examined the interrelationship between language and mathematics (Varley et al., 2005). Mathematics shares some characteristics with language. It is a rule-based symbolic system, with a lexicon of abstract symbols (digits, and signs representing the various mathematical operations) and a number of rules. For example, addition and multiplication are commutative operations in which the order of digits does not matter. However, subtraction and division are non-commutative and $7 - 3$ and $3 - 7$ or $25 \div 5$ and $5 \div 25$, result in very different outcomes, in the same way as 'the lion killed the man' and 'the man killed the lion' describe different events. A relationship between language and mathematics may also exist at a deeper level. Hauser et al. (2002a) suggest that both capacities derive from a common recursive mechanism that may be unique to the human mind. All normally developing and healthy adult humans have language, whilst mathematics is a cultural acquisition and, as the Pirahã people show, if you live in a culture with no tradition of mathematics, the ability will not develop. Perhaps then, the universal characteristics of natural language provide a template for the acquisition of other related symbolic-rule-based functions. If syntax-like operations in mathematics are in some way parasitic upon the grammatical mechanisms of language, then people with severe agrammatic aphasia might show syntactic mathematical impairments.

In a study involving three men with agrammatic aphasia (SA, SO and PR), we examined general mathematical abilities and performance on maths problems that involved sensitivity to syntactic features. All three were competent calculators. They were able to complete all basic mathematic operations and could add and subtract fractions such as $3/6 - 2/9$. On problems involving syntactic features, they performed well on non-commutative subtraction and division problems despite their failure on parallel reversible sentence structures in spoken and written language. Participants were given paired expressions in which the larger integer appeared in first position in half of the problems, producing a positive number result in subtraction and a whole number in division, and in second position in the remaining half, producing a negative result in subtraction and a fractional result in division (e.g. $59 - 13$; $13 - 59$; $60 \div 12$; $12 \div 60$). Similarly, they were sensitive to the structural features of embedded mathematical structures represented in problems with brackets (e.g. $(5 \times (6 + 2))$). Finally, they were able to use generative, recursive principles in maths that were not evident in their language production. For example, there is an infinite number of values between the numbers 1 and 2, and each participant was able to serially generate numbers in response to the instruction, 'write a number bigger than 1, but smaller than 2'.

These results indicated a clear dissociation between structural principles necessary for natural language and those of mathematics. These men with agrammatic aphasia were not agrammatic in mathematics, and the structural principles necessary for calculation were independent of those for natural language, at least in an adult cognitive system. This finding suggests new possibilities for intervention in language disorders. For example, if an individual retains structural knowledge in one symbolic system, can that insight be used to bootstrap or scaffold impaired performance in a second function? Hence, if somebody with severe agrammatic aphasia can no longer distinguish the difference between 'the man kills the lion' and 'the lion kills the man' but is able to calculate the results of '7 − 2' and '2 − 7', can this mathematical awareness be used to regain insight into sentence structure (Byrne and Varley, in preparation)?

These findings also shed light on a long-standing debate within aphasiology as to whether aphasia can also be viewed as a loss of ability to manipulate symbols more generally (or *asymbolia*). Henry Head (1926) suggested that aphasia was more than a language impairment. The evidence that some people with aphasia also have difficulties with calculation or understanding the categories and values represented within playing cards indicated that aphasia represented a generalized disturbance of manipulating symbols (Saygin et al., 2003). However, evidence of clear dissociation between maths and language suggests that the notion of aphasia as asymbolia cannot be sustained. One of the agrammatic calculators (SO) was a very competent mathematician prior to his stroke. In a follow-up study, we examined whether he retained an ability to solve algebraic problems. In particular, we compared his ability to solve algebraic expressions containing either solely numeric or solely abstract variables (i.e. $(5 \times 2 - 3 \times 2) \div 2 = ?$ and $(cb - ab) \div b = ?$). SO's performance on the two forms of problem was not significantly different and indicated a sophisticated ability to manipulate highly abstract symbolic representations (Klessinger et al., 2007).

Taken together, the results of these experiments provide little support for the cognitive view of language. In an adult, with an established cognitive architecture, it appears that sentences of natural language are not the medium for thinking certain forms of thought, and that the syntactic processes of mathematics are autonomous from those of language. Similarly, the evidence from the calculation and algebra studies provides no support for the claim that aphasia necessarily involves a loss of ability in other symbolic systems. But this does not entail that the cognitive view is flawed and unworthy of further theoretical or experimental exploration. First, although there is no evidence of language mediation in theory of mind, causal reasoning and maths, perhaps there are other cognitive domains for which language mediation will be crucial. Reorientation might be one area for fruitful research, given the findings of experiments on healthy adults and young children. Second, the question of the role of language in creating a capacity for certain forms of cognition cannot be answered by research into aphasia. Only research involving people with developmental disabilities of language can begin to address this question. Third, our investigations have addressed the role of grammar and sentences in thinking and reasoning but leave unanswered questions regarding the role of lexicon in creating distinctively human cognition.

The relationship between research into the cognitive abilities of people with language impairment and debates in cognitive science is not one-way. Although the evidence from pathologies of language can be used to illuminate complex questions within the cognitive sciences, there is also payback in terms of enhanced understanding of the cognitive implications of language impairment. Self-directed speech and private inner speech are powerful tools in supporting thinking and problem solving. Both are used to rehearse options or conduct simulations before committing to a particular course of action. Faced with a complex, multi-stepped problem, we can identify the sequence of stages necessary to move through to resolution. Self-directed speech is not evident in people with severe language impairment, and on the basis of the small amount of research conducted into the issue, inner speech appears also to be reduced. Even if natural language words and sentences are not the substance of thoughts, they might be very useful in scaffolding our thinking. If this is the case, people with language impairment, in addition to their interpersonal communicative disruption, also face a reduction in a valuable cognitive tool.

Finally, there is the possibility that investigations into the role of language in other cognitive domains might provide new insights into intervention. If it can be established that a domain of cognition that shares some of the characteristics of language is intact, then it might be possible to develop new therapies for both developmental and acquired language disorders. For example, it might be possible to bootstrap or piggyback an impaired language process onto a functionally similar process that is intact. Retained insight into non-commutative mathematical operations might allow the development, or regaining, of insight into the structural properties of a sentence. The language and thought debate might appear abstract and esoteric and a long way from the concerns of the language clinic, but setting your sights on a distant horizon can sometimes take you along new paths and lead to radically new knowledge.

Acknowledgements

I am grateful to SA, SO, MR and PR for their enthusiastic participation in the experimental work reported here. The research reported in this chapter is supported by an Economic and Social Research Council Professorial Fellowship.

References

Astington JW, Jenkins JM (1999) A longitudinal study of the relation between language and theory-of-mind development. Developmental Psychology 35: 1311–20.

Baddeley A (1986) Working Memory. Oxford: Oxford University Press.

Baldo JV, Dronkers NF, Wilkins D et al. (2005) Is problem solving dependent on language? Brain and Language 92: 240–50.

Berk L (1994) Why children talk to themselves. Scientific American November: 78–83.

Byrne C, Varley R (in preparation) Bootstrapping from mathematics to language: a novel intervention for syntactic comprehension difficulties in aphasia.

Carruthers P (1996) Language, Thought and Consciousness: An Essay in Philosophical Psychology. Cambridge: Cambridge University Press.

Conrad R (1971) The chronology of the development of covert speech in children. Developmental Psychology 5: 398–405.

Cromer RF (1991) Language and Thought in Normal and Handicapped Children. Oxford: Blackwell.

De Villiers JG, Pyers JE (2002) Complements to cognition: a longitudinal study of the relationship between complex syntax and false-belief-understanding. Cognitive Development 17: 1037–60.

Delazer M, Girelli L, Semenza C et al. (1999) Numerical skills and aphasia. Journal of the International Neuropsychological Society 5(3): 213–21.

Fodor J (1983) The Modularity of Mind. Cambridge, MA: MIT Press.

Gardner RA, Gardner BT (1969) Teaching sign language to a chimpanzee. Science 165: 664–72.

Gentner TQ, Fenn KM, Margoliash D et al. (2006) Recursive syntactic pattern learning by songbirds. Nature 440: 1204–7.

Goldin-Meadow S, Zheng M-Y (1998) Thought before language: the expression of motion events prior to the impact of a conventional language system. In: P Carruthers, J Boucher (eds), Language and Thought: Interdisciplinary Themes. Cambridge: Cambridge University Press.

Goodglass H, Denes G, Calderon M (1974) The absence of covert verbal mediation in aphasia. Cortex 10: 264–9.

Gordon P (2004) Numerical cognition without words: evidence from Amazonia. Science 306: 496–99.

Hauser MD, Chomsky N, Fitch WT (2002a) The faculty of language: what is it, who has it, and how did it evolve? Science 298: 1569–79.

Hauser MD, Weiss D, Marcus G (2002b) Rule learning by cotton-top tamarins. Cognition 86: B15–22.

Head H (1926) Aphasia and Kindred Disorders of Speech, Volumes 1 and 2. London: Cambridge University Press.

Heaton RK, Chelune GJ, Talley JL et al. (1993) Wisconsin Card Sorting Test. Odessa, TX: Psychological Assessment Resources.

Hermelin B, O'Connor N (1990) Factors and primes – a specific numerial ability. Psychological Medicine 20: 163–9.

Hermer-Vasquez L, Spelke E, Katsnelson A (1999). Sources of flexibility in human cognition; dual-task studies of space and language. Cognitive Psychology 39: 3–36.

Kaminski J, Call J, Fischer J (2004) Word learning in a domestic dog: evidence for 'fast mapping'. Science 304: 1682–3.

Kertesz A (1988) Cognitive function in severe aphasia. In: L Weiskrantz (ed.), Thought without Language. Oxford: Oxford University Press.

Klessinger N, Szczerbinski M, Varley R (2007) Algebra in a man with severe aphasia. Neuropsychologia 45: 1642–8.

Learmonth AE, Newcombe NS, Huttenlocher J (2001) Toddlers' use of metric information and landmarks to reorient. Journal of Experimental Child Psychology 80: 225–44.

Mithen S (1996) The Prehistory of the Mind. London: Thames & Hudson.

O'Connor N, Cowan R, Samella K (2000) Calendric calculation and intelligence. Intelligence 28: 31–48.

Pica P, Lemer C, Izard V et al. (2004) Exact and approximate arithmetic in an Amazonian indigene group. Science 306: 499–503.

Pinker S (1994) The Language Instinct. London: Allen Lane, Penguin Press.

Raby CR, Alexis DM, Dickinson A et al. (2007) Planning for the future by western scrub-jays. Nature 445: 919–21.

Raven J, Raven C, Court JH (1998) Standard Progressive Matrices. San Antonio, TX: Harcourt.

Santos LR, Nissen AG, Ferrugia JA (2006) Rhesus monkeys, *Macaca mulatta*, know what others can and cannot hear. Animal Behaviour 71: 1175–81.

Saygin AP, Dick F, Wilson SW et al. (2003) Neural resources for processing language and environmental sounds: evidence from aphasia. Brain 126: 928–45.

Schaller S (1995) A Man without Words. Berkeley: University of California Press.

Seyfarth RM, Cheney DL (1990) The assessment by vervet monkeys of their own and other species' alarm calls. Animal Behaviour 40: 754–64.

Siegal M, Varley R (2002) Neural systems involved in 'theory of mind'. Nature Reviews Neuroscience 3: 463–71.

Sovrano VA, Bisazza A, Vallortigara G (2003) Modularity as a fish (*Xenotoca eiseni*) views it: conjoining geometric and nongeometric information for spatial reorientation. Journal of Experimental Psychology 29(3): 199–210.

Terrace HS, Petitto LA, Sanders RJ et al. (1979) Can an ape create a sentence? Science 206: 891–902.

van der Lely H, Rosen S, McClelland A (1998) Evidence for a grammar-specific deficit in children. Current Biology 8: 1253–8.

Varley R (2002) Science without grammar: scientific reasoning in severe agrammatic aphasia. In: P Carruthers, S Stich, M Siegal (eds), The Cognitive Bases of Science. Cambridge: Cambridge University Press.

Varley R, Siegal M (2000) Evidence for cognition without grammar from causal reasoning and 'theory of mind' in an agrammatic aphasic patient. Current Biology 10: 723–6.

Varley R, Siegal M, Want SC (2001) Severe grammatical impairment does not preclude 'theory of mind'. Neurocase 7: 489–93.

Varley R, Klessinger N, Romanowski CAJ et al. (2005) Agrammatic but numerate. Proceedings of the National Academy of Sciences 102: 3519–24.

von Frisch K (1954) The Dancing Bees: An Account of the Life and Senses of the Honey Bee. London: Methuen.

Vygotsky L (1962) Thought and Language. Cambridge, MA: MIT Press.

Wechsler D (1981) Wechsler Adult Intelligence Scale – Revised. San Antonio, TX: The Psychological Corporation.

Whitehouse AJO, Maybery MT, Durkin K (2006) Inner speech impairments in autism. Journal of Child Psychology and Psychiatry 47: 855–65.

Winsler A, Naglieri J (2003) Overt and covert problem solving strategies: developmental trends in use, awareness, and relations with task performance in children aged 5 to 17. Child Development 74: 659–78.

CHAPTER 3

Aphasia therapy and Cognitive Neuropsychology: a promise still to be fulfilled?

JANE MARSHALL

Department of Language and Communication Science, City University

Introduction

Cognitive Neuropsychology began to make an impact on aphasia therapy in the 1980s. It promised many benefits (see Whitworth et al., 2005). The language processing models provided a clear (and reasonably simple) means of conceptualizing the stages involved in typical language tasks, such as producing and understanding single words. In so doing, they provided a framework against which the abilities of aphasic people could be investigated. Furthermore, carefully designed assessments were becoming available with which to probe those abilities (e.g. Kay et al., 1992). These enabled therapists to formulate hypotheses about which processing mechanisms were impaired or intact, and so helped determine targets for intervention.

There were further advantages. The approach stimulated a plethora of single-case studies, involving a detailed assessment of the person's difficulties, followed by the administration and evaluation of individually tailored therapy packages. For the practising clinician, these offered a rich new resource. Previous therapy studies, particularly those involving large-group designs, often failed to specify the treatment used. So, even if results were positive, clinicians were none the wiser about how they were achieved (see similar arguments in Howard, 1986 and Pring, 2004, 2005). The Cognitive Neuropsychological therapy studies were different. Here, the therapy descriptions provided the level of detail needed for replication (see Luzzatti et al., 2000 for a good example).

Language Disorders in Children and Adults: New Issues in Research and Practice.   Victoria Joffe, Madeline Cruice, Shula Chiat.
© 2008 John Wiley & Sons, Ltd. ISBN 978-0-470-51839-7

Cognitive Neuropsychology also introduced a different type of therapy evaluation. The processing models made it possible to predict the changes that should occur as a result of therapy, so motivating the selection of outcome measures. They also made it possible to identify control measures that were not predicted to change, for example, because they assessed components of the language system that were 'untouched' by the therapy tasks (see Byng and Coltheart, 1986 for an early example). This laid the foundations for experimental designs that gave therapy a fair chance of showing an effect, while also allowing researchers to speculate about the processing origins of that effect.

Well, it could not last. Quite soon after the appearance of Cognitive Neuropsychology, the first wave of party-poopers came along (e.g. Caramazza, 1989). They rightly argued that models of language processing are not models of remediation, and that processing 'diagnoses' did not, in themselves, prescribe the therapy. A key observation here was the fact that people with apparently similar impairments responded differently to the same therapy, for example, with some benefiting and others not (e.g. Hillis and Caramazza, 1994). There was the further difficulty that, even if therapy worked, it was often difficult to determine why or to know if our processing assumptions were correct (see Nickels and Best, 1996 for similar arguments). Unexpected therapy gains contributed to this problem. For example, Best and Nickels (2000) offered the same therapy to four people with anomia. The task involved selecting the first letter of a blocked word then responding to a phonemic cue generated from that letter by a computerized aid. Only one of the participants had the processing skills required for this task, in that he could reliably identify the first letters of words and benefit from phonological cues. Yet, surprisingly, all four showed effects of therapy. Findings like these suggest that the same therapy may work in different ways for different people, making it difficult to know how any task affects the processing system.

A number of commentators have suggested that the problem of explaining therapy is particularly acute in the case of box-and-arrow models, mainly because they are static (e.g. Shallice, 2000). This contrasts with connectionist models that have the capacity to learn. Indeed, there have been a number of computer simulations of rehabilitation involving such models (e.g. Plaut, 1996; Welbourne and Lambon-Ralph, 2005). Here, the model is first trained to perform a language function, such as reading aloud. The model is then 'lesioned' and retrained. Of interest is to what extent the model can re-acquire its original skills, and the effects of different variables on learning. These simulations enable us to experiment with therapy ideas without risking the recovery of our clients. Some have also produced suggestive findings. For example, Plaut (1996) found that training with atypical words resulted in better generalization than training with typical words. However, a major concern is whether such studies have much to say about real therapy with real people. Just because the models behave in a particular way is no guarantee that our clients will follow suit.

Many of the above arguments concern the theoretical relationship between processing models and therapy. Others are more purely practical, and these will be the focus of this chapter. One issue is whether Cognitive Neuropsychology has led to genuine therapeutic advances. A concern here is that a detailed and time-consuming assessment may be followed by a therapy that seems only thinly connected to the processing diagnosis, and which could equally have been generated by common sense. Let us apply this criticism to a recent study. Rapp (2005) worked with three people who had acquired dysgraphia. One was thought to have problems in accessing the Orthographic Output Lexicon, which stores written word forms, while the others had a deficit in the graphemic buffer, which retains accessed forms prior to their production. Despite their different impairments, the same therapy was attempted, largely consisting of spelling to dictation and delayed copying of the target words. This approach seemed vindicated by the fact that all three participants improved. Furthermore, the gains were congruent with the diagnoses, in that generalization to untreated words only occurred for those with buffer-level impairments. However, we are left with the nagging question of how much the Cognitive Neuropsychological analysis contributed to the intervention, given that the therapies ended up being the same.

A second concern is whether Cognitive Neuropsychological approaches are feasible in the routine clinical setting. There is contrary evidence here. On the one hand, we know that Cognitive Neuropsychological tests like the Psycholinguistic Assessment of Language Processing in Aphasia (PALPA) (Kay et al., 1992) are widely used in UK clinical practice (Katz et al., 2004). On the other hand, we know that provision for aphasic people in the United Kingdom is often so minimal that detailed investigation and therapy hardly seem possible. For example, Enderby and Petherham (2002) found that aphasic people across 11 health care sites received, on average, less than 7 hours contact time.

The problem of feasibility is exemplified by a quote from a recent Cognitive Neuropsychological therapy study:

> 'A comprehensive assessment of spelling . . . includes examination of spontaneous writing, written naming, writing to dictation, copying and oral spelling. It requires the use of controlled word lists that allow for independent evaluation of various lexical features, such as word frequency, imageability grammatical class, spelling regularity, word length, morphological complexity and, in addition, non word spelling. Assessment of oral spelling, typing, spelling with anagram letters and copying may also be indicated to discern whether central or peripheral spelling processes are impaired'
>
> Schmalzl and Nickels, 2006, pp. 4–5

Hard-pressed clinicians working within the time constraints of the modern National Health Service cannot possibly meet these requirements (even if convinced that they were justified). Yet, the problem is not confined to assessment. The treatments described in Cognitive Neuropsychological studies often involve new tasks and materials that are individualized for the client (see Robson et al., 1999 for an example). So even when such treatments are carefully described, replication will be hampered by the non-availability of these resources.

The third and perhaps most serious concern is that therapies based on Cognitive Neuropsychology do not pay sufficient attention to real-life goals. The argument here is that a focus on language processing models discourages thinking about how the client actually uses language, for example, in his or her family, social or working life. Instead, treatment goals become abstracted and model based. In line with this, the experimental measures often bear very little relation to language as it is actually used, examples being writing to dictation, lexical decision and picture naming.

This chapter will take each of these critiques in turn. It will argue that all either have been answered or could be with some modification to our practice. In so doing, it will attempt to show that Cognitive Neuropsychology can be applied in routine settings and in ways that pay serious attention to the real-life goals of our clients.

Emperor's new clothes?

Has Cognitive Neuropsychology injected anything new into the practice of aphasia therapy? In other words, is it possible to point to novel therapy techniques and approaches that seem genuinely indebted to the application of language processing models?

Well, I think that we can. An example is in the domain of sentence therapy. Sentence production models (e.g. Garrett, 1982) encouraged clinicians to think about the aspects of processing that underpin the surface form, such as the specification of verb–argument relationships. This stimulated new therapy approaches. One was 'mapping therapy', which focussed on how the meaning relations commanded by the verb are conveyed in sentence structures (e.g. see Jones, 1986; Byng, 1988). This therapy has been successfully replicated, in varying guises, both with single cases and small groups (see reviews in Marshall, 1995; Mitchum et al., 2000; Conroy et al., 2006). There is even evidence that it might be helpful for children with sentence-level problems (Bryan, 1997).

There have also been clear benefits for lexical treatments. For example, a number of studies use Cognitive Neuropsychological assessment to identify processing strengths that are then cunningly exploited in therapy. Take the familiar study by Nickels (1992) (and see Nickels, 1995). TC had global aphasia following a left middle cerebral artery stroke. He had fluent but highly anomic speech and impaired comprehension. Reading aloud was also difficult, with semantic errors. The ability to employ grapheme-to-phoneme conversion (GPC) as evidenced by non-word reading was very limited.

Two positive features emerged from testing. First, TC's spoken naming was responsive to phonological cues. Second, he could still write some words. These strengths offered a way into therapy. Nickels decided to focus on the training of GPC skills. On the face of it, this was an unlikely choice. However, her rationale was that if TC could pronounce written forms, or even just their first letter, this could provide a bridge to speech. In effect, Nickels was hoping that when faced with a word-finding block, TC might visualize the written word then apply a reading strategy to say that word.

A big part of the therapy involved the use of relay words. Every letter was linked to a personally selected relay word (so M was linked to a friend's name, Martin). TC was taught to segment the initial letter of his relay words and convert that into a phoneme (i.e. M converted into /m/). Further stages developed this into a cueing mechanism:

- Stage 1: link a written target word with the relay word (so 'map' is linked to Martin);
- Stage 2: use the relay word to generate a phonological cue (/m/); and
- Stage 3: use the phonological cue to say the target word.

The final component of therapy applied the cueing mechanism to naming. TC was shown a picture. If he could not think of its spoken name, he was encouraged to visualize the written word. He then had to think about the first letter of that word and convert it into a phoneme, so providing a phonological cue for naming.

Post-therapy testing suggested that therapy had been effective. There were significant gains in spoken naming, with scores improving from 12% correct pre-therapy to 62% correct post-therapy. Furthermore, these gains were well maintained, in that he achieved 58% correct in naming 5 months after therapy had ceased. Perhaps most encouraging is the suggestion that he was able to apply his self-cueing strategy to improve word retrieval in conversation.

The study of TC offers a good example of a novel therapy that was founded on Cognitive Neuropsychological analysis, and with results that seem to justify that analysis. It does, however, raise the second problem of feasibility. The very fact that therapy was so individualized begs the question of whether it could be used with other people (although see DePartz, 1986 for a similar case). Replicating the therapy in the routine setting would pose further practical problems, not only because of the number of sessions required, but also because of the need for carefully graded and individualized materials. Here, therefore, is a tantalizing therapy that is clearly described and apparently effective, yet still not readily transportable into practice.

Clinical feasibility

As already outlined, most Cognitive Neuropsychological therapy studies entail a phase of very detailed assessment, of perhaps 10 different tests,

followed by an individualized programme of therapy and evaluation. The
latter may call upon further new tasks and materials and a whole new
episode of testing. Not only does the administration of the programme
require considerable contact time, but there must also be a good deal of
'backroom work' on the part of the clinician to develop the tests and
materials. Put against the therapy regimes typically available in the United
Kingdom, this seems like a tall order. Clearly, if Cognitive Neuropsychological approaches are to be truly replicable, we need to move from these
pure, highly individualized, time-intensive approaches into the quick and
dirty realities of clinical practice. How can research get us there?

In the first stage, we still need the individual study. This develops the
therapy approach and offers some indication that it might be useful, at
least with the person tested. We then need to establish the broader applicability of the treatment. An ideal mechanism for this is the case-series
design, in which a group of people are given the same therapy, but their
results are analysed individually (see proposals in Howard, 2003).

Case-series studies can also be used to refine the assessment regime.
In effect, we should be asking, 'what are the minimal tests that we need
on which to base therapy decisions?' Ideally, prognostic tests that can
identify clients who are most likely to benefit should be included. Fillingham et al. (2006) explored the prognosticators for an errorless anomia
treatment by correlating results on pre-therapy background assessments
with the size of the therapy effect. Interestingly, they found that scores on
cognitive tests, such as the Wisconsin Card Sorting Test, were more predictive than language measures. An alternative approach offers brief, 'home-
opathic' doses of the therapy (in the form of cues), and then checks
whether the cueing effect is predictive of therapy outcomes. Best and colleagues (Best et al., 2002; Hickin et al., 2002) took this approach. Their
study involved eight people with aphasia, all of whom had word-finding
difficulties. The first stage explored each person's response to a range of
phonological and orthographic cues. This was followed by a treatment
study, in which the cue techniques were extended into therapy. All except
one of the participants showed a significant therapy effect, and the size of
this effect correlated with the original response to cues. This suggests that
a cueing assessment could be a helpful prognosticator for the described
treatment.

A further outcome from case-series studies should be a manual of the
therapy that can be made available to practising clinicians. For example,
this could include the hierarchy of therapy tasks, sets of stimuli, facilitation
techniques and indicators of when to progress. The manual could also
contain diagnostic and prognostic tests, with notes to guide interpretation
and measures to assess outcome.

Case-series studies can lay the foundation for the collection of Class 1
evidence. Here, a large group of participants is recruited, all of who meet
the selection criteria for the therapy. They are randomly allocated either
to an experimental group, which receives the manualized therapy, or to a

control group, which receives an alternative treatment or a no-treatment placebo. Pre- and post-therapy measures indicate whether the experimental therapy outperforms its competitors or the no-treatment condition.

The above programme of research would provide clinicians with:

- an economical assessment regime, which broadly identifies clients' strengths and weaknesses and indicates whether an individual is likely to benefit from a given therapy;
- manualized therapies, which can be taken off the shelf and either administered wholesale or adapted for individual needs (e.g. by including personalized stimuli); and
- evidence that the approaches are successful and therefore worth attempting in the clinic; initially, this may be restricted to single-case and case-series evidence; it could, however, be extended to Class 1 evidence.

These steps would help tackle the problem of feasibility. In particular, they would give clinicians the resources that they need to transport Cognitive Neuropsychogical therapies into practice.

Making a difference to everyday language

In their introduction to the PALPA, Kay et al. (1992) acknowledge that 'there is a substantial gap between the assessment of language processing as a mental activity and language used as a means of communication in everyday life' (p. 1). Such a gap lays open the possibility that a focus on language processing generates interventions that have floated away from the everyday language concerns of our clients.

The first point to make in response to this has been said before, but is worth saying again. The Cognitive Neuropsychological approach is just one aspect of what we do. The therapist will also be advising family and friends, developing compensatory strategies and helping the person deal with the psychological consequences of their stroke (see Lesser and Algar, 1995 for an example of how Cognitive Neuropsychology can be integrated with other therapy approaches). However, a potential objection still remains. Cognitive neuropsychological therapy may be only one aspect of a complex intervention, but we still need to demonstrate that it is a useful aspect that contributes to the person's well-being.

A further response argues that just because a therapy is founded on Cognitive Neuropsychological theory and employs rather abstract clinical tasks does not preclude functional consequences. The argument here is that if therapy changes a person's processing capacities, even in a small way, there should be benefits for their language use. However, Cognitive Neuropsychological therapy studies have been slow to provide us with evidence of this, mainly because they rarely use functional outcome measures.

So what progress has been made in this area? A number of studies *have* integrated functional objectives into their design, and have attempted to measure the effects of therapy on everyday language. An example is that of Hickin et al. (2007). Here, two people with aphasia received therapy, aiming to improve word production. The stimuli comprised 100 standard items, selected by the researchers, and 20 personal items, chosen by the participants. In the first phase of therapy, pictures of the items were presented for naming. If this was not possible, a series of phonological or orthographic cues were provided, which revealed increasing portions of the word form. An element of choice was also incorporated into the therapy (e.g. where the person had to select the first letter of a word from a choice of two) in the hope that this would increase the depth of processing. The second stage of therapy aimed to promote the communicative use of the 120 words. This employed more naturalistic tasks such as making shopping lists, reminiscing, telling anecdotes and holding conversations.

The outcome measures used by Hickin et al. aimed to find out not only whether therapy improved picture naming, but also whether there was a carry-over into an everyday language activity, in this case, conversation. In terms of picture naming, both participants improved significantly, although only one showed generalization to untreated words. The activity assessment involved analysing samples of pre- and post-therapy conversations. Encouragingly, one participant showed gains on this, in that the noun content of his conversational turns increased, and errors declined. Less encouragingly, there were no changes for the other participant. Interestingly, progress in conversation occurred only for the person who had achieved generalized picture-naming gains.

Another example of therapy with a functional focus is the study of RMM (Robson et al., 1998). RMM had severe jargon aphasia. Her speech was almost totally unintelligible, and apparently unmonitored; for example, she made no overt attempts at self-correction and displayed surprise (and even fury) when not understood. In some ways, writing was equally disadvantaged. For example, written naming was at floor. However, there were hints of some 'covert' access to orthography. When asked to copy words and non-words following a delay, RMM showed a significant advantage for words, suggesting that she was drawing on some preserved knowledge of written word forms. RMM also seemed aware of her writing errors and attempted to correct them, again pointing to some retained orthographic knowledge.

There were three stages of therapy. The first aimed to establish a functional vocabulary of written words (the list was drawn up in consultation with two of RMM's close friends). This phase used tasks that are thought to restore access to entries in the Orthographic Output Lexicon, including anagram sorting, delayed copying and written naming with a cue. The results of this therapy were typical for these types of treatments: words that had been practised improved, while control words did not (assessment took the form of written picture naming). Everyday writing was not formally assessed. However, there was not even a glimmer that RMM was using her writing communicatively. For example, her friends reported that she never attempted to resolve communication breakdowns by writing her practised words.

The second and third phases of therapy attempted to promote the *use* of writing. Further naming tasks aimed to expand the vocabulary of words that could be written, but these were now integrated with tasks that required RMM to write her practised words for communicative purposes. Examples were responding to conversational questions, conveying information about recent events in her life and labelling locations on a map of her local area. The therapists also invited RMM to link her practised words to messages that she might want to convey. Here, a message was shown to RMM, such as 'the laundry is late' (RMM lived in a nursing home and was plagued by laundry problems). RMM was then shown three pictures (e.g. shirt, shoes, walking stick), all of which illustrated practised words, but only one of which was linked to the message. She was asked to select the linked picture and write its label. Discussion emphasized the connection between the word and the message and how one could at least partially convey the other.

Assessments suggested that these phases of therapy increased the range of RMM's written vocabulary (although still only for practised words) and enabled her to use those words communicatively. For example, she was more able to use her written words to answer conversational questions. Her friends were even able to supply examples of everyday writing, for example, when RMM wrote 'hair' to indicate that the hairdresser had not called.

In the above studies, skills are first established through rather abstract clinical tasks, such as picture naming, and then generalized to functional use. An alternative model is proposed by Duchan and Black (2001). They argue that intervention should begin with a discussion about the 'life goals' of the client. In effect, we should find out what he or she hopes to achieve from any given episode of therapy, and we should do this in our earliest contacts with the client. The goal directs the focus of both assessment and therapy. So, assessment aims to identify the client's current level of attainment and why further progress is blocked. Reasons here may include language processing limitations and external barriers. For example, a client may be experiencing difficulties in conversation because of an auditory comprehension impairment, and because his conversational partners are using language that is too complex for his processing capacities. Therapy then attempts to remove, or at least lower, the barriers.

The proposal of Duchan and Black is attractive not only because of its clinical applicability, but also because it potentially dismantles false divisions between 'functional'- and 'impairment'-centred approaches. Therapy is directed from the outset by a functional goal. Yet this does not preclude the use of model-driven thinking, both in the assessment and intervention phases. The proposal also helps with feasibility, particularly in the assessment phase. It argues that, rather than assessing the entire language system, clinicians should test areas that relate to the person's goal.

A recent therapy study took this approach (Panton and Marshall, 2008). 'Ray' had aphasia following a left hemisphere stroke. Despite problems in all language modalities, Ray's priority for therapy was writing. His goal was to develop note-writing skills, which were needed in his role as a political counsellor.

A note-taking assessment was developed that was consistent with his goal. This involved listening to and writing down tape-recorded messages. Figure 3.1 shows one of the messages used in the assessment and Ray's attempt to write it down.

Ray's difficulties with this task were obvious, particularly with the longer words (such as 'compensation', 'disciplinary' and 'committee'). There was some evidence that he was using strategies (such as the abbreviation IT for Industrial Tribunal). However, there were also aspects that were not very strategic, such as the needless repetition of 'Michael' and the apparent attempt to write down the greeting. Ray also seemed to grind up on problematic words (coN, com and comm were repeated attempts to write 'committee') rather than moving on or substituting these.

Further assessments aimed to uncover the processing origins of Ray's writing difficulties. These involved four, fairly brief, writing-to-dictation tasks using controlled word lists. Results suggested that Ray's problems lay primarily in his Orthographic Buffer. The signs of this impairment were:

- a significant influence of word length on writing, but not of frequency or imageability;

'Hi Ray Its Michael Brown here. Thank you for your correspondence and enclosures about the tribunal. I'd like to get your permission to set up a committee to talk about the disciplinary hearing. We need to arrange the agenda and talk about possible compensation. Can you call my mobile phone and suggest a time that would be good for you. My number is 07942 9111321.'

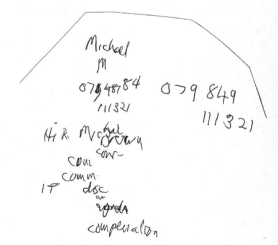

Figure 3.1 Message used in the note-taking assessment and Ray's attempt to record it.

- a characteristic error pattern, involving letter deletions, substitutions, additions and transpositions; these errors show that the word has been accessed, but with only hazy and possibly fading information about the spelling; and
- word position effects, with errors typically occurring in medial positions.

Therapy consisted of 12 1-hour sessions, which reflected the typical regime available in Ray's NHS setting. It was two-pronged. One aspect attempted to remediate the buffer impairment. Sixty words were identified, relating to Ray's home and working life. Thirty of these were included in therapy, and 30 acted as untreated controls. The therapy tasks aimed to stabilize the spelling of the treated words and were influenced by previous accounts of buffer-level treatments (e.g. Rapp and Kane, 2002; Raymer et al., 2003). These included copying the target words, copying the words after a delay, spelling words from letter-by-letter dictation and completing partially obscured words. Ray was encouraged to segment words into syllables prior to spelling, in the hope that this would reduce the stress on buffer storage. He was also asked to check his responses for errors and, where necessary, attempt correction. These tasks were carried out twice a week with the clinician, with intervening worksheets that Ray completed at home.

The second aspect of therapy aimed to develop note-writing strategies. The main therapy task involved listening to messages and writing down the key information (different messages were used in assessment and therapy). Prior to attempting the task, Ray and the therapist discussed strategies that he could use, for example:

- not attempting to write everything down, but only key words;
- using abbreviations;
- using symbols;
- replacing long/difficult words with simpler ones; and
- attempting to produce a recognizable attempt at the word, without necessarily achieving the correct spelling.

After writing down each message, Ray and the therapist would discuss which strategies he had used and whether he had been effective in recording the information.

Therapy was evaluated by re-administering the note-taking assessment. This showed that Ray was able to write far more correct words after therapy than before, and make more effective use of strategies such as abbreviation and word substitution. Importantly, these gains made his notes more comprehensible to neutral judges. Ray also improved on a second evaluation task, in which he was asked to spell the 60 treatment and control words to dictation. This pointed to some improvement in buffer functioning.

This study shows that applying Cognitive Neuropsychological principles to therapy is entirely compatible with a functional approach. Crucially, this was possible because intervention was driven from the outset by the client's goal. The researchers did not aim to find out which parts of Ray's system were failing and then try to correct those parts. Rather, the starting place was to discuss with Ray what he wanted to target in therapy. The Cognitive Neuropsychological analysis then explored why Ray could not achieve his goal, and what processing changes might bring him closer to its attainment.

Conclusions

I have argued that Cognitive Neuropsychology has made, and will continue to make, a genuine contribution to the practice of aphasia therapy. We do, however, need to help clinicians apply Cognitive Neuropsychological therapies in their setting. In order to do this, we need to supplement single-case studies with designs that test 'manualized' approaches with groups of individuals. These designs also need to prune the assessment stage, so that clinicians can rapidly identify a person's processing profile and link that profile to a therapy.

I have also argued that we need to provide more evidence that Cognitive Neuropsychological approaches can facilitate everyday language activities. I have suggested that this requires a model of intervention that is driven from the outset by the person's life goals. This model will ensure that our assessments are directed towards the areas of language that most concern the individual. It also makes it likely that we will be integrating processing therapy with practical and strategic tasks.

Some readers may spot a seeming contradiction here. On the one hand, I am arguing for 'quick and dirty' techniques, whereby the clinicians can carry out some reasonably constrained investigations and, on the basis of the findings, select a package of off-the-shelf therapy. On the other hand, I am arguing for the investigation of necessarily individualized life goals and the integration of a personally tailored programme of Cognitive Neuropsychological therapy and functional strategies.

I do not, in fact, think that there is a contradiction. Therapy should always address the priorities and goals of the individual, and so will always be personally planned. Yet, within this, the clinician should be able to call upon ready-made techniques to investigate and treat the processing impairment. So, for example, having identified that writing is a goal, the clinician should be able to turn to a package of assessments and interpretive notes to explore the writing impairment. There should also be a manual of writing therapies from which the clinician can select the approach that most closely addresses that impairment. Of course, he or she may still tailor the approach for the particular client, for example, by working on a personally relevant vocabulary or by selecting the tasks and cues that the individual finds most helpful. He or she will probably also integrate this therapy with strategies and environmental modifications that tackle the other barriers faced by the individual.

Do the themes raised in this chapter apply to kids? It seems to me that the need for time efficiency is even greater in the developmental domain. For example, children are unlikely to be tolerant of extensive testing. We might also wonder whether such testing will reveal the kind of clear-cut patterns that can emerge with adults. A number of acquired cases have shown remarkably 'pure' impairments that can be localized to very specific domains of the model (see Francis et al., 2001 for an example). Such findings seem improbable with kids. Here, impairments are impacting upon a developmental system, and so are likely to have wide-reaching consequences. Therefore, even if we test until the cows come home, we may not get very emphatic data. Rather, clinicians need guidance about economical assessment that will provide them with enough insight to progress into therapy. Similarly, the need for functional and goal-driven approaches is just as strong for children as it is for adults. As with adults, we need to be clear about what language gains would make a difference for the child and drive our assessment and therapy from that starting point.

Finally, I think that children present us with a real opportunity. As stated at the beginning of this chapter, we still have very limited understanding about how therapy affects the operation of the language system. Observing the effects of carefully targeted therapy with both adults and children might help us here, since this allows us to explore the possibilities of change for both a 'fixed' and a developing system. We can also see whether treatments that have been helpful for adults have comparable benefits with children. If they do, we might be onto something.

References

Best W, Nickels L (2000) From theory to therapy in aphasia: where are we now and where to next? Neuropsychological Rehabilitation 10: 231–47.

Best W, Herbert R, Hickin J et al. (2002) Phonological and orthographic facilitation of word retrieval in aphasia: immediate and delayed effects. Aphasiology 16: 151–68.

Bryan A (1997) Colourful semantics. In: S Chiat, J Law, J Marshall (eds), Language Disorders in Children and Adults. London: Whurr, pp. 143–61.

Byng S (1988) Sentence processing deficits: theory and therapy. Cognitive Neuropsychology 5: 629–76.

Byng S, Coltheart M (1986) Aphasia therapy research: methodological requirements and illustrative results. In: E Hjelmquist, L-G Nilssen (eds), Communication and Handicap: Aspects of Psychological Handicap and Technical Aids. North Holland: Elsevier, pp. 191–213.

Caramazza A (1989) Cognitive neuropsychology and remediation: an unfulfilled promise? In: X Seron G, Deloche (eds), Cognitive Neuropsychology and Cognitive Rehabilitation. Hillsdale, NJ: Lawrence Erlbaum Associates, pp. 383–98.

Conroy P, Sage K, Lambon-Ralph M (2006) Towards theory driven therapies for aphasic verb impairments: a review of current theory and practice. Aphasiology 20: 1159–85.

De Partz M-P (1986) Re-education of a deep dyslexic patient: rationale of the method and results. Cognitive Neuropsychology 3: 149–77.

Duchan J, Black M (2001) Progressing towards life goals: a person centred approach to therapy. Topics in Language Disorders 21: 37–49.

Enderby J, Petherham B (2002) Has aphasia therapy been swallowed up? Clinical Rehabilitation 16: 604–8.

Fillingham J, Sage K, Lambon-Ralph M (2006) The treatment of anomia using errorless learning. Neuropsychological Rehabilitation 16: 129–54.

Francis D, Riddoch M, Humphreys G (2001) Cognitive rehabilitation of word meaning deafness. Aphasiology 15: 749–66.

Garrett M (1982) Production of speech: observations from normal and patho-logical language use. In: A Ellis (ed.), Normality and Pathology in Cognitive Functions. London: Academic Press, pp. 19–76.

Hickin J, Best W, Herbert R, Howard D, Osborne F. (2002) Phonological Therapy for Word Finding Difficulties: A Re-evaluation. Aphasiology 16: 981–99.

Hickin J, Herbert R, Best W et al. (2007) Lexical and functionally based treatment: effects on word retrieval and conversation. In: S Byng, J Duchan, C Pound (eds), The Aphasia Therapy File, Volume 2. Hove: Psychology Press, pp. 69–82.

Hillis A, Caramazza A (1994) Theories of lexical processing and rehabilitation of lexical deficits. In: MJ Riddoch, GW Humphreys (eds), Cognitive Neuropsychology and Cognitive Rehabilitation. Hove: Lawrence Erlbaum Associates, pp. 449–84.

Howard D (1986) Beyond randomised controlled trials: the case for effective case studies on the effects of treatment in aphasia. British Journal of Disorders of Communication 21: 89–102.

Howard D (2003) Single cases, group studies and case series in aphasia therapy. In: I Papathanasiou, R De Bleser (eds), The Sciences of Aphasia: From Therapy to Theory. Oxford: Pergamon Press, pp. 245–58.

Jones E (1986) Building the foundations for sentence production in a non-fluent aphasic. British Journal of Disorders of Communication 21: 63–82.

Katz R, Hallowell B, Code C et al. (2004) A multinational comparison of aphasia management practice. International Journal of Language and Communication Disorders 35: 303–14.

Kay J, Lesser R, Coltheart M (1992) The Psycholinguistic Assessment of Language Processing in Aphasia. Hove: Psychology Press.

Lesser R, Algar L (1995) Towards combining the cognitive neuropsychological and the pragmatic in aphasia therapy. Neuropsychological Rehabilitation 5: 67–96.

Luzzatti C, Colombo C, Frustaci M et al. (2000) Rehabilitation of spelling along the sub-word-level routine. Neuropsychological Rehabilitation 10: 249–78.

Marshall J (1995) The mapping hypothesis and aphasia therapy. Aphasiology 9: 517–39.

Mitchum C, Greenwald M, Berndt R-S (2000) Cognitive treatments of sentence processing disorders: what have we learned? Neuropsychological Rehabilitation 10: 311–36.

Nickels L (1992) The autocue? Self-generated phonemic cues in the treatment of a disorder of reading and naming. Cognitive Neuropsychology 9: 155–82.

Nickels L (1995) Reading too little into reading? Strategies in the rehabilitation of acquired dyslexia. European Journal of Disorders of Communication 30: 37–50.

Nickels L, Best W (1996) Therapy for naming disorders (Part 1): principles, puzzles and progress. Aphasiology 10: 21–47.

Panton A, Marshall J (2008) Improving spelling and everyday writing after a CVA: a single case therapy study. Aphasiology 22(2): 164–83.

Plaut D (1996) Relearning after damage in connectionist networks: towards a theory of rehabilitation. Brain and Language 52: 25–82.

Pring T (2004) Ask a silly question: two decades of troublesome trials. International Journal of Language and Communication Disorders 39: 285–302.

Pring T (2005) Research Methods in Communication Disorders. London: Whurr.

Rapp B (2005) The relationship between treatment outcomes and the underlying cognitive deficit: evidence from the remediation of acquired dysgraphia. Aphasiology 19: 994–1008.

Rapp B, Kane A (2002) Remediation of deficits affecting different components of the spelling process. Aphasiology 16: 439–54.

Raymer A, Cudworth C, Haley M (2003) Spelling treatment for an individual with dysgraphia: analysis of generalisation to untrained words. Aphasiology 17: 607–24.

Robson J, Pring T, Marshall J et al. (1998) Written communication in undifferentiated jargon aphasia: a therapy study. International Journal of Language and Communication Disorders 33: 305–28.

Robson J, Marshall J, Pring T et al. (1999) Phonological naming therapy in jargon aphasia: positive but paradoxical effects. The Journal of the International Neuropsychological Society 4: 675–86.

Schmalzl L, Nickels L (2006) Treatment of irregular word spelling in acquired dsygraphia: selective benefit from visual mnemonics. Neuropsychological Rehabilitation 16: 1–37.

Shallice T (2000) Cognitive neuropsychology and rehabilitation: is pessimism justified? Neuropsychological Rehabilitation 10: 209–17.

Welbourne S, Lambon-Ralph M (2005) Using computational, parallel distributed processing networks to model rehabilitation in patients with acquired dyslexia: an initial investigation. Aphasiology 19: 789–806.

Whitworth A, Webster J, Howard D (2005) A Cognitive Neuropsychological Approach to Assessment and Intervention in Aphasia. Hove: Psychology Press.

CHAPTER 4

Speech-language therapy and evidence-based practice

BARBARA DODD

Department of Language and Communication Science, City University, and Perinatal Research Centre, University of Queensland

Introduction

Evidence-based practice has become a crucial issue for all health and social care professions. It has the potential to improve intervention for people with communication disorders, increase resources for services and enhance perception of the profession. If that potential is to be realized, however, the profession of speech-language therapy needs to consider the best ways to provide evidence proving efficacy. The methodologies developed to evaluate other health professions may not always be appropriate. The ability to communicate is complex, integrating anatomical, physiological, cognitive, linguistic and psychological elements. Consequently, clinical intervention in speech-language therapy is multifaceted and complicated. Clinicians need to integrate and apply theory from medicine, education, psychology and linguistics, as well as speech-language pathology. The available research literature, however, reflects the professions' relatively limited research tradition. There are large gaps in our knowledge base.

This chapter will argue that the need to demonstrate that practice in speech-language therapy is based on evidence is beyond dispute. For example, the ability to demonstrate the clinical benefit of intervention is increasingly necessary to secure a share of available health resources (Murcott, 2005). How best to provide valid evidence, however, requires debate. The assumptions inherent in definitions of evidence-based practice need to be examined in the context of speech-language therapy. Further, research methodologies that generate valid evidence are likely to

Language Disorders in Children and Adults: New Issues in Research and Practice. Victoria Joffe, Madeline Cruice, Shula Chiat.
© 2008 John Wiley & Sons, Ltd. ISBN 978-0-470-51839-7

differ according to the stage of development of a profession's knowledge base, the types of impairments targeted in intervention and the types of intervention implemented. That is, while the concept provides opportunities for speech-language therapy, the profession should have reservations about accepting a medical model of evidence-based practice.

Consequently, this chapter will focus on two important issues:

- What type of research questions should be asked in speech-language therapy?
- What clinical research methodologies are appropriate to establish the clinical evidence base in speech-language therapy?

Defining evidence-based practice

Justice (2006), in the introduction to a new journal, stated that the following types of knowledge are essential for evidence-based practice in speech-language therapy: high-quality research studies and systematic reviews in the scientific literature; clinical expertise that reflects theoretical knowledge and clinical experience; client preferences; and institutional norms and policies that affect clinical decision making. The most widely cited definition of evidence-based practice, however, focuses on research evidence. Evidence-based practice is 'the conscientious, explicit and judicious use of current best evidence in making decisions about the care of individual patients' (Sackett et al., 1997, p. 2).

Other definitions have different emphases. For example, the American Speech-Language-Hearing Association (ASHA) placed individual clinician's measurement of the outcome of their intervention at the centre of evidence-based practice, although their definition also stresses the importance of research evidence. They stated that the professional role of speech-language therapists is to 'Participate in outcomes measurement activities and use data to guide clinical decision making and determine effectiveness of services provided in accordance with the principles of evidence-based practice' (ASHA, 2001, I-29). This statement recognizes that the knowledge base in speech-language therapy does not yet allow clinicians to rely on the research literature to identify best practice for all populations served.

The research literature in speech-language therapy

The assumption that relevant, high-quality research exists to support best practice in speech-language therapy is often not true. The profession is relatively young, and it has a short research tradition compared with more established health professions like medicine. Nevertheless, only two types of literature are specified as providing valid evidence: randomized control trials and systematic reviews. Randomized control trials are considered the gold standard for evaluating clinical interventions across health service provision (Reilly et al., 2004). In an ideal randomized control trial, clients are randomly allocated to treatment and non-treatment groups and outcome compared using double-blind assessment. Double blinding means that neither the assessing clinician nor the client has any idea if they have received intervention.

The paradigm has its strengths for some types of intervention in medicine, such as drug trials. For example, a new drug regime using antibiotics for the treatment of stomach ulcers was developed in the 1980s (Marshall and Warren, 1983). Stomach ulcers can be accurately diagnosed because they can be seen. The administration of the treatment, as long as clients comply with swallowing the pills appropriately, can be accurately measured in terms of the drug's content and amount. That is, the researchers evaluating the benefits of the drug regime have a homogeneous client population, half of whom receive exactly the same treatment and half who are given placebos. The outcome is fairly immediate and measured by whether or not the ulcer heals. The design is made stronger because clients do not know if they have received the drug or the placebo and nor does the clinician who is assessing whether the ulcer has healed. The randomized control trial provides a simple, straightforward, strong measure of efficacy of a single, known treatment for a specific, easily diagnosed physiological condition.

While there are some exceptions, in general, there are problems implementing randomized control trials in speech-language therapy. Speech-language therapy usually deals with developmental and acquired communication disorders of unspecified aetiology using a wide range of intervention techniques that are often untested by research in varying service delivery contexts. Outcome of intervention can be measured in many different ways over varying periods of time post-therapy. Randomized control trials are not easily adapted to take account of a number of factors intrinsic to the practice of speech-language therapy. Some of the most important factors are now examined in more detail.

The population

People with communication disorders are a heterogeneous group, and heterogeneity within diagnostic categories poses enormous problems for research into treatment outcomes (Pring, 2004). Causal factors, maintenance factors, symptomatology and response to a specific treatment approach differ, especially for diagnostic categories such as aphasia or developmental language disorders. Communication is such a complex behaviour, it is consequently often difficult to predict outcome of a specific treatment. Clients with communication disorders are not passive recipients of a drug. Motivation, carer support and other environmental factors such as schooling and living conditions affect response to therapy. One important lesson to emerge from research into evidence-based practice in speech-language therapy so far is that most positive randomized control trial findings are for studies of well-defined, homogeneous diagnostic groups such as dysfluency, voice and acquired motor disorders (Pring, 2004).

The treatment

Pring (2004, p. 291) argued that 'the problem of choosing which treatment approach to adopt is daunting because, so far, there is only emerging evidence about which therapeutic approach should be used with specific types of disorder' defined in terms of symptomatology. The inadequate knowledge base on the effectiveness of clinical interventions leads to student speech-language therapists despairing of ever being taught 'how to' treat specific disorders and clinicians implementing a 'one-size-fits-all' approach to diagnostic categories that include disparate populations of communication disorder (e.g. aphasia, developmental language disorder). Currently, randomized control trials of service provision where the intervention is unspecified (e.g. 'tabletop activities'; Glogowska et al., 2000) not only usually provide negative findings, but they also fail to evaluate an intervention and therefore add nothing to the knowledge base.

Double blinding

Double blinding is rarely possible in research designs for speech-language therapy, although the use of a single-blind strategy (reassessment by a 'blind' clinician) can strengthen outcomes research. An alternative approach is to compare two intervention approaches in a crossover design. For example, Crosbie et al. (2005) compared two approaches for children with phonological disorders. The children were randomly allocated to two groups, half receiving 16, 30-minute sessions of phonological contrast therapy first, and half the same dosage of core vocabulary therapy. After a 4-week break, they then received the other intervention. This design not only allowed comparison of two different intervention approaches, but comparison of rate of improvement according to type of phonological disorder for each treatment approach.

Outcome measures

Outcome measures pose a particularly thorny difficulty for research in speech-language therapy because how and when outcome is measured affects results. Two metrics for describing the same language ability can provide different findings. For example, when Wandschneider et al. (submitted) compared the narrative samples of children born premature with that of controls, the two groups did not differ when the sample was segmented by T-units (i.e. independent clause and any attached dependent clauses), but they did when mean length of ulterance was calculated, because the second measure includes mazes (false starts, self-corrections, repetitions, etc.). Apart from the difficulty posed by choices for description of language behaviour, researchers must choose between measuring whether clients have acquired the intervention target, increased general language competence on standardized assessments, generalized intervention targets to functional communication, or have enhanced functional communication.

Another research decision concerns whether outcome measures should be done immediately post-therapy or at follow-up over months or years. For example, Nancollis et al. (2005) found that a pre-school intervention program focusing on phonological awareness successfully taught the treated group onset-rime skills. The reason for targeting phonological awareness was that it is a well-accepted precursor for literacy. The advantage, however, failed to positively influence literacy abilities 3 years later, despite maintenance of enhanced onset-rime time abilities. This finding raises the question of how efficacy and efficiency should be evaluated. Outcomes in speech-language therapy are more complicated than judging whether a drug has effectively treated a physiological condition.

It was for reasons like these that Mobley (2000) argued that randomized control trials were 'totally inappropriate' for speech-language therapy. The problems of implementing randomized control trials in speech-language therapy are demonstrated by studies reporting negative findings (e.g. Glogowska et al., 2000) that are often published in high-profile medical journals that affect clinician morale, perception of speech-language therapy services and policy decisions about the allocation of resources. Pring's (2004, p. 292) critique concluded that, given the current stage of development of speech-language therapy's knowledge base, randomized control trials studies of therapy provision 'are studies of a well intentioned lottery in which different, unproven treatments are offered to clients with different disorders'.

It is not surprising, then, that systematic reviews and meta-analyses of evidence-based practice in speech-language therapy report rather discouraging findings (e.g. Law et al., 2004). Systematic reviews summarize the available literature on a specific clinical issue where the methodology used provided unbiased results, determined by the use of explicit inclusion and exclusion criteria and precise statistical methodologies. Bernstein Ratner (2006) argued that the knowledge base derived from systematic reviews of available clinical interventions in speech-language therapy is not only often incomplete, it may be wrong and is certainly biased, for the following reasons. Clinical research reporting negative findings is very difficult to publish, biasing the literature towards positive results. Further, for research studies to be published, participants must have 'pure disorders' that do not necessarily reflect a real-life clinical population. For example, in a study on children with speech disorder, children who have a co-morbid language difficulty (at least one-third of the population) should be excluded (Broomfield and Dodd, 2004). That is, the available best-practice evidence may not have been gathered on populations typical of clinicians' caseloads. Bias is also introduced by the inclusion and exclusion criteria used in studies that allow admission of a paper to the evidence base (e.g. excluding studies that do not have double blinding or a no-treatment control group).

Most importantly, unlike those in medicine, systematic reviews of the speech-language therapy literature often amalgamates findings from reports that investigated different populations using different interventions. For example, one meta-analysis of children with speech disorder amalgamated findings from trials that had used between 6 and 80 hours of therapy, that occurred between once and three times a week, and used very different treatment approaches (i.e. articulation of individual speech sounds, auditory discrimination or teaching phonological contrasts) with children who had heterogeneous symptomatology (Law et al., 2004). It would be difficult, then, for clinicians to determine what should be the target in therapy for individual children and how therapy should be scheduled.

Research questions in evidence-based practice for speech-language therapy

The question of whether speech-language therapy 'works' (e.g. Glogowska et al., 2000) is too large, too vague and provides information that does not allow enhanced practice. Rather, the evidence base can only be built by asking a smaller, more specific question: which intervention approach (that specifies content, amount and service delivery) works best with a well-specified diagnostic group?

Bernstein Ratner (2006) poses three important clinical research questions. Is one treatment more cost-effective than another treatment? Is a particular treatment clinically cost-effective, as well as statistically significantly effective? In evaluating a particular intervention, how and why does it change communication behaviour, and who, precisely, will benefit from this intervention? These questions raise the issue of the role of clinicians in building the evidence base. One benefit of the current emphasis on evidence-based practice has been to blur the distinction between research and practice. Excellence in clinical research is probably best achieved by an interaction between practice and theory. Practice should motivate theory and it is the ultimate test of theory.

The following example of a single-case study treatment design, conducted by Franklin et al. (2002), illustrates this argument. MB, an 83-year-old woman suffered a middle cerebral artery infarction that resulted in aphasia and right hemiparesis. No difficulties were apparent in her comprehension of everyday speech 4 months later, but she had marked spoken and written expressive problems. Her spontaneous speech was described as showing 'many phonemic paraphasias as well as neologistic words and phrases' (Franklin et al., 2002, p. 1092). Few previous studies had investigated an acquired disorder of phonological production characterized by inconsistent phonological errors occurring on all tasks requiring spoken output, particularly those using longer words. MB was diagnosed with reproduction conduction aphasia (as opposed to repetition conduction aphasia, where single words are intact but imitation is impaired) because her comprehension was relatively unimpaired but she had difficulty producing single words.

A number of underlying deficits might explain MB's inconsistent speech errors, including representation of words' phonology at the lexical level or post-lexical impairment in phonological encoding for output. Franklin et al. (2002) hypothesized that the outcome of treatment would provide evidence about the nature of the deficit, as well as assessing the efficacy of a specific treatment approach. Twice-weekly 30-minute treatment sessions, carried out at home, focused on improving MB's self-monitoring. Phoneme discrimination was targeted in the first phase of therapy. MB had few difficulties mastering the tasks (e.g. spoken-to-written phoneme matching). The second phase of treatment involved three stages, where MB first judged her clinician's word production accuracy in picture naming (e.g. harrot for carrot was an error trial), identified the phoneme error (the initial sound /h/) and correctly produced the picture name (carrot). Once she demonstrated her ability to perform this task, she was required to perform it on tape recordings of her own picture naming and then 'live' in single-word naming and words in sentences.

The outcome of treatment was significant improvement in all output modalities, including naming in single words and sentences, repetition, reading of real and non-words, and storytelling. Importantly, there was generalization from treated to untreated words. The effect of therapy was maintained at 4 months post-intervention. In-depth analyses comparing pre- and post-intervention data (including non-word production, word length effects, syllable structure frequency, lexical item specificity and phoneme generalization) indicated that MB's difficulties could be attributed to a post-lexical deficit in phonological encoding.

The example given demonstrates the interaction between theory and practice. A clinical case motivated treatment that clarified the nature of the deficit underlying the communication difficulty. The results informed theory concerning models of speech output. The results also provide the impetus for future research to test the clinical applicability of the finding across clients. Clinical practice, then, can contribute to the knowledge base, emphasizing the important role of clinicians' expertise for research building the evidence base.

Clinicians' expertise

Sackett et al. (1996) argued that application of research evidence might be inappropriate for individual cases and needed to be evaluated by clinicians who have specific expertise. The knowledge and skills listed by Hill and Romich (2002) for clinical expertise in augmentative and alternative communication are relevant for other areas of speech-language therapy. Their list of competencies included: knowledge and skills in using systematic observation, identification of outcome measures; skill in preparing, monitoring, documenting and analysing goals, objectives, procedures and progress; and the ability to evaluate levels of evidence, and to use that evidence to ensure more effective practice. These competencies are dependent upon clinicians' grasp of theory.

Clinicians need to understand each treatment's 'mechanism of action' to adequately evaluate differing interventions (Bernstein Ratner, 2006). Understanding how and why a particular therapy approach changes a client's communication behaviour also allows clinicians to adapt an intervention program to meet a specific client's needs. The role of speech-language therapists is not to implement a recipe, but to use available information to guide the clinical approach used with an individual client.

The expertise of clinicians varies, however, according to their education and work experience. Approaches to the education of speech-language pathologists, particularly clinical practice, have only recently become a focus of research and debate (e.g. Brumfitt, 2005). Didactic teaching approaches are being challenged by problem-based learning courses that provide skills in dealing with the rapidly advancing knowledge base and integrating new information into clinical management. Reported benefits of problem-based learning include better retention of knowledge and information and enhanced integration of theory to practice (Whitworth et al., 2004). The most recent meta-analysis to evaluate problem-based learning confirmed previous positive findings (Dochy et al., 2003). Education for speech-language therapists should not only teach information literacy, it should provide students with strategies for evaluating the growing knowledge base critically and implementing that knowledge clinically.

The nature and length of workplace experience is also crucial for the acquisition of clinical expertise. Employers' and speech and language therapy's professional associations' recognition of the need to build clinician expertise includes mentoring, continuing professional development courses and special interest groups. There is evidence, however, that formal continuing medical education workshops that are presented didactically do not change clinician behaviour (Davis et al., 1999). More effective methods involve active learning that addresses known barriers to learning and where there is one-to-one communication, small group learning and follow-up (Thomas et al., 2006). Recently reported difficulties in recruiting and retaining speech-language therapists serving the school-age population (Edgar and Rosa-Lugo, 2006) underline the need for research on how to best support clinicians so that expertise can be gained and maintained. That expertise can then be used to identify relevant research questions and generate clinical studies.

Methodology: assembling evidence in speech-language therapy

Pring (2004) argued that it was premature to rely on evidence from randomized control trials for best practice in speech-language therapy. He suggested that the development of evidence-based practice consists of a series of phases. For example, Robey and Schultz (1998) provide a five-phase model of clinical outcome research, where each phase must be successfully completed before researchers move on to the next step of the process:

1. Clinical reports and case studies of a treatment show a potential therapeutic effect with no harmful side effects, indicating that further investigation is worthwhile.
2. The treatment is refined in terms of population, exclusion criteria, outcome measures, amount of therapy and type of service delivery. The theory underpinning treatment should be explained.
3. Large-scale efficacy studies evaluate the treatment to provide stronger evidence of its worth. Efficacy studies test the therapy under optimal rather than clinical conditions that can provide more intensive therapy, more objective assessment of effects and a more homogeneous population. The treatment given is standard (e.g. involves training of clinicians) and described in detail, allowing replication by other researchers. While a randomized control trial design might be used, it is not obligatory.
4. Clinical effectiveness is evaluated within a speech-language therapy service. Effectiveness studies test the therapy under clinical conditions – that is, what happens in clinics as opposed to what happens in an efficacy trial that is most likely done by research teams in universities. The advantage of effectiveness studies is that the treatment approach is assessed in field conditions where the client base, delivery and content are determined by the context of the service.
5. Finally, effectiveness trials evaluate the cost benefit of the intervention and assess consumer satisfaction and the effects on clients' quality of life.

Some researchers consider intervention case studies to be the best design for gaining evidence evaluating practice in speech-language pathology (e.g. Whitworth et al., 2005). Case studies provide precise information about the client, the disorder, the intervention and the outcomes in terms of acquisition, generalization and maintenance, and provide a perspective on individual differences in symptomatology and varying response to therapy. Case studies allow more in-depth testing and provide better information about the course of intervention and the clinical decisions made. Reliability and validity can be provided by multiple single-case study designs, where a series of treatment cases test one intervention approach that is adapted for individual clients (Howard, 1986).

For some diagnostic categories, either no relevant research literature exists or it is contradictory, leading to clinicians' reliance on their own expertise and the opportunity to build the knowledge base by recording the outcome of intervention case studies systematically and without bias (O'Rourke, 1998). For example, Apel and Self (2003) report on a university-based speech and hearing clinic's move to evidence-based practice. Clinical educators measured the outcome of particular intervention approaches, entering results on a database that listed the purpose of the study, the clinical population concerned, the method used, the outcome measures chosen and the significance of the results, including effect size. As the database grows, it should provide evidence to support or refute the choice of clinical procedures for specific populations. Speech-language services might contribute to evidence-based practice by adopting a similar procedure (Apel and Self, 2003; Wambaurgh and Bain, 2002).

Conclusions

Two criticisms of evidence-based practice recur across the health care professions (e.g. O'Rouke, 1998). Some clinicians believe it consumes time and money that should be spent on client care; and evidence-based practice can be perceived as restricting those delivering care, preventing clinicians from adopting treatments of unproved efficacy even when their clinical experience suggests it may be beneficial. There is also emerging research that has identified methodological difficulties in randomized control trials done in the 'field' (Tognini et al., 1991; Huibers et al., 2004). Methodological problems involving recruitment of primary health clinicians and randomization and retention of clients have cast doubt on the validity of the findings of some randomized control trials. Finally, the current use of the approach should be debated, given the nature of communication disorders, the type of interventions available and the knowledge base in speech-language therapy.

Another generic difficulty with the medical model of evidence-based practice is that the concept of the disease model leads to the 'objectification' of a client, transforming the whole person into a set of physiological processes, one of which is malfunctioning, and is treated independently of an individual's personality, social status and life demands. For that reason, the World Health Organization changed its classification system of speech-language therapy to reflect the social context, including impairment, activity and participation. This classification has more universal applicability than the disease model (impairment, disability and handicap), which may be impracticable in many health care systems, particularly those of developing countries.

Nevertheless, the profession has no choice about evidence-based practice. Funding is already becoming dependent on the need to demonstrate that speech-language therapy intervention is effective and cost efficient. Apart from that imperative, there are good reasons to become involved in the development of evidence-based practice because it fits with:

- recommendations to make education in speech-language therapy more about problem-centred, lifelong learning and less about memorizing a static body of knowledge;
- continuing professional education encouraging more focused and productive reading and data handling;
- confidence in clinical decision making, by allowing easier justification of decisions to patients and managers and other professions;
- more rapid application of research findings to clinical practice;
- the purchaser–provider split: purchasers may insist on good evidence that a service or procedure has been proven to be effective, meaning that client advocacy is dependent upon research findings; and
- prioritizing explicit outcomes in intervention.

The profession of speech-language therapy needs to foster the next generation of dedicated clinical researchers whose work will allow a better understanding of the nature of specific communication disorders. Those research findings can underpin clinical research that should not just be an audit of whether speech-language therapy 'works'. Clinical research needs to address the gaps in knowledge by investigating the interacting factors of differential diagnosis, intervention content and service delivery models.

As yet, many diagnostic categories are too broad to allow the development of specific intervention approaches that are matched with well-defined sets of symptoms. Diagnostic categories with the highest incidence, like 'specific language impairment' or 'aphasia', combine populations that differ in severity, type of underlying deficit and symptomatology, including co-morbidity of different language abilities. Basic research is needed that would augment understanding of the types of impairment associated with subgroups within these generic categories. For example, the developmental disorder with the highest incidence is functional speech disorder, affecting 6.4% of all children (Broomfield and Dodd, 2004). Despite these children being well recognized as a heterogeneous group, research assessing intervention outcome most often uses only one approach (Law et al., 2004), including participants with marked differences in symptomatology. It is not surprising, then, that those studies provide contradictory findings since outcome for individual children will vary according to the nature of their speech impairment. Development of novel intervention approaches is dependent upon the investigation of the nature of the disorder, which allows differential diagnosis.

The content of intervention is not often well specified in studies measuring outcome (e.g. Glogowska et al., 2000; Law et al., 2004). Consequently, it is difficult to build knowledge about effective and efficient therapy approaches. Therapy for communication disorders is not like a pharmaceutical where the content and dosage can easily be measured with precision. Not only must descriptions of intervention specify targets and method of instruction, but measurement of whether what is taught is learned must also precede measurement of generalization to functional communication. It also seems important that the behaviour targeted is precisely defined. Targeting 'input' or 'motor skill' oversimplifies the complexity of the mental abilities involved in language comprehension and production. Acquisition of knowledge about what constitutes effective and efficient therapy is likely to be dependent on outcome studies targeting specific abilities (e.g. Franklin et al., 2002).

Finally, little is currently known about the effect of service delivery (Kahmi, 2006). Evidence-based practice in speech-language therapy requires in-depth understanding of the effects of agent of therapy, dosage, scheduling, age (for children) and stage (for acquired impairment) of client, and where intervention should best occur (e.g. classroom or clinic). Kahmi (2006) argued that these factors may be more important than content of therapy. While this seems unlikely, until research studies have determined the effect of different service delivery decisions, service provision is vulnerable. Policy makers can issue guidelines (e.g. amount of therapy allowed) that limit the effectiveness of intervention for speech and language impairment.

It seems obvious that these three factors – differential diagnosis, intervention content and service delivery – interact. All three aspects need to be considered in research into both developmental and acquired disorders to build knowledge of best practice. Accurate and specific differential diagnosis underpins advances in appropriate intervention, which must be delivered using appropriate dosage and scheduling by a skilled agent of intervention. If knowledge about one of these components is deficient, the outcome for the client is likely to be diminished. There would seem, then, to be an enormous need for both basic and applied research before speech-language therapy can be adequately evaluated in the same way as many medical treatments.

References

American Speech-Language-Hearing Association (ASHA) (2001) Scope of Practice in Speech-Language Therapy. I-29–I-32. Rockville, MD: ASHA.
Apel K, Self T (2003) Evidence-based guidelines: the marriage of research and clinical services. ASHA Leader 8(16): 6–7.

Bernstein Ratner N (2006) Evidence-based practice: an examination of its ramifications for the practice of speech-language pathology. Language, Speech and Hearing Services in Schools 37: 257–68.

Broomfield J, Dodd B (2004) Children with speech and language disability: caseload characteristics. International Journal of Language and Communication Disorders 39: 303–24.

Brumfitt S (2005) Innovations in Professional Education for Speech and Language Therapists. London: Whurr.

Crosbie S, Holm A, Dodd B (2005) Intervention for children with severe speech disorder: a comparison of two approaches. International Journal of Language and Communication Disorders 40: 467–91.

Davis D, O'Brien M, Freemantle N et al. (1999) Impact of formal continuing medical education: do conferences, workshops, rounds and other traditional continuing medical education activities change physicians behaviours and health care outcomes? Journal of American Medical Association 282: 867–74.

Dochy F, Segers M, Van den Bossche P et al. (2003) Effects of problem-based learning: a meta-analysis. Learning and Instruction 13: 533–68.

Edgar D, Rosa-Lugo L (2006) The critical shortage of speech-language pathologists in the public school setting: features of the work environment that affect recruitment and retention. Language Speech and Hearing Services in Schools 38: 31–46.

Franklin S, Buerk F, Howard D (2002) Generalised improvement in speech production for a subject with reproduction conduction aphasia. Aphasiology 16: 1087–114.

Glogowska M, Roulstone S, Enderby P et al. (2000) Randomised controlled trial of community based speech and language therapy in preschool children. British Medical Journal 321: 908–9.

Hill K, Romich B (2002) AAC evidence-based clinical practice: a model for success. AAC Institute Press 2(1): 1–6.

Howard D (1986) Beyond randomised control trials: the case for effective case studies of the effects of the treatment of aphasia. British Journal of Disorders of Communication 21: 89–102.

Huibers M, Bleijenberg G, Beurskens A et al. (2004) An alternative trial design to overcome validity and recruitment problems in primary care research. Family Practice 21: 213–18.

Justice L (2006) Evidence-based practice briefs: an introduction. EPB Briefs 1(1): 1–2.

Kahmi A (2006) Prologue: combining research and reason to make treatment decisions. Language Speech and Hearing Services in Schools 37: 255–7.

Law J, Garret Z, Nye C (2004) The effect of treatment for children with developmental speech and language delay/disorder: a meta-analysis. Journal of Speech, Language, and Hearing Research 47: 924–43.

Marshall BJ, Warren RR (1983) Unidentified curved bacilli in the stomach of patients with gastric and peptic ulceration. Lancet, 1: 1273–5.

Mobley P (2000) Research renaissance. The RCSLT Bulletin 7: 577.

Murcott T (2005) The Whole Story: Alternative Medicine on Trial? New York: Macmillan.

Nancollis A, Lawrie B, Dodd B (2005) Phonological awareness intervention and the acquisition of literacy skills in children from deprived social backgrounds. Language Speech and Hearing Services in Schools 36: 325–35.

O'Rourke A (1998) An Introduction to Evidence-Based Practice, http://www.web. edu/library (accessed 8 April 2008).

Pring T (2004) Ask a silly question: two decades of troublesome trials. International Journal of Language and Communication Disorders 3: 285–302.

Reilly S, Douglas J, Oates J (2004) Evidence Based Practice in Speech Therapy. London: Whurr.

Robey R, Schultz M (1998) A model for conducting clinical outcome research: an adaptation of the standard protocol for use in aphasiology. Aphasiology 12: 787–810.

Sackett D, Rosenberg W, Muir Gray J et al. (1996). Evidence based medicine: what it is and what it isn't. British Medical Journal 312: 71–2.

Sackett D, Richardson W, Rosenberg W et al. (1997) Evidence Based Medicine. London: Churchill-Livingstone.

Thomas D, Johnston B, Dunn K et al. (2006) Continuing medical education, continuing professional development and knowledge translation: improving care of older patients by practicing physicians. American Journal of Geriatrics 54: 1610–18.

Tognini G, Alli C, Avanzini F et al. (1991) Randomised clinical trials in general practice: lessons from a failure. British Medical Journal 303: 969–71.

Wambaugh JL, Bain B (2002) Using research in your clinical practice. ASHA Leader 1: 10–12.

Wandschneider S, Crosbie S, Hemsley G et al. (submitted). What t-units don't tell you. Journal of Speech, Language, and Hearing Research.

Whitworth A, Franklin S, Dodd B (2004) Case based problem solving for speech and language therapy students. In: S Brumfitt (ed.), Innovations in Professional Education for Speech and Language Therapists. London: Whurr, pp. 29–50.

Whitworth A, Webster J, Howard D (2005) A Cognitive Neuropsychological Approach to Assessment and Intervention in Aphasia: A Clinicians Guide. London: Psychology Press.

CHAPTER 5
Minding the gap between research and practice in developmental language disorders

VICTORIA JOFFE

Department of Language and Communication Science, City University, London

The journey of a thousand miles begins with one step.

Lao Tzu

Introduction

Evidence-based practice (EBP) in speech and language therapy has become the standard to which we all aspire, the Holy Grail for which we hanker. The profession has adopted the principle and is trying to apply it to its practice with children and adults in both health and education. Its importance may be judged from its prominence in recent articles, books and conferences (see, e.g. the publication by Reilly et al., 2004, a special journal edition of *Advances in Speech-Language Pathology* and the appearance of a new journal – *Evidence-Based Communication Assessment and Intervention*). Professional bodies in the United Kingdom and in many other countries internationally all make specific reference to the implementation of such practice in the work of speech and language therapists. The Royal College of Speech and Language Therapists (RCSLT), for example, has incorporated aims relating to EBP into its current strategic plan. Similarly, the American Speech and Hearing Association, the Canadian Association of Speech-Language Pathologists and Audiologists, and Speech Pathology Australia have integrated the principles of EBP into their policy documents and competency-based standards. In addition, the recent and continuing shift towards patient choice in medical care (shown

Language Disorders in Children and Adults: New Issues in Research and Practice. Victoria Joffe, Madeline Cruice, Shula Chiat.
© 2008 John Wiley & Sons, Ltd. ISBN 978-0-470-51839-7

in documents such as 'Commissioning a Patient-Led NHS' (Department of Health, 2005) and 'Payment by Results' (Deparment of Health 2006) increases the need for service providers to demonstrate their worth and show what they do actually works!

These trends are indicative of a health care system where health care providers need to demonstrate their effectiveness in order to be commissioned. Speech and language therapy services in both health and education increasingly have to justify their existence and show the efficacy and efficiency of proposed speech and language therapy in the context of other competing treatments (e.g. the Dore programme, an exercise-based treatment for dyslexia and attention-deficit hyperactivity disorder – see Bishop, 2007 for further discussion). Speech and language therapists are required to be more accountable to stakeholders and service users about the ways in which they work and the results they obtain. This increased accountability subsists in the context of an increasing demand for speech and language therapy services.

The challenge for EBP comes at a difficult time for speech and language therapy. The demands upon clinicians have increased, making it difficult for them to appraise their methods. The profession itself is relatively young and has not fully developed its evidence base (Pring, 2004, 2005; Reilly et al., 2004). Pring (2005) asserts that 'a shortage of research and a lack of research training have led to a profession that is uncritical of its knowledge base and unscientific in some of its practices' (p. 257). The diversity of client groups, heterogeneity within these groups and complexity of the disorders makes the adoption of generic treatments problematic (Johnson, 2006). Some have argued that randomized control trials (RCTs), the gold standard methodology of EBP, have little place in speech and language therapy (Bernstein Ratner, 2005, 2006; Johnston, 2005). A further obstacle is the alarming divide that appears to exist between clinicians and researchers. The clinician may have little time to read or apply research to their practice. In a survey exploring speech pathology practice in Australia, whilst 93% of respondents agreed that time allocated for reading the literature is important, 69% reported having no such allocated time in work to do so (Vallino-Napoli and Reilly, 2004). As a result, research findings may be perceived as being irrelevant to clinical practice (Threats, 2002).

This chapter explores what we mean by EBP and how it can be applied to the speech and language therapy profession, particularly in the area of developmental language disorders. It argues that we have a limited view of EBP, which makes its adoption in clinical practice almost impossible. A fuller understanding of its principles and possibilities can enhance its use in clinical decision making. Three school-based intervention studies are discussed as exemplars of intervention that can be implemented by clinicians, arguably within a routine working day in a clinical or educational context. These examples not only highlight some of the obstacles faced by clinical researchers in conducting research in the clinical domain, but also present the possibilities available to them in conducting EBP research. The responsibility of undertaking EBP lies with both the clinical researcher and practitioner. EBP encompasses research using a variety of research methodologies, all of which can be used by clinicians and researchers to build on our existing body of evidence. The question, however, that first needs to be asked is . . .

. . . What is EBP?

The current emphasis on EBP can be regarded as a step towards narrowing the gap between research and practice. However, what is meant by EBP and how well is it understood? The term itself brings to mind (besides white coats and rats) large research studies conducted under laboratory conditions with little relevance or application to clinical practice. It is unsurprising that clinicians feel that such research cannot contribute to their clinical practice. A consideration of what is meant by EBP in its broadest terms provides an opportunity for both the clinical researcher and clinician to conduct intervention studies to enhance the clinical decision-making process and add to the evidence base: a win-win situation for all – service users, service providers, clinicians and clinical researchers.

The popular and often quoted definition of EBP is that of Sackett et al.:

> Evidence based medicine is the conscientious, explicit, and judicious use of current best evidence in making decisions about the care of individual patients.
>
> Sackett et al., 1996, p. 71

The emphasis here is on the application of research evidence. The interpretation and adoption of evidence-based medicine to speech and language therapy has been deemed by many as challenging, and not always appropriate (see e.g. Dodd (Chapter 4 this volume) on the problems of accepting a medical model of EBP for speech and language therapy). At the root of this mistrust of EBP is the misconception that it is solely dependent on the use of RCTs, where clients are randomly assigned to treatment or no-treatment groups. Although Sackett et al. (1996) view RCTs as the gold standard for evaluating therapy, they also say that evidence-based medicine is not restricted to RCTs but involves finding the best and most appropriate evidence to inform clinical decision making. RCTs are not the only way to establish an evidence base. Indeed, their applicability to speech and language therapy has been questioned (Wertz, 2002; Johnston, 2005; see Dodd (Chapter 4 this volume) for further discussion on RCTs in speech and language therapy). There are a range of other methodologies that can be employed, and that are accessible to both clinicians and researchers. The incorporation of these different types of methodologies is important in building a solid evidence base in a relatively young profession with complex and diverse clinical populations. (Ylvisaker et al., 2002).

Robey and Schultz's (1998) five-phase clinical outcome research model, described in Dodd's chapter (Chapter 4, this volume), details the range of methodologies available. The role of clinical reports, single-case studies and small group studies (Phases 1 and 2) are appropriate in the initial testing and refining of therapies: a period of discovery and refinement. Single-subject experimental designs have been more widely used with adult client groups (see Marshall, Chapter 3 this volume, for further discussion) and are not as frequently employed in the developmental arena. It is at Phase 3 that RCTs are essential, testing the *efficacy* of the treatment, that is, testing the treatment that has already been trialled and refined in Phases 1 and 2, under ideal or optimal conditions. RCTs are studies where clients who meet strict subject selection criteria are randomly assigned to treatment and no-treatment conditions, and usually include large samples to ensure sufficient statistical power. If these studies yield positive results, research moves to Phases 4 and 5, where the *effectiveness* of the treatment is investigated, that is, testing the therapy under real-world, typical clinical conditions and exploring patient and carer satisfaction, as well as assessing its cost-effectiveness or overall *efficiency*. Large sample sizes are still required, but this can be achieved not only by RCTs, but also through single-case studies with multiple replications or single-group studies (Wertz, 2002). Whilst scales of the quality of evidence (e.g. American Academy of Neurology, 1994) typically deem RCTs to be Class 1 evidence, other methodologies are also included. Class 2 evidence includes well-designed observational studies with controls, which could include single-case studies; Class 3 evidence includes expert opinion and case reports. Some hierarchies even place well-controlled single-case designs with appropriate replications together with RCTs as 'Category 1' evidence (Chambless and Ollendick, 2001). Other frameworks (e.g. Birch and Davis Associates Inc., 1997) include systematic reviews (comprehensive review of the scientific literature on a specific clinical question) as the highest level of evidence. A meta-analysis is a type of systematic review that draws on quantitative methods to combine results from studies that meet specific methodological criteria in order to assess and critically appraise them (see, e.g. Law et al., 2003). Models such as Robey and Schultz's illustrate how different sources of evidence can *all* contribute to the evidence for therapy. They also show how clinicians can contribute to the evidence. They can carry out single-case studies and small group studies in Phases 1 and 2, and can participate in effectiveness studies in the later stages. Indeed, only RCTs of the efficacy of therapy may be beyond the working clinician. An integration of all methodologies, where appropriate, if robustly rationalized, rigorously conducted and objectively evaluated, is the best way forward for the profession to build a strong evidence base. This view is consistent with Sackett et al., who maintain that:

The practice of evidence based medicine means integrating individual clinical expertise with the best available external clinical evidence from systematic research. By individual clinical expertise we mean the proficiency and judgment that individual clinicians acquire through clinical experience and clinical practice. Good doctors use both individual clinical expertise and the best available external evidence, and neither alone is enough. Without clinical expertise, practice risks becoming tyrannised by evidence, for even excellent external evidence may be inapplicable to or inappropriate for an individual patient.

Sackett et al., 1996, p. 71

This emphasis on combining clinical expertise and research evidence is important and underlines the symbiotic roles of the clinician and clinical researcher in amassing a robust evidence base. The survival of the profession relies on the collaboration between clinicians and clinical researchers. But what of the continued claims that . . .

' . . . Clinicians are from Uranus, Researchers are from Pluto' (Meline and Paradiso, 2003, p. 275)

In reality, there appears to be an alarming gap between clinicians and researchers; for example, surveys in Australia and the United Kingdom have found gaps between research and practice in child speech disorders (McLeod and Baker, 2004; Joffe and Pring, 2008). Meline and Paradiso (2003) attribute this to the different environments in which they work and the different languages they speak. Clinicians rarely use the research literature as a starting point for clinical decision making, preferring to rely on subjective observations of the performance of previously treated clients (Threats, 2002). Kamhi (1999) characterizes clinicians as pragmatists swayed more by observable changes in their practice than by research findings. This view is supported by McLeod and Baker (2004), who found that many clinicians read little of the research literature. In turn, clinical researchers often produce research with little application to routine clinical practice. Most research findings are published in academic journals, with no certainty that their results will be disseminated to clinicians and transferred to clinical practice (Law, 2000). Yet, the responsibility for conducting and applying EBP lies with practitioners and researchers. According to the standards of proficiency for all speech and language therapists, set out by the Health Professions Council in the United Kingdom, all speech and language therapy graduates should be able to conduct EBP. To ensure that this is the case, we need to worry less about the planetary origins of clinicians and researchers and facilitate an easier collaboration between the two. As Kazdin (2001) notes, and as Robey and Schultz's model implies, there is a place for clinical hunches and intuitions. These are valuable starting points for clinical research that is ecologically valid and meaningful for clinical practice (see Johnson, 2006 for a useful tutorial on getting started in EBP for clinicians working in the area of child language disorders). Researchers in turn need ways of disseminating research evidence that is accessible to clinicians (Justice and Fey, 2004). It would be helpful for researchers to spend more time in clinical settings, and for clinicians to have more research training. Such collaborative practice is beneficial to both sides: clinicians have access to clients that researchers need, whilst researchers can share their research expertise. A commitment to EBP then becomes an advantageous conduit to reducing the gap between research and practice.

The evidence is not uniformly weak in speech and language therapy. In some areas, quite strong evidence is available, as in the case of the Lidcombe Programme for stuttering in children (see Jones et al., 2005 for details of an RCT). The area of child speech disorder also provides good evidence for some treatment methods with some groups of children, for example, the use of core vocabulary (Crosbie et al., 2005), the involvement of parents (Bowen and Cupples, 1999, 2004; Gibbard, 1994) and metaphonological therapy (Gillon, 2000, 2002; Hesketh et al., 2000). This evidence appears to translate well into clinical confidence. In a survey of speech and language therapy practice in child speech disorder in the United Kingdom, a majority of therapists (nearly 80%) reported feeling confident about selecting therapy, and a majority (60%) felt that there was good evidence for its effectiveness (Joffe and Pring, 2008). On the other hand, a substantial minority felt confident about their therapy choices despite being ambivalent about the evidence, suggesting that their confidence emanates from their clinical experience rather than research evidence and reinforces the presence of a gap between research and practice. This gap may arise because clinicians give research findings a low priority and have little time to read, as discussed above. It may also be a product of contradictory research findings in intervention studies, for example, in the conflicting outcomes reported by Gillon (2000) and Hesketh et al. (2000). Positive outcomes reported by Gillon (2000), in what can be regarded as an efficacy study, were not replicated in a study by Denne et al. (2005), which – one could argue – is more of an effectiveness study. Clearly, even in areas where research evidence exists, the picture is more complex than what appears on the surface, and further work is needed. The existence of research *per se* is also not, in itself, a sufficient proof of evidence. The quality of the research needs to be considered carefully; not all evidence is created equally (Wertz, 2002). The picture is even less positive for developmental language disorders, which makes up a significant proportion of the workload of a typical community speech and language therapist (Pearson, 1995; Hall, 1996; RCSLT, 2005). A recent Cochrane review of paediatric speech and language disorders found a limited number of studies showing positive evidence, with a specific lack of evidence in the case of receptive language disorders (Law et al., 2004). However, the overall conclusions of this review have been criticized for including only clients with primary speech and language disorders, only children between the ages of 2 and 3 years, and considering only studies that used RCTs (Johnston, 2005). As noted previously, several hierarchies of evidence consider a range of intervention methodologies to be appropriate in the building of a strong evidence base. We should not wait for a utopian context in which to conduct sufficiently large RCT studies or other interventions that we deem as perfectly meeting all criteria for 'Class 1' evidence. The danger with this is that it leads to inertia and fails to move us forward in any way in solidifying a robust evidence foundation. Intervention studies that fulfil the criteria for lower levels of evidence, and that meet the criteria stipulated by Robey and Schultz's (1998) Phases 1 and 2, can be highly informative and provide insights into clinical practice and future refinements in clinical research.

We now turn to examples of three group studies of intervention in developmental language disorders in the education context. These studies are used here primarily as vehicles to illustrate some of the major issues and debates surrounding EBP in speech and language therapy. Each is argued to be efficient with regard to time and resources, to be pedagogically and contextually realistic, ecologically valid, theoretically motivated, and to show some changes in performance. The limitations of each study provide insights into the problems of conducting intervention studies in the education context with the school-age child, and provide a useful platform for further discussion. Key issues arising from these studies will be highlighted. We now turn to . . .

. . . The intervention studies

Study 1: narrative and vocabulary training in language-impaired secondary school-age children (Joffe, 2006)

Background

Research into language development and disorders has routinely focused on preschool and primary children. In contrast, this study involved secondary school-age students with language impairment. Whilst most children have acquired basic linguistic regularities by the age of 3 (Rice, 2004), their understanding and use of language becomes increasingly complex and abstract throughout later childhood and adolescence (Nippold, 1998, 2007; Berman, 2004). In addition, adolescents experience fundamental changes in cognitive, social and educational development, and the move from primary to secondary education coincides with a more peer-focused orientation (Moshman, 1999). At secondary school, adolescents are required to integrate their linguistic, cognitive and social skills into coherent meaningful discourse. They enter Piaget's formal operational stage of development, becoming capable of sophisticated reasoning and higher-level logical and abstract cognitive processing (Piaget, 1963). These changes pose significant challenges for young people using language to meet social and educational demands. The limited research on language development in adolescence is mirrored by the lack of clinical research with language-impaired adolescents. This reflects the shortage of speech and language therapy provision for this population, reported in the United Kingdom (Law et al., 2000; Leahy and Dodd, 2002; Lindsay et al., 2002) and further afield (McKinley and Larson, 1989; Larson et al., 1993; Paul, 2001; Hollands et al., 2005). A significant proportion of secondary school-age students have language and communication impairments that impede access to the school curriculum (Larson et al., 1993; Conti-Ramsden et al., 2001). Few currently receive any speech and language therapy, despite strong evidence for the long-term effects of speech, language and communication impairments into adolescence and adulthood (Johnson et al., 1999; Snowling et al., 2001; Clegg et al., 2005; see Rutter, Chapter 7 this volume; Lindsay and Dockrell, Chapter 8 this volume), and despite some evidence that it can be effective (Ebbels, 2007; Larson et al., 1993; Leahy and Dodd, 2002; Stringer, 2006).

The study addresses this gap in service provision through an exploratory study of the effectiveness of two interventions (narrative and vocabulary enrichment) designed to enhance the language and communication abilities of secondary school-age students.

Narrative therapy was chosen as it has been found to be effective with younger children (Davies et al., 2004), and is an integral part of everyday life. Storytelling is frequently used in school and in social settings as a means of communicating our thoughts, beliefs and personal experiences and as a means of gaining peer group acceptance. Grove (1998) observes how storytelling facilitates social inclusion and helps develop a sense of self and a connection with others. Difficulties with interpreting oral narratives may impact adversely on children's social relationships, with the child becoming socially isolated (Davies et al., 2004). The language of the classroom is also heavily dependent on narrative (Milosky, 1987; Allen et al., 1994). All four key stages of the National Curriculum in the United Kingdom emphasize storytelling skills, speaking fluently and appropriately in different contexts, and adapting language for a range of purposes and audiences (Department for Education and Employment, 2000a,b). Oral storytelling is also crucial in the National Literacy Strategy, which emphasizes comprehension and composition at text level (Department for Education and Employment, 1998). Narrative is considered by some to be the bridge between oral language and literacy (Allen et al., 1994; Kaderavek and Sulzby, 2000).

Storytelling makes heavy demands on receptive and expressive language, requires complex syntax and semantics, abstract and imaginative thinking, general knowledge, a range of pragmatic and discourse skills, and draws upon a set of internal organizational rules (Nippold, 1998, 2007). Unsurprisingly, individuals with language impairments have significant difficulties with storytelling (Roth and Spekman, 1986; Liles, 1993; Paul and Smith, 1993; Wetherell et al., 2007). Narrative ability is crucial to academic success and has been found to be a significant predictor of persistent language difficulties and later academic performance (Roth and Spekman, 1986; Bishop and Edmundson, 1987; Fazio et al., 1993; Botting, 2002). This link to educational outcomes makes it a highly functional therapeutic tool. It has sound ecological validity, can be undertaken in a highly structured way and targets receptive and expressive linguistic skills. However, there is limited evidence for its effectiveness as a therapy tool.

Vocabulary enrichment was chosen as the second therapy programme. Growth in vocabulary is an important aspect of development during adolescence (Nippold, 1998, 2004, 2007). Lack of vocabulary is a significant barrier for children with language impairments (Crystal, 1987), particularly in secondary schools (Sim, 1998). Vocabulary development involves the ability to retrieve words with speed and accuracy (Dockrell and Messer, 2004), use complex, abstract and low-frequency words, elaborate semantic networks to facilitate literacy (Ravid, 2004), and define complex vocabulary (Nippold et al., 1999). It is central to cognitive development and literacy (Cunningham and Stanovich, 1997). Despite its obvious importance, little direct time is devoted to vocabulary instruction in school (Dockrell and Messer, 2004). There is some evidence to suggest that vocabulary training is effective in improving language performance (Sim, 1998; Nippold, 1999; Law et al., 2003; Parsons et al., 2005; Nash and Snowling, 2006).

Aim

The study investigated the effectiveness of narrative and vocabulary enrichment intervention programmes to enhance the language and communication abilities of secondary school-age children.

Procedure

Fifty-four secondary school-age students, with a mean age of 12.8 years (age range 10.00–15.3 years), with language and communication impairments were randomly assigned to the narrative and vocabulary groups. Forty-seven boys and seven girls participated in the study.

A range of language and literacy assessments were administered pre- and post-intervention. A post-intervention questionnaire was also used to evaluate the students' perceptions of the interventions' effectiveness. The assessments were conducted by therapists who did not conduct the intervention, and were therefore blind to group membership.

The narrative therapy was adapted from Shanks (2000, 2003), and incorporated the understanding and telling of stories with a focus on story structure, story description and inferential understanding. The students were told a variety of stories and were taught about story structure (beginning, middle and end) and key components (place, time, action, motivations, character, climax and resolution). Students were also encouraged to make their own stories using all these components and to think about sequencing their ideas in a logical order. The vocabulary enrichment was curriculum-based, as recommended by Paul (2001). It included the teaching of key concepts through word associations, mind mapping, word building, and the use of the dictionary and thesaurus. Topic areas relevant to this age group were used, including current affairs, famous people, employment seeking, exam preparation and the media. Specific vocabulary items from the National Curriculum in geography, mathematics, history, information technology and science were targeted. The students were encouraged to categorize new vocabulary into related groups through brainstorming and word webs to help them remember new words more easily. They were encouraged to use synonyms, antonyms, multiple meanings, definitions, and categorization and classification games to explore word meanings and word boundaries. Each intervention consisted of two sessions of 50 minutes per week for 6 weeks (12 sessions in total). These were delivered by speech and language therapy students in schools to groups of one to six children.

Results

The group, as a whole, showed significant improvements in receptive vocabulary, recalling sentences, naming and idiomatic comprehension. There were no significant differences in performance between the two groups. It was predicted that the narrative group would outperform the vocabulary group on narrative assessments, but this was not upheld. According to the student questionnaires, 74% of the children felt the programme had helped them with talking and understanding, and more than half of them reported that it helped with their reading and writing, with work in the classroom and in getting on with friends. Forty-one percent wanted more of these lessons. Thus, the majority of children reported some important benefits from the intervention.

Discussion

The study raises important points for future research. There was no control group – a major drawback in this study – so we cannot be certain that the change was due to therapy. However, language impairments in adolescents are pervasive, and their test scores rarely change this much in so short a period. The lack of a 'no-treatment group' is problematic; yet including one in education has ethical implications and is often met with resistance from clinicians and school staff. There are, however, ways around this problem, which meet the needs of research but are ethically acceptable. A delayed-treatment group can be used in clinical settings by including participants on existing waiting lists. They can act as a control group, and then receive the intervention later. Other research designs avoid the need for a 'no-treatment' group. These include crossover designs, where groups of participants get different therapies at different times, and multiple-baseline designs, where participants act as their own controls

(Owen et al., 1994; Pring 2005). For example, in a multiple-baseline design looking at the effectiveness of language therapy targeting subject–verb–object sentence construction, measures could be taken of vocabulary and mean length of utterance. One may predict significant improvement in mean length of utterance but not vocabulary if improvement was directly related to the therapy. This design is appropriate for single-case studies and could be incorporated with relative ease as part of a clinician's routine clinical practice. A baseline period of no intervention (see Study 2) can also be used to control for maturation, a period which can coincide with existing waiting lists.

Returning to the findings of the study, whilst significant changes were evident in some measures post-intervention, others fell just short of statistical significance (receptive grammar, semantics and spelling). This raises issues about the outcome measures used to chart changes in performance. First, we need to challenge the notion that the *only* change we accept is the one deemed statistically significant, that is, the change that occurs at the 0.05 level of confidence when conducting statistical significance tests (Meline and Paradiso, 2003). Kazdin (1999) and others (see, e.g. Meline and Schmitt, 1997; Meline and Wang, 2004) propose that, in addition to statistical significance, consideration be given to clinical significance, which is described as the practical or applied value of the intervention for everyday life. This is an interesting distinction as the two can at times be at odds with each other. A change in performance that is statistically significant (e.g. in receptive vocabulary as measured by the British Picture Vocabulary Scale (BPVS; Dunn et al., 1997) in this study) may have little clinical value and make little change in the client's life, and therefore have little clinical significance. Johnson (2006) advises the routine use of effect sizes, the statistical measure of practical significance (Cohen 1988) and confidence intervals, which relate to the precision with which these effect sizes have been estimated, as key tools to explore the practical significance of the changes observed. Tests of statistical significance like *t*-tests and analysis of variance are affected by sample size, whereas effect sizes are not (see Meline and Schmitt, 1997; Meline and Paradiso, 2003; Meline and Wang, 2004 for further discussion on this point). Effect sizes are useful in determining how many participants are needed in any study to obtain a statistically significant finding. Clinical or practical significance, however, is a subjective concept, and consideration also needs to be given to who is best at evaluating change. It may not always be appropriate for the clinician to assess clinical change, and the roles of the client, teaching staff, parent and other family members in this endeavour need to be considered. The best evaluation of outcomes should incorporate both measures of statistical and clinical significance, and that the latter be taken from a variety of vantage points including the client and family. A strength of this study was that it gathered the views of the students themselves about the therapy through questionnaires. Service user involvement in evaluating change and in the clinical decision-making process is recommended as good practice (Ylvisaker et al., 2002). Sackett et al. (1996) also discuss the role of patient choice in EBP. The observations of teachers and parents would also be useful, and the inclusion of their views as outcome measures give added credence to any statistically significant changes found.

The use of standardized measures alone as outcome measures is problematic for a number of reasons. First, there are often difficulties in finding a standardized measure relevant to the age range and content of the specific intervention given. For example, clinical assessment tools for the adolescent client group are scarce (Tomblin et al., 1992). Furthermore, in a vocabulary training study focusing on the teaching of specific vocabulary items, one needs to question the suitability of using the BPVS as the only measure of vocabulary change. It is completely possible, even probable, that vocabulary knowledge may improve for the specific vocabulary items taught, and even for some non-treated items related in some way to the treated words, without notable changes in the standard scores for a test like the BPVS (and the knowledge of words like 'festoon', 'digit' or 'arable', for example). A more appropriate assessment in this case may be the use of a vocabulary checklist containing the items specifically targeted in the therapy rather than the more generic BPVS. In Study 1, there were no changes evident on the standardized test of narrative ability. We did not include a non-standardized measure of storytelling so we were unable to explore any changes that might have been observed on another measure more directly reflecting the therapy. This is clearly evident in Intervention 2 (below), where changes in storytelling were only seen on a non-standardized measure of story generation. The most comprehensive and ideal assessment battery would incorporate both standardized and non-standardized measures. Non-standardized measures do not have sufficient construct validity or reliability to be used in isolation, and do not provide any age-related normative information. There is, however, the need to streamline the number of assessments used in the clinical context, and the challenge for clinicians is to be selective and choose a combination of standardized and non-standardized assessments that are sufficiently sensitive to identify changes resulting from therapy, as well as providing the necessary normative information often required. These issues of economical assessment in both the adult and child domains are also raised by Marshall (Chapter 3) in this volume. Clinicians need to be bolder in choosing what assessments to use, and should feel comfortable in using informal assessments to measure change.

Of further importance is the attempt to assess more broadly how therapy impacts on a child's life. This may include, for example, the adoption of educational outcomes, such as the National Curriculum standard assessment tests – conducted at the end of Year 6 (10 years of age) and 9 (13 years of age) in English, Maths and Science – which are mandatory assessments for all pupils in England and provide a measure of performance relative to the local and national standards of educational achievement.

The inclusion of educational outcomes strengthens our credibility in schools with teachers, school administrators and local education authorities, whose focus is often on individual end-of-year performance and national league tables.

Study 2: narrative therapy in primary school language-impaired children (Jennings, 2006)

Background

Study 1 highlighted the role and importance of narrative in children's language development. Research has provided some evidence for the effectiveness of narrative therapy in improving primary school-age children's language abilities. Davies et al. (2004) reported on a narrative therapy study delivered by speech and language therapists and teaching staff to groups of 5-year-old children with language learning difficulties. Results showed that the training was effective in improving the children's language skills. Swanson et al. (2005) conducted narrative therapy individually over a 6-week period (three sessions of 50 minutes per week) with 10 7- to 8-year-old children with specific language impairment (SLI), and also reported increased performance in some areas of language post-treatment. Improvements were noted in what they termed narrative quality, which included incorporation of more story grammar components, with no significant improvements reported in measures of grammar, sentence imitation and sentence repetition. Neither of these studies, however, included a baseline or control group, which makes it difficult to ascertain whether the changes observed were due to the therapy *per se*, or simply due to maturation or another variable.

Aim

This study aimed to explore the effectiveness of narrative therapy in four children with SLI in a routine clinical context.

Procedure

Four male primary school-age students, with a mean age of 8.10 years (age range 8.8–9.00 years), with SLI participated in the study. Participants were assessed on a battery of standardized narrative and language assessments and a non-standardized story generation task, at baseline, pre-therapy and post-therapy points. The non-standardized story generation task explored the number of narrative episodes, number of cohesive devices and story grammar components (Merritt and Liles, 1987). The assessments were administered by different researchers at each assessment point, so that the assessors were blind to whether the performance was pre- or post-therapy. Therapy consisted of twice-weekly 40-minute sessions for 6 weeks, and was adapted from a narrative therapy resource based on a story grammar approach (Shanks, 2003; Shanks and Rippon, 2003).

Results

Due to loss of data for one child, results are only reported for three participants. The only statistically significant improvements noted were on the non-standardized measure of story generation. Significant improvements were made in the number of clauses (Figure 5.1) and narrative episodes used (Figure 5.2). Story grammar components post-therapy increased, but the change fell just short of significance (Figure 5.3). Figures 5.4–5.6 illustrate the increased use of individual story grammar components by each participant on the story generation task. Whilst Participant A used a variety of all story grammar components over time, Participants

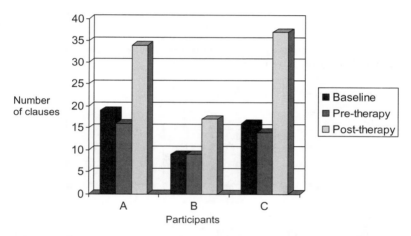

Figure 5.1 Number of clauses for each participant at baseline, pre- and post-therapy on the story generation task.

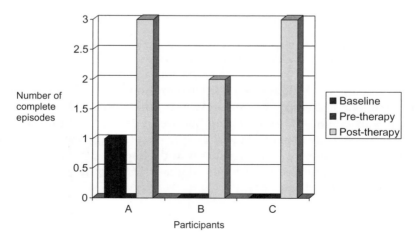

Figure 5.2 Number of complete episodes for each participant at baseline, pre- and post-therapy on the story generation task.

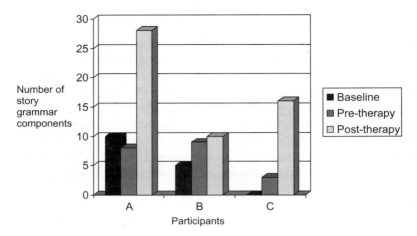

Figure 5.3 Number of story grammar components for each participant at baseline, pre- and post-therapy on the story generation task.

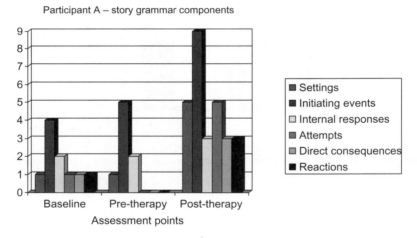

Figure 5.4 Individual story grammar components across assessment points for Participant A in the story generation task (raw scores).

B and C demonstrated a marked increase in the use of all story grammar components post-therapy, where previously, their use of these had been minimal. Participant A also increased his use of each story grammar component post-therapy. This reflected a shift post-therapy towards a more structured and cohesive story (Hudson and Shapiro, 1991). Excerpts of Participant C's narratives reflect this increase in story grammar components post-therapy (Table 5.1).

Discussion

This is a small-scale pilot study, and its results cannot be generalized to other children with language impairment. Nevertheless, it is a useful addi-

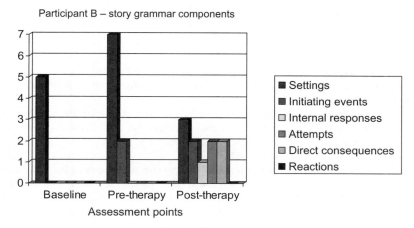

Figure 5.5 Individual story grammar components across assessment points for Participant B in the story generation task (raw scores).

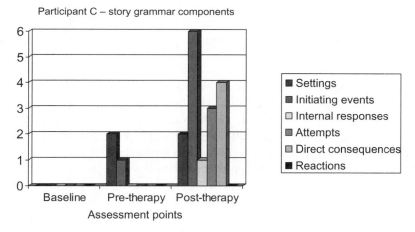

Figure 5.6 Individual story grammar components across assessment points for Participant C in the story generation task (raw scores).

tion to the evidence that storytelling can enhance language in language-impaired children (Shanks, 2000, Davies et al., 2004; Swanson et al., 2005; Stringer, 2006; Suttie, 2007). The clinician carried out the therapy with her regular client group in a typical clinical setting. A larger replication would be possible within an existing clinical caseload and would serve to strengthen the findings. Other clinical colleagues were used to conduct the assessments, which meant that the assessments were undertaken by clinicians not involved in the intervention and who were blind to the timings of the assessment points. Study 1 also used assessors who were blind to group membership. The inclusion of blind assessment is an

Table 5.1 Excerpts of Participant C's narratives at baseline, pre- and post-therapy points

---

Baseline
'A naughty dog is like a dog which bites and he barks you and he makes scratches on you. And he makes your arm bleed. When a dog bites you it hurts badly . . .'
Pre-therapy
'. . . When a dog bites you you get a cut and he can bite your face. He can bite your hand and he'll make you have a cut, a bad cut. And the dog starts chasing you for the rest of your life . . .'
Post-therapy
'A naughty dog bit someone on the leg and the person went to hospital. And the naughty dog was locked up in his cage. And the naughty dog have to think about what he has done. And the naughty dog was locked up in his cage for five days. Then when the person came back from hospital the person was okay and the person be able to walk and he was feeling much better . . .'

---

important protocol when undertaking research in clinical practice as it, crucially, controls for experimenter bias.

This intervention shows the potential for change in performance with a relatively small amount of group-based therapy delivered in the education context. It is far too small a study to generalize findings; however, it can be replicated by other clinicians. If replications are conducted accurately and with care, data from single-case and small group studies can be combined to produce more robust evidence. A difficulty with replicating studies is that insufficient details of the intervention are often given. Therapy is often described as 'traditional therapy' or using 'tabletop activities'. Journals may not allow sufficient space for more detailed accounts of the therapy, and it is difficult to replicate a study without them. In these cases, researchers and clinicians should be encouraged to contact authors for more details, and researchers should make available session plans and descriptions of the therapy to ensure treatment fidelity. Intervention studies could come with treatment manuals containing guidelines on how to administer the therapy (Ollendick and King, 2004). This is not to provide 'cookbook' therapy but to reduce the frustrations often felt by clinicians wanting to follow a treatment without having sufficient details.

The final intervention study again demonstrates that change can occur with amounts of therapy that are within the reach of clinicians working in clinical and educational contexts.

Study 3: imagery training in primary school language-impaired children (Maric, 2006; Joffe et al., 2007)

Background

Children with SLI have story comprehension deficits. They experience difficulties recalling literal information as well as integrating information within the story and inferring information that is not explicitly stated (Bishop and Adams, 1992; Norbury and Bishop, 2002; Botting and Adams, 2005). Their difficulties are not restricted to the verbal domain, and their ability to answer questions about stories is poorer than that of age-matched controls for stories presented visually as well as for spoken text (Bishop and Adams, 1992). Research with typically developing children, poor comprehenders and poor readers have shown that the use of mental imagery aids comprehension of stories (Pressley, 1976; Gambrell and Bales, 1986; Oakhill and Patel, 1991). According to the dual-coding theory, meaning can be represented by two separate coding systems: one system (verbal) specializing in language and the other (non-verbal or imagery system) dealing with non-linguistic events (Paivio, 1971, 1983, 1991; Sadoski and Paivio, 2001, 2004). These two systems can operate independently (e.g. activity in one but not the other: reading without mental images), in parallel (e.g. separate activity in both at the same time: reading with unrelated images), as well as in a connected integrated way (e.g. reading with related images) to reorganize and manipulate information (Sadoski and Paivio, 2001, 2004). Visual imagery as a comprehension strategy can be explained by the 'conceptual pegs hypothesis'. Key images serve as mental 'pegs' to which associated information is hooked for storage and retrieval (Sadoski et al., 1991).

Aim

This study explored the effectiveness of using mental imagery to improve literal and inferential comprehension in children with SLI.

Procedure

Nine children (two girls and seven boys) with SLI, with a mean age of 9.6 years (age range 8.3–11.8 years), were trained to produce mental images for sentences and stories in five 30-minute sessions. Their performance was compared with that of an age-matched control group consisting of 16 typically developing children (12 girls, 4 boys), with a mean age of 9.10 years (age range 8.6–11.3 years), who were recruited from the same mainstream primary school as the SLI group and had similar cultural and linguistic backgrounds. The ability of the SLI group to answer literal and inferential questions on short narratives was assessed pre- and post-intervention and compared with the performance of the typically developing controls. Imagery training took place in five 30-minute sessions over a 3-week period totalling 2½ hours of therapy. Only the SLI group received training. Paragraphs of one to five sentences in length were used. Children were told that 'a good way to remember things is to make up pictures in your head'. They were encouraged to use picture cues to visualize the sentences, first by breaking them into parts (e.g. visualize first '**pig**' and then '**large pink pig**' from the sentence stimulus: '**the large pink pig**

was eating hot brown potatoes') (see Joffe et al., 2007 for further details of the training).

Results

The SLI group showed greater improvement from pre- to post-training on both literal and inferential questions compared with the controls. Improvement was most pronounced for literal questions. These improvements were not evident in the control group (Figures 5.7–5.9).

Discussion

The enhanced performance of the SLI group in story comprehension after a relatively short period of visual imagery training is exciting. This increased performance was not evident in a control group who did not receive the

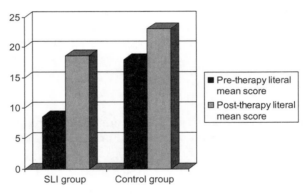

Figure 5.7 Performance on literal questions for both groups pre- and post-therapy.

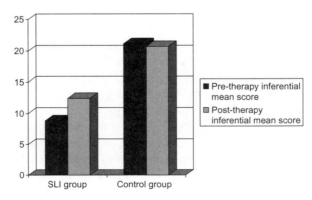

Figure 5.8 Performance on inferential questions for both groups pre- and post-therapy.

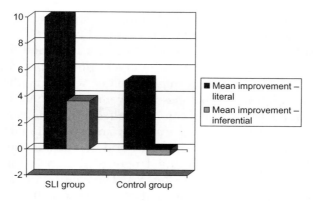

Figure 5.9 Improvement over time for both literal and inferential questions.

same training. It is a problem using typically developing children as a control group, as they are less likely to change and therefore are not a fair comparison group. It would be far better to use an alternative design to control for treatment effects, for example, the use of a baseline as was used in the second study reported above, a comparison of two different therapies, as was used in Study 1, or the inclusion of a control group of SLI children. The latter can either consist of children on the waiting list, or can be a delayed-treatment group that gets the same treatment but at a later point in time.

General discussion

All three of the intervention studies cited had only one post-therapy assessment immediately after the intervention. A second follow-up assessment would be useful to assess the maintenance of the taught skills over time. This assessment could fit in quite neatly with a planned review appointment (see Gillon, 2002 for an example of a design with two post-therapy assessment points). Some studies only report changes to have occurred at a final follow-up assessment, suggesting that children may need time to consolidate and generalize skills learned (McIntosh et al., 2007). Longer-term maintenance of change would be strong evidence to rationalize our services to stakeholders and service providers, and more importantly, touches on the very essence of the changes that we hope, as a profession, to engender, that is, long-term impact.

All the interventions described were undertaken in schools, delivered by speech and language therapists or students within modest time frames. None are first-class evidence according to the levels of evidence introduced previously, but they are examples of research at Phases 1 and 2 of Robey and Schultz's (1998) five-phase outcome research model. Replications by clinicians are feasible and would produce a more robust evidence base for these interventions. Their limitations highlight the problems of producing research evidence in realistic clinical contexts. Acknowledging and addressing these problems can refine research methodologies and lead to a better research base. Each intervention was provided by therapists; however, future research might explore whether other personnel (e.g. teaching staff, carers) may be equally effective. Some evidence suggests, for example, that parents can be as effective as clinicians in treating young children with expressive vocabulary and syntactic difficulties (Law et al., 2004). This is an important question to consider in light of the increasing demands of speech and language therapy support and the burden this places on existing resources. The sharing of responsibilities and delegation of tasks is an important consideration – not to diffuse our expertise – but rather to protect and strengthen them by knowing the areas in which we can delegate (with supervision and support) and those in which we need to be actively and directly involved. A critical evaluation of the current evidence base provides the opportunity to consider other . . .

. . . Exciting challenges and directions for future research and practice

We have already touched on the range of possible outcome measures that can be used to chart change. The main focus of standardized assessments is at the level of the impairment, for example, using the BPVS to explore the extent of a vocabulary deficit. The International Classification of Functioning, Disability and Health (ICF), a conceptual framework proposed by the World Health Organization (2001), provides a highly useful and relevant scaffold for exploring change at different levels of functioning (Threats, 2000, 2002; Threats and Worrall, 2004). This has three levels of focus: impairment, activity and participation. Whilst the first focuses on the functioning and impairment of speech, language and communication at the individual level, activity and participation allow us to explore how the impairment impacts on the client's life in the wider community and across a range of different contexts. This classification system is not only able to inform assessment, but also intervention. We should consider not only how effectively current assessments reflect the functional impacts of the impairment, but also, furthermore, how much of our intervention itself targets levels beyond impairment and assesses performance across different contexts. If the highest goal of EBP is that an intervention improves a client's quality of life (Threats, 2002), then assessments are needed at the levels of activity and participation, and performance should be evaluated in the different contexts in which the children most frequently find themselves (e.g. school classroom, playground, youth club, home). Measures of quality of life have been used much more routinely with adults with acquired disorders (see, e.g. Cruice et al. (Chapter 6 this volume) on evaluating quality of life by investigating the views not only of the clients but also of their caregivers, and Marshall (Chapter 3 this volume) for an example of a functional therapy within a cognitive neuropsychological approach). Attempts are, however, being made to broaden the range of outcomes used and evaluate quality of life in children (see, e.g. Markham and Dean, 2006). McLeod (2004) has produced an assessment of activity and participation for children with speech disorders, the Speech Participation and Activity-Children, which contains questions about the impact of having a speech impairment and is directed to children with speech impairments, their siblings, parents, friends, teachers and significant others (see McLeod, 2006 for an example of its application to the management of a child with a speech disorder). Washington (2007) recently argued for the usefulness of the ICF framework with children with SLI, both in the management and evaluation of outcomes. This is an exciting area for future development, one in which developmental clinicians have only just begun to wet their toes.

Whilst most current research in developmental language disorders focuses on quantitative analyses, the potential of employing more qualitative research methodologies should not be missed. These might include the use of interviews and/or focus groups to explore the views of clients, caregivers and teachers (see Owen et al., 2004; Lindsay and Dockrell, Chapter 8 this volume). Qualitative research could also involve the use of other modalities such as pictures or photography. Abigail Beverly, in this volume, uses her artwork, to a profound effect, to reveal the impact of having a language impairment on her life.

The use of dynamic assessment provides another potentially useful outcome measurement. Within this approach, instead of focusing on a static level of achievement (the child's independent performance on a standardized measure), the target of investigation is the child's potential for learning, the difference between the two reflecting the child's developmental potential and termed by Vygotsky (1978) as the 'zone of proximal development' (see Hasson and Joffe, 2007 for further discussion of the role of dynamic assessment in speech and language therapy). The concept of 'responsiveness to intervention' is a similar construct used in special education, and has at its roots the dual application of high-quality instruction and continuous monitoring of performance (Mellard et al., 2004; see Sampson Graner et al., 2005 for an overview on the use of responsiveness to intervention in practice). A further challenge is to examine individual differences in responses to therapy that may be masked in group studies, a point emphasized by Dockrell and Law (2007). This leads to the questions of why and for whom an intervention works. Most research studies report on group rather than individual performances. Group scores mask individual variations, and they tell us little about how different individuals within the group perform. Clinicians are in the ideal position to look more closely at individual performances and ask not only whether an intervention is effective, but also with which clients it works best. This has the potential of not only providing more details of the intervention and the client's abilities, but may also provide insights into the complex dynamics between language processing, language impairment and the therapeutic process. Pawson and Tilley (1997) provide an interesting review of the application of the generative realist approach to evaluation. Whereas a positivist account asks whether an intervention works, the realist approach explores the more searching questions about how it works and why it works for some clients and not for others (see Mathews, 2003). There are many exciting and different approaches that clinical research can adopt that are accessible to both the clinical researcher and clinician and have the potential to provide valuable research evidence. What is required is willingness on both sides to share expertise and engage full throttle in collaborative partnership.

Conclusions

In this chapter, I have argued that EBP should be adopted in its broadest sense in our everyday work with developmental language disorders. It is only through combining research evidence and clinical expertise that a true and solid evidence base can be built. The participation of both the clinical researcher and clinician is necessary. Clinicians are in the best position to be both providers and consumers of research evidence. For clinicians, each client is potentially a single-case study. It requires a change of perspective and openness on both sides for a true collaborative enterprise. We cannot, and should not, wait for the perfect context in which to conduct the perfect study. The danger here is that we will never get started and will fall further behind in the construction of a suitable evidence base. We need to explore a range of research methodologies across all the levels of evidence. Research studies must be rigorously conducted and objectively evaluated, but must also be meaningful within clinical and educational contexts. Clinicians and researchers must learn to work in partnership. The relationship between researcher and clinician is potentially a match made in heaven, and the joint enterprise of building an evidence base can be the main vehicle for closing the gap between research and practice. To end as we began, if indeed every journey of a thousand miles does start with one step, then such endeavours will ensure that we are well on the road, and will not need so much to be warned to . . . mind that gap.

Acknowlegements

Thanks go to the Toyne Baby Triathlon and Afasic for funding intervention Study 1, and to all participating children, schools, parents, therapists and SLT students involved in all three interventions. The intervention described in Study 1 was devised by the author in collaboration with K Bright, L Finn and L Green. The author is indebted to Professor Tim Pring for his useful comments and discussion on the chapter.

References

Allen M, Kertoy M, Sherbllom J et al. (1994) Children's narrative productions: a comparison of personal event and fictional stories. Applied Psycholinguistics 15: 149–76.

American Academy of Neurology (1994) Assessment: melodic intonation therapy. Neurology 44: 566–8.

Berman R (2004) Between emergence and mastery: the long developmental route of language acquisition. In: RA Berman (ed.), Language Development across Childhood and Adolescence. Amsterdam: John Benjamins Publishing Company, pp. 9–34.

Bernstein Ratner N (2005) Evidence-based practice in stuttering: some questions to consider. Journal of Fluency Disorders 30(3): 163–88.

Bernstein Ratner N (2006) Evidence-based practice: an examination of its ramifications for the practice of speech-language pathology. Language, Speech, and Hearing Services in Schools 37: 257–67.

Bishop DVM (2007) Curing dyslexia and attention-deficit hyperactivity disorder by training motor co-ordination: miracle or myth? Journal of Paediatrics and Child Health 43(10): 653–5.

Bishop DVM, Edmundson A (1987) Language-impaired 4-year-olds: distinguishing transient from persistent impairment. Journal of Speech and Hearing Disorders 52: 156–73.

Bishop DVM, Adams C (1992) Comprehension problems in children with specific language impairment: literal and inferential meaning. Journal of Speech and Hearing Research 35: 119–29.

Birch and Davis Associates Inc. (1997) The State of the Science: Medical Rehabilitation. Falls Church, VA: Birch and Davis Associates, Inc.

Botting N (2002) Narrative as a tool for the assessment of linguistic and pragmatic impairments. Child, Language, Teaching and Therapy 18(1): 1–21.

Botting N, Adams C (2005) Semantic and inferencing abilities in children with communication disorders. International Journal of Language and Communication Disorders 40: 49–66.

Bowen C, Cupples L (1999) Parents and children together (PACT): a collaborative approach to phonological therapy. International Journal of Language and Communication Disorders 34: 35–55.

Bowen C, Cupples L (2004) The role of families in optimizing phonological therapy outcomes. Child Language Teaching and Therapy 20: 245–60.

Chambless DL, Ollendick TH (2001) Empirically supported psychological interventions: controversies and evidence. Annual Review of Psychology 52: 685–716.

Clegg J, Hollis C, Mawhood L et al. (2005) Developmental language disorders – a follow-up in later adult life. Cognitive, language and psychosocial outcomes. Journal of Child Psychology and Psychiatry 46(2): 128–49.

Cohen J (1988) Statistical power analysis for the behavioural sciences, 2nd edn. Hillsdale, NJ: Lawrence Erlbaum and Associates.

Conti-Ramsden G, Botting N, Simkin Z et al. (2001) Follow-up of children attending infant language units: outcomes at 11 years of age. International Journal of Language and Communication Disorders 36: 207–19.

Crosbie S, Holm A, Dodd B (2005) Intervention for children with severe speech disorder: a comparison of two approaches. International Journal of Language and Communication Disorders 40: 467–91.

Crystal D (1987) Teaching vocabulary: the case for a semantic curriculum. Child, Language, Teaching and Therapy 3: 40–56.

Cunningham A, Stanovich K (1997) Early reading acquisition and its relation to reading experience and ability ten years later. Developmental Psychology 33(6): 934–45.

Davies P, Shanks B, Davies K (2004) Improving narrative skills in young children with delayed language development. Educational Review 56(3): 271–86.

Denne M, Langdown N, Pring T et al. (2005) Treating children with expressive phonological disorders: does phonological awareness therapy work in the clinic? International Journal of Language and Communication Disorders 40: 493–504.

Department for Education and Employment (1998) The National Literacy Strategy. London: DfEE.

Department for Education and Employment/Qualifications and Curriculum Authority (2000a) The National Curriculum – handbook for primary teachers in England (Key stages 1 and 2). London: The Stationery Office.

Department for Education and Employment/Qualifications and Curriculum Authority (2000b) The National Curriculum – handbook for secondary teachers in England (Key stages 3 and 4). London: The Stationery Office.

Department of Health (2005) Commissioning a patient-led NHS. http://www.dh.gov.uk/en/Publicationsandstatistics/Publications/PublicationsPolicyAndGuidance/DH_4116716.

Department of Health (2006) Code of Conduct for Payment by Results. http://www.dh.gov.uk/en/Publicationsandstatistics/Publications/PublicationsPolicyAndGuidance/DH_4127045.

Dockrell J, Messer D (2004) Lexical acquisition in the early school years. In: RA Berman (ed.), Language Development across Childhood and Adolescence. Amsterdam: John Benjamins Publishing, pp. 35–52.

Dockrell J, Law J (2007) Measuring and understanding patterns of change in intervention studies with children: implications for evidence-based practice. Evidence-Based Communication Assessment and Intervention 1(2): 86–97.

Dunn LM, Dunn LM, Whetton C et al. (1997) British Picture Vocabulary Scale, 2nd edn. Windsor: NFER-Nelson.

Ebbels S (2007) Teaching grammar to school-aged children with specific language impairment using stage coding. Child Language Teaching and Therapy 23(1): 67–93.

Fazio B, Naremore R, Connell P (1993) Tracking children from poverty at risk for specific language impairment: a 3-year longitudinal study. Journal of Speech and Hearing Research 39: 611–24.

Gambrell LB, Bales RJ (1986) Mental imagery and the comprehension-monitoring performance of fourth- and fifth-grade poor readers. Reading Research Quarterly 21: 454–64.

Gibbard D (1994) Parental based intervention with preschool language delayed children. European Journal of Disorders of Communication 29: 131–50.

Gillon G (2000) The efficacy of phonological awareness intervention for children with spoken language impairment. Language, Speech and Hearing Services in Schools 31: 126–41.

Gillon GT (2002) Follow-up study investigating the benefits of phonological awareness intervention for children with spoken language impairment. International Journal of Language and Communication Disorders 37: 381–400.

Grove N (1998) Literature for All. London: David Fulton Publishers Ltd.

Hall DMB (ed.) (1996) Health for All Children. Report of the Third Joint Working Party on Child Health Surveillance. Oxford: Oxford University Press.

Hasson N, Joffe VL (2007) The case for dynamic assessment in speech and language therapy. Child Language Teaching and Therapy 23(1): 9–25.

Hesketh A, Adams C, Nightingale C et al. (2000) Phonological awareness therapy and articulatory training approaches for children with phonological disorders: a comparative outcome study. International Journal of Language and Communication Disorders 35: 337–54.

Hollands K, van Kraayenoord C, McMahon S (2005) Support to adolescents experiencing language difficulties: a survey of speech-language pathologists. Advances in Speech-Language Pathology 7(3): 113–29.

Hudson J, Shapiro L (1991) From knowing to telling: the development of children's scripts, stories and personal narratives. In: A McCabe, C Peterson (eds), Developing Narrative Structure. Hillsdale, NJ: Lawrence Erlbaum Associates, pp. 89–136.

Jennings T (2006) The effects of narrative therapy on language ability in children with specific language impairment. Dissertation (MSc), Department of Language and Communication Science, City University, London.

Joffe VL (2006) Enhancing language and communication in language-impaired secondary school-aged children. In: J Ginsborg, J Clegg (eds), Language and Social Disadvantage. London: Wiley Publishers, pp. 207–16.

Joffe VL, Pring T (2008) Children with phonological problems: a survey of clinical practice. International Journal of Language and Communication Disorders 43(2): 154–64.

Joffe VL, Cain K, Maric N (2007) Comprehension problems in children with specific language impairment: does mental imagery training help? International Journal of Language and Communication Disorders 42(6): 648–64.

Johnson CJ (2006) Getting started in evidence-based practice for childhood speech-language disorders. American Journal of Speech-Language Pathology 15: 20–35.

Johnson CJ, Beitchman JH, Young A, Escobar M, Atkinson L, Brownlie EB, Douglas L, Tabak N, Lam I, Wang M (1999) Fourteen year follow-up of children with and without speech/language impairments: speech/language stability and outcomes. Journal of Speech, Language, and Hearing Research 42: 744–61.

Johnston J (2005) Letters to the editor. Re: Law, Garrett and Nye (2004a). The efficacy of treatment for children with developmental speech and language delay/disorders: a meta-analysis. Journal of Speech, Language, and Hearing Research 48: 1114–20.

Jones M, Onslow M, Packman A et al. (2005) A randomised control trial of the Lidcombe Programme for early stuttering. British Medical Journal 331: 659–61.

Justice L, Fey M (2004) Evidence-based practice in schools: integrating craft and theory with science and data. The ASHA Leader 4–5: 3–32.

Kaderavek JN, Sulzby E (2000) Narrative production by children with and without specific language impairment: oral narratives and emergent readings. Journal of Speech, Language, and Hearing Research 43: 34–49.

Kamhi AG (1999) To use or not to use: factors that influence the selection of new treatment approaches. Language, Speech and Hearing Services in Schools 30: 92–8.

Kazdin AE (1999) The meanings and measurements of clinical significance. Journal of Consulting and Clinical Psychology 67: 332–9.

Kazdin AE (2001) Bridging the enormous gaps of theory with therapy research and practice. Journal of Clinical Child Psychology 30: 59–66.

Larson V, McKinely N, Boley D (1993) Clinical forum: adolescent language. Service delivery models for adolescents with language disorders. Language Speech and Hearing Services in Schools 24: 36–42.

Law M (2000) Strategies for implementing evidence-based practice in early intervention. Infants and Young Children 13: 32–40.

Law J, Lindsay G, Peacey N et al. (2000) Provision for Children with Speech and Language Needs in England and Wales: Facilitating Communication between Education and Health Services. London: DfEE/DoH.

Law J, Garrett Z, Nye C (2003). Speech and language therapy interventions for children with primary speech and language delay or disorder. Cochrane Database of Systematic Reviews, Issue 3. Art. No.: CD004110. DOI: 10.1002/14651858. CD004110.

Law J, Garrett Z, Nye C (2004) The efficacy of treatment for children with developmental speech and language delay/disorder: a meta-analysis. Journal of Speech, Language, and Hearing Research 47: 924–43.

Leahy M, Dodd B (2002) Why should secondary schools come second? RCSLT Bulletin 601: 11–13.

Liles B (1993) Narrative discourse in children with language disorders and children with normal language: a critical review of the literature. Journal of Speech and Hearing Research 36: 868–82.

Lindsay G, Soloff N, Law J et al. (2002) Speech and language therapy services to education in England and Wales. International Journal of Language and Communication 37: 273–88.

Maric N (2006) An exploration of visual imagery training on development of reading comprehension in children with specific language impairment (SLI). Dissertation (MSc), Department of Language and Communication Science, City University, London.

Markham C, Dean T (2006) Parents' and professionals' perceptions of quality of life in children with speech and language difficulty. International Journal of Language and Communication Disorders 41: 189–212.

Mathews J (2003) A framework for the creation of practitioner-based evidence. Educational and Child Psychology 20(4): 60–7.

McIntosh B, Crosbie S, Holm A et al. (2007) Enhancing the phonological awareness and language skills of socially disadvantaged preschoolers: an interdisciplinary programme. Child Language Teaching and Therapy 23(3): 267–86.

McKinley N, Larson V (1989) Students who can't communicate: speech-language services at the secondary level. National Association of Secondary School Principals Curriculum Report 19: 1–8.

McLeod S (2006) An holistic view of a child with unintelligible speech: insights from the ICF and ICF–CY. Advances in Speech-Language Pathology 8(3): 293–315.

McLeod S (2004) Speech pathologists' application of the ICF to children with speech impairment. Advances in Speech-Language Pathology 6(1): 75–81.

McLeod S, Baker E (2004) Current clinical practice for children with speech impairment. In: BE Murdoch, J Goozee, B-M Whelan et al. (eds), 26th World Congress of the International Association of Logopedics and Phoniatrics. Brisbane: University of Queensland.

Meline T, Schmitt J (1997) Case studies for evaluating significance in group designs. American Journal of Speech-Language Pathology 6: 33–41.

Meline T, Paradiso T (2003) Evidence-based practice in schools: evaluating research and reducing barriers. Language, Speech and Hearing Services in Schools 34: 273–83.

Meline T, Wang B (2004) Effect-size reporting practices in AJSLP and other ASHA journals 1999–2003. American Journal of Speech-Language Pathology 13: 202–7.

Mellard DE, Deshler DD, Barth A (2004) LD identification: it's not simply a matter of building a better mousetrap. Learning Disability Quarterly 27(4): 229–42.

Merritt D, Liles B (1987) Story grammar ability in children with and without language disorder: story generation, story retelling and story comprehension. Journal of Speech and Hearing Research 30: 539–52.

Milosky LM (1987) Narratives in the classroom. Seminars in Speech and Language 8(4): 329–43.

Moshman D (1999) Adolescent Psychological Development. Rationality, Morality and Identity. Mahwah, NJ: LEA Publishers.

Nash H, Snowling M (2006) Teaching new words to children with poor existing vocabulary knowledge: a controlled evaluation of the definition and context methods. International Journal of Language and Communication Disorders 41(3): 335–54.

Nippold M (1998) Later Language Development. The School-Age and Adolescent Years. Austin, TX: Pro-ed.

Nippold M (1999) Word definition in adolescents as a function of reading proficiency: a research note. Child, Language, Teaching and Therapy 15(2): 171–6.

Nippold M (2004) Research on later language development: international perspectives. In: RA Berman (ed.), Language Development across Childhood and Adolescence. Amsterdam: John Benjamins Publishing Company, pp. 1–8.

Nippold M (2007) Later Language Development. School-Age Children, Adolescents, and Young Adults, 3rd edn. Austin, TX: Pro-ed.

Nippold M, Hegel S, Sohlberg M et al. (1999) Defining abstract entities: development in preadolescents, adolescents and young adults. Journal of Speech, Language, and Hearing Research 42: 473–81.

Norbury C, Bishop DVM (2002) Inferential processing and story recall in children with communication problems: a comparison of specific language impairment, pragmatic language impairment and high-functioning autism. International Journal of Language and Communication Disorders 37: 227–51.

Oakhill J, Patel S (1991) Can imagery training help children who have comprehension difficulties? Journal of Research in Reading 14: 106–15.

Ollendick TH, King N (2004) Empirically supported treatments for children and adolescents: advances toward evidence-based practice. In: PM Barrett, TH Ollendick (eds), Handbook of Interventions That Work with Children and Adolescents. Prevention and Treatment. London: John Wiley & Sons, Ltd, pp. 3–25.

Owen AS, Owen OL, Pannbacker MH et al. (1994) Research strategy and design. In: MH Pannbacker, GF Middleton (eds), Introduction to Clinical Research in

Communication Disorders. San Diego, CA: Singular Publishing Group, pp. 103–18.

Owen R, Hayett L, Roulstone S (2004) Children's views of speech and language therapy in school: consulting children with communication difficulties. Journal of Child, Language, Teaching and Therapy 20(1): 55–73.

Paivio A (1971) Imagery and Verbal Processes. New York: Holt, Rinehart and Winston.

Paivio A (1983) The mind's eye in arts and science. Poetics 12: 1–18.

Paivio A (1991) Dual coding theory: retrospect and current status. Canadian Journal of Psychology 45: 255–87.

Parsons S, Law J, Gasciogne M (2005) Teaching receptive vocabulary to children with specific language impairment: a curriculum-based approach. Child, Language, Teaching and Therapy 21(1): 39–59.

Paul R (2001) Language Disorders from Infancy through Adolescence. Assessment and Intervention 2nd Edition. St Louis, MO: Mosby.

Paul R, Smith RL (1993) Narrative skills in 4-year-olds with normal, impaired, and late-developing language. Journal of Speech and Hearing Research 36: 592–8.

Pawson R, Tilley N (1997) Realist Evaluation. London: Sage.

Pearson VAH (1995) Speech and language therapy: is it effective? Public Health 109: 143–53.

Piaget J (1963) The Origins of Intelligence in Children. New York: W.W. Norton & Company, Inc.

Pressley GM (1976) Mental imagery helps eight-year-olds remember what they read. Journal of Educational Psychology 68: 355–9.

Pring T (2004) Ask a silly question: two decades of troublesome trials. International Journal of Language and Communication Disorders 39(3): 285–302.

Pring T (2005) Research Methods in Communication Disorders. London: Whurr.

Ravid D (2004) Derivational morphology revisited: later lexical development in Hebrew. In: RA Berman (ed.), Language Development across Childhood and Adolescence. Amsterdam: John Benjamins Publishing Company, pp. 53–81.

Reilly S, Douglas J, Oates J (eds) (2004) Evidence Based Practice in Speech Pathology. London: Whurr.

Robey R, Schultz M (1998) A model for conducting clinical outcome research: an adaptation of the standard protocol for use in aphasiology. Aphasiology 12: 787–810.

Roth FP, Spekman NJ (1986) Narrative discourse: spontaneously generated stories of learning-disabled and normally achieving students. Journal of Speech and Hearing Disorders 51: 8–23.

Royal College of Speech and Language Therapists (RCSLT) (2005). RCSLT Statutory Company Information. London: RCSLT.

Rice M (2004) Growth models of developmental language disorders. In: ML Rice, SF Warren (eds), Developmental Language Disorders: From Phenotype to Etiologies. Mahwah, NJ: Lawrence Erlbaum Associates, pp. 207–40.

Sackett D, Rosenberg W, Muir Gray J et al. (1996) Evidence based medicine: what it is and what it isn't. British Medical Journal 312: 71–2.

Sadoski M, Paivio A (2001) Imagery and Text: A Dual Coding Theory of Reading and Writing. Mahwah, NJ: Lawrence Erlbaum Associates.

Sadoski M, Paivio A (2004) A dual coding theoretical model of reading. In: RB Ruddell, NJ Unrau (eds), Theoretical Models and Processes of Reading, 5th edn. Newark, DE: International Reading Association, pp. 1329–62.

Sadoski M, Paivio A, Goetz ET (1991) Commentary: a critique of schema theory in reading and a dual coding alternative. Reading Research Quarterly 26: 463–84.

Sampson Graner P, Faggella-Luby M, Fritschmann N (2005) An overview of responsiveness to intervention. What practitioners ought to know. Topics in Language Disorders 25(2): 93–105.

Shanks B (2000) Telling tales. The RCSLT Bulletin 583: 9–10.

Shanks B (2003) Only a story? Speech and Language Therapy in Practice Spring: 10–13.

Shanks B, Rippon R (2003) Speaking and Listening Through Narrative: A Pack of Activities and Ideas to Target at Key Stage 1, 2nd edn. Keighley: Black Sheep Press.

Sim I (1998) One plus one equals three! Improving vocabulary acquisition and learning in pupils with speech and language impairments. Child, Language, Teaching and Therapy 14(1): 83–93.

Snowling MJ, Adams JW, Bishop DVM et al. (2001) Educational attainments of school leavers with preschool history of speech-language impairments. International Journal of Language and Communication Disorders 36(2): 173–83.

Stringer H (2006) Facilitating narrative and social skills in secondary school students with language and behaviour difficulties. In: J Ginsborg, J Clegg (eds), Language and Social Disadvantage. London: Wiley Publishers, pp. 199–206.

Suttie E (2007) Whole class narrative intervention. RCSLT Bulletin 663: 14–15.

Swanson LA, Fey ME, Mills CE et al. (2005) Use of narrative-based language intervention with children who have specific language impairment. American Journal of Speech-Language Pathology 14: 131–43.

Threats TT (2000) The World Health Organization's revised classification: what does it mean for speech-language pathology? Journal of Medical Speech-Language Pathology 8: 13–18.

Threats TT (2002) Evidence-based practice research using a WHO framework. Journal of Medical Speech-Language Pathology 10(3): 17–24.

Threats TT, Worrall L (2004) Classifying communication disability using the ICF. Advances in Speech-Language Pathology 6: 53–62.

Tomblin JB, Freese PR, Records NL (1992) Diagnosing specific language impairment in adults for the purpose of pedigree analysis. Journal of Speech, Language, and Hearing Research 35: 832–43.

Vallino-Napoli L, Reilly S (2004) Evidence-based health care: a survey of speech pathology practice. Advances in Speech-Language Pathology 6(2): 107–12.

Vygotsky L (1978) Mind in Society. Cambridge, MA: Harvard University Press.

Washington KN (2007) Using the ICF within speech-language pathology: application to developmental language impairment. Advances in Speech-Language Pathology 9(3): 242–55.

Wertz RT (2002) Evidence-based practice guidelines: not all evidence is created equal. Journal of Medical Speech-Language Pathology 10(3): 11–15.

Wetherell D, Botting N, Conti-Ramsden G (2007) Narrative in adolescent SLI: a comparison with peers across two different narrative genres. International Journal of Language and Communication Disorders 42(5): 583–605.

World Health Organization (2001) ICF: International Classification of Functioning, Disability and Health. Geneva: World Health Organization.

Ylvisaker M, Coelho C, Kennedy M et al. (2002) Reflections on evidence-based practice and rationale clinical decision making. Journal of Medical Speech-Language Pathology 10(3): 26–33.

CHAPTER 6

Comparing and contrasting views: building consensus around quality of life with aphasia

MADELINE CRUICE,[1,2] RUTH HILL,[1] LINDA WORRALL,[2] AND LOUISE HICKSON[2]

[1]Department of Language and Communication Science, City University, London
[2]Communication Disability Centre, School of Health and Rehabilitation Sciences, University of Queensland, Australia

Introduction

In aphasiology, there is little published research on what quality of life is like for people who have aphasia. There are seminal papers on the consequences of aphasia on life that have been gathered through interviews with clients and relatives, but to the best of our knowledge, there are none that explicitly investigate 'quality of life'. Despite this, there is an ever-increasing need in speech and language therapy for clinicians to understand, and to provide intervention in the context of, the broader life quality issues for clients. This chapter begins to address this gap in our knowledge base, by sharing with readers the findings of quality of life interviews conducted with 30 Australian men and women with chronic aphasia after stroke.

Communicating with and interviewing persons with language impairment can be a challenge. When patients or clients with aphasia are unable to communicate their views, it is routine to rely on relatives and others to provide that information. However, we should be cautious about asking family members and friends to comment on the aphasic person's *quality*

Language Disorders in Children and Adults: New Issues in Research and Practice.   Victoria Joffe, Madeline Cruice, Shula Chiat.
© 2008 John Wiley & Sons, Ltd. ISBN 978-0-470-51839-7

of life, as recent research shows that significant others score their partners' health-related quality of life *lower* than the persons would themselves (Cruice et al., 2005; Hilari et al., 2007). Further research is needed to determine whether we can rely on relatives and others to provide reliable information about someone's quality of life, and also to explore where and why different views might arise. This chapter takes the first step in that direction, sharing findings from interviews with 28 family members and two friends who partnered the aphasic men and women mentioned above. These significant others took part in the capacity of a 'proxy respondent', answering interview questions as if they were the aphasic person. Comparing and contrasting these perspectives (aphasic person versus other) will enable us to build consensus on what quality of life is like for men and women with aphasia after stroke.

Quality of life

Quality of life has only seen recent introduction to the health and social sciences, and then to different degrees amongst the professional fields. Within speech and language therapy, quality of life research has been undertaken in primarily five populations: head and neck cancer, aphasia, Parkinson's disease, traumatic brain injury and voice (see Cruice et al., 2000 for a review). More recent research has developed in multiple sclerosis, although not specifically on communication and swallowing changes. Research with these individuals has been fundamentally *exploratory*, seeking to describe a sample's life quality on specific questionnaires or surveys.

On the other hand, paediatric quality of life is less systemically researched, and less empirical work has been undertaken. The populations typically investigated are those that are high mortality, high cost and high care, such as oncology, transplant, asthma, epilepsy, diabetes and rheumatism (Pal, 1996). In paediatric speech and language therapy, recent research by Markham and Dean (2006) reveals insights into children and adolescents' quality of life with speech and language difficulties. The main source of information has been the parents or the care staff and not the child/teenager's views of their quality of life. Interestingly, social determinants of life quality, such as family and friends, are more highly acknowledged and valued in paediatric research than in adults (Pal, 1996), most likely due to the significant influence in the child's development. Researching quality of life with children and teenagers raises many issues around age and development, the changing nature of children, and cognitive capacity, verbal proficiency and reading ability to name a few (Rosenbaum and Saigal, 1996), and serve as useful reminders to apply similar scrutiny to adult quality of life investigation.

Quality of life with aphasia

Delving into quality of life issues of people with communication disabilities raises more questions than we currently have answers for. What does quality of life mean to people with aphasia after stroke? What should we be focusing on in speech and language therapy intervention that will improve or maintain the person's quality of life? What outcome measures can we use to capture this? What are health systems and social services prepared to pay for in relation to quality of life? In order to build our knowledge base and answer these questions, we can look towards existing conceptual, quantitative and qualitative research within aphasiology as a starter.

In 1999, LaPointe suggested that we consider quality of life with aphasia as a number of life dimensions: physical, toxicity, body image and mobility, communication, psychological, interpersonal, spiritual and financial. Taylor Sarno (1997) describes quality of life with aphasia as viewed as a 'total human response to an unexpected and unwanted life event' (p. 675). This is given meaning that is influenced by an individual's 'personality, psychology, life expectations and achievement, system of beliefs and values, and philosophy in life' (Taylor Sarno, 1997, p. 676). In 2002, Cruice proposed that quality of life with aphasia could be defined not only in personal terms, but also in terms of physical, social, emotional and mental health, and psychological well-being. In 2003, three quantitative studies of aphasic people's quality of life were published (Cruice et al., 2003; Hilari et al., 2003; Ross and Wertz, 2003). These demonstrated that aphasic people's emotional distress, involvement in activities, functional communication ability and co-morbidity (health conditions) predicted their quality of life (Cruice et al., 2003; Hilari et al., 2003), and that independence, social relationships and the environment distinguished aphasic from non-aphasic quality of life (Ross and Wertz, 2003). Turning back in time to the 1990s, we also find direction from two seminal pieces of qualitative research on the impact of aphasia on life (Le Dorze and Brassard, 1995; Zemva, 1999). These two papers (a combined total of 29 people with aphasia and their 29 relatives) reported the handicapping effects of aphasia to be altered communication, changes in communication situations, physical dependency, changes in interpersonal relationships, loss of autonomy, restricted activities, fewer social contacts, changed social life, stigmatization, difficulty controlling emotions, and negative feelings of anxiety, irritation, stress, annoyance and loneliness. Thus, it would seem that change, restriction and dependency, and emotions, activities, communication and the physical aspects of life are important in quality of life with aphasia after stroke, and are topics that may arise during explicit and structured interviews on quality of life.

Differences of opinion

Given that we do not have an agreed understanding or definition of what quality of life actually is or means in health care, it is unsurprising to learn that the views of patients, relatives, friends and health professionals differ on quality of life questionnaires (Addington-Hall and Kalra, 2001). Within aphasiology, we can anticipate that relatives and friends may show a particular bias in prospective quality of life interviews. For example, we know from Le Dorze and Brassard's work (1995) that relatives and friends are concerned with changes in roles, worries about finances, and concerns over their own and the aphasic person's health, which are different to the issues raised by aphasic participants in that study. Similarly, family members seem to focus more on handicap after aphasia, whereas clinicians tend to focus more on disability (Oxenham et al., 1995).

In quality of life stroke studies, family members or others are often used as proxy respondents for language and/or cognitively impaired research participants, who are excluded on the basis of their aphasia or other difficulties (see Segal and Schall, 1994 or de Haan et al., 1995). It is not entirely clear though what level of bias these family members and others introduce into the results. Do they say the same things as the patient would say? Do they score the patient the same on tests and questionnaires as the patient would score himself or herself? The best way to answer these questions is to gather the opinions of both parties from non-communication-impaired couples and compare their assessment scores. From a substantial body of research in the general quality of life field, we know that others not only have a general tendency to report *lower* or *worse* quality of life on assessment (Addington-Hall and Kalra, 2001), but also that others' views are not always consistent. That is, they may score the person lower in one quality of life domain such as physical health, but score the person roughly similar on another domain such as daily activities (Addington-Hall and Kalra, 2001).

Within aphasiology, two recent significant studies confirm that family members and friends follow this same general pattern. Hilari and colleagues (2007) found that family members and friends of 50 men and women with chronic aphasia (aged 32–80 years, mean of 7.1 years post-stroke) rated their aphasic partners with more affected (worse) health-related quality of life (tapping physical, psychosocial, communication and energy domains) than the aphasic men and women rated themselves. Cruice and colleagues (2005) found that family members and friends of 30 men and women with chronic aphasia (aged 57–88 years, mean of 3.4 years post-stroke) rated their aphasic partners with lower global and physical health-related quality of life (tapping physical functioning, general or overall health, pain and vitality).

When comparing proxies and self-reports in the quality of life field, it is argued that it is not just significant differences that are important, but also the correlation or association between the sets of scores. For example, a high correlation suggests 'excellent agreement' (e.g. 0.8) between the data sets, meaning that the family members and others are *consistently rating lower* than the aphasic individuals. A medium to low correlation suggests only 'fair agreement' (e.g. 0.5) between the data sets, meaning that there is less consistency, with some rating higher and some rating lower, or some are rating lower by one point on the scale and others are rating lower by two to three points on the scale, for example. From both these studies, it seems that family and friends are the most consistent when reporting on questions that pertain to overall and physical life quality, that is, they all underrate. However, it is more difficult to identify a clear pattern or trend in how they report on psychosocial aspects, communication, feelings and daily activities (Cruice et al., 2005; Hilari et al., 2007), and impossible to predict how they will report on social life aspects such as social functioning, activities, support and relations with others (Cruice et al., 2005). These differences of opinion are equally likely to present in qualitative interviews, and form the basis for the analysis and discussion of this chapter.

Current study

This section of the chapter reports the details of the 60 participants involved in the study, the structured interview questions, the procedure for the study and the analysis used to examine the interview responses. Two different ways of comparing and contrasting the data are explained: the first as 30 individual pairs, the second as two group samples: client and proxy. Carrying out both comparisons demonstrates just how strikingly *different* methodologies can impact on the findings from the *same* interview data.

Thirty Australian individuals (16 women, 14 men) with mild to moderate aphasic impairment and normal to moderate mobility took part. Participants were drawn from metropolitan hospitals, university clinics, stroke groups, other research studies and state stroke associations. The average age of the aphasic participants was 71 years, in the range 57–88 years. Aphasic participants were, on average, 41 months post-stroke (range 10–108 months), and had a mean education of 11 years (range 6–20 years). Education was calculated in terms of years spent in schooling, higher education and training. Aphasic individuals had a range of occupations including: engineer; manager of caravan park/betting agency/bank/radio station; housewife; harness maker; police officer; nursing assistant; teacher; ferry boat driver; and more.

Aphasic individuals had to meet the following criteria to be included in the study:

- speak English as their first language;
- demonstrate aphasia at time of stroke and self-report ongoing aphasic difficulties;

Table 6.1 Language abilities of aphasic participants as measured by the WAB

	Mean	Standard deviation	Range
WAB AQ	74.4	18.6	21.9–95.8[a]
Fluency	15	4.2	4–20
Comprehension	8.5	1.3	6–10
Repetition	6.9	2.9	0–10
Naming	6.7	2.4	0–9.5

[a] Four participants were above the standard WAB cut-off of 93.8 but still displayed higher-level linguistic impairments.
WAB AQ, Western Aphasia Battery Aphasia Quotient.

- have a reliable yes/no response (no less than 16/20 on the *Western Aphasia Battery* (WAB) yes/no questions; Kertesz, 1982);
- have moderate auditory comprehension ability at time of interviewing (no less than 5/10 on the WAB comprehension subtest);
- have no concomitant neurological disease;
- have normal to moderate mobility (participants requiring a wheelchair were excluded to minimize the impact of physical impairment on quality of life);
- be almost 12 months post-stroke or more;
- live independently in the community; and
- have a family member or friend agree to act as a proxy respondent.

Using the WAB Aphasia Quotient (AQ) scores as a basis for severity of linguistic impairment, Table 6.1 illustrates that the aphasic individuals were largely fluent, with good auditory comprehension, and average repetition and naming skills. The range of AQ scores indicates mild to moderate-severe linguistic impairment; however, the majority of scores fell between 60 and 89, meaning primarily mild to moderate linguistic impairment. Using the WAB profiles, 15 individuals had anomic aphasia, eight had conduction aphasia, three had Broca's type aphasia and Wernicke's type aphasia each, and one individual had transcortical sensory aphasia.

Aphasic individuals self-selected their family member or friend as a proxy,[1] and were simply instructed to choose 'someone who knows you well and can answer questions about your quality of life'. However, family members and friends were still required to meet the following criteria to be included in the study:

[1] There are two ways of acting as a proxy respondent. The first is to comment on someone else's life, for example, Wendy comments on her husband John's life as she sees it from her perspective. The second way is to comment on someone else's behalf, that is, Wendy says what she thinks John would say to the question. This study used the *second* interpretation of proxy.

- speak English as first language;
- live independently;
- have a negative history of cerebrovascular or neurological disease (one spouse excluded after interviewing on basis of having had a stroke himself);
- not take medication for clinical depression; and
- have regular contact of some form with the person with aphasia that was more frequent than monthly.

Twenty-three women and six men took part in this study ($N = 29$). Thirty members were originally contacted, but one family member was later excluded on the basis of having had a stroke. Proxies comprised 16 spouses, nine children (primarily daughters), two friends, one sibling and one daughter-in-law. They had a mean age of 57 years (range 27–80 years), and an average of 11.7 years education (range 5–18 years). Proxies knew participants for, on average, 40 years (range 3–70 years). Twenty-six proxies had daily contact with participants, two had weekly and one had fortnightly contact. In terms of the most common type of contact, 21 proxies lived with the participants, five phoned and three visited. Family members and friends were also asked to indicate their main support role in their relationship with their aphasic partner, choosing from tangible support, emotional support, social support and informational support. Fifteen proxies indicated their main role as emotional support, four as informational support, three as tangible support and seven could not choose a main support role. Proxies had a range of occupations including: home duties; manager (airline training, advertising productions, bakery, primary industries); teacher; clerk/secretary; nurse; social worker; labourer, cable joiner, machinist, tool maker; and gem sorter.

Respondents (aphasic individuals and family members/friends) were separately interviewed in their own homes using six open-ended questions in a structured interview with a speech and language therapist. Interviews were conducted on the same day to ensure that respondents did not confer with each other. The first five questions were drawn from Farquhar's work (1995) of elderly Londoners' quality of life, and a sixth question specifically targeting communication was added (see below). Family members and friends were instructed to respond to the question as they thought their aphasic counterpart *would* respond, not as they thought the person *should* respond. Whilst this should/would emphasis seems a pedantic semantic difference, it is important to differentiate the two in proxy quality of life research. For example, if Wendy were to judge her husband John's social life, she could think that because he has lots of people drop by the house and his mates take him out fishing once a week, that he *should* say his social life is good. However, because Wendy knows John well and knows that he feels unequal in the group and feels 'looked after' by his mates, this impacts on how he feels about his social life, and he *would* say his social life was not good. Thus, questions were rephrased for family members and friends to encourage them to think in this manner. For example, in his interview, John was asked, 'What things give your life quality?' When interviewing John's wife, she was asked, 'Wendy, what things would *John* say give his life quality?' It is important to note that even though questions were rephrased and probe reminders were given during the interviews, some proxy respondents found it difficult to follow this line of thinking, and the language they used when responding sometimes suggests they were reflecting their own views on what *should* be the answer. Responses to the questions were not timed and the respondents were instructed to provide as little or as much information as they wanted. Because respondents were engaged in a large study with numerous assessments being carried out (see Cruice et al., 2003), their responses were not probed so as to keep respondent burden to a minimum. People's responses were audiotaped or sometimes recorded online, and transcribed by the original researcher (Cruice).

Structured interview questions

1. How would you describe the quality of your life? And why do you say that?
2. What things give your life quality?
3. What things take quality away from your life?
4. What would make the quality of your life better?
5. What would make the quality of your life worse?
6. Does communication have an impact on the quality of your life? If yes, then how?

Data analysis

Two sets of data were generated: that from aphasic participants and that from family members and friends. The aphasic data was coded and analysed first as a group. Second, the family and friend data was analysed, with each family member or friend matched to their aphasic partner (generating 30 pairs of data), and their response was coded in relation to the concepts and categories that had already been identified in their aphasic partner's response. Third, additional information from the family member and friend data that was not matched against their aphasic partner was coded and analysed as its own group. These three sets of coding and analyses enabled us to ask the following two research questions of the data:

1. How good are individual family members and friends at commenting on their partners' quality of life, that is, how much of what each one says is what their aphasic partner has also said? (individual matches)
2. How good are family members and friends in general at commenting on aphasic individuals' quality of life in general? (overall group data comparison)

Using content analysis, the research assistant started with the aphasic data, and read each of the 30 responses to a question (e.g. Question 2) and categorized a word or a group of words as a *unit of data* (Patton, 1990; Step 1). A unit of data could be a word, a phrase, a clause or a sentence that had a distinct semantic meaning. Example units of data from aphasic respondents from Question 2 include: 'movies'; 'I go to the pictures'; and 'get at my machine, do all me sewing'. Then, looking at all 30 responses for a question, units of data that were semantically related were identified and coded as *concepts* (Step 2). For example, 'movies' and 'I go to the pictures' were coded under 'Entertainment'. Concepts that were further semantically similar were identified and merged to form a *category* (Step 3). For example, 'Entertainment' became one concept underneath the umbrella category of 'Activities' and included other concepts of 'Outdoor activities', 'Social activities', 'Personal interests' and 'Occupational interests' from the Question 2 aphasic data.

To ensure that data was coded only once, strict definitions were written about what comprised each concept and each category. This would enable another person to code the data in the same way as the research assistant. An example definition of a concept is provided: Entertainment – 'these activities must involve mainstream entertainment mediums and be the primary foci of interest for the individual (with the view that any additional or potential interactions with people are secondary to the activity itself)'. Once all the data for each question had been coded, it was visually represented as a mind map using the Mind Manager Pro software(Mindjet (UK) Ltd, Tackley, Oxon, UK). The mind map for each question included all the categories, concepts and units of data that had been coded, and thus enabled the researchers to make judgements about the importance of the categories and concepts within the data. For example, there were 27 units of data coded under 'Activities' in Question 2 aphasic data, compared with four units of data coded under 'Home'[2]. Finally, the mind maps for each question were scrutinized and compared across the questions, and categories that appeared across the questions were identified to create superordinate themes. For example, 'Activities' appeared in Questions 1, 2, 3, 4 and 6 from the aphasic data, and thus became a strong theme within the data. In conclusion, this system of coding and analysis resulted in three distinct sets of maps: (1) maps that represented all of the aphasic participants' data; (2) maps that represented the matched units of data between each aphasic person and their proxy; and (3) maps that represented the additional content that proxies said during interviews that was not matched to their individual partner. Tallies of units of data per concept and per category were recorded on the maps. In this manner, we are able to compare what aphasic

---

[2] The reader will note that tallies of units of data per concept and per category were recorded. The usefulness of this quasi-quantitative method for recoding qualitative data will become apparent when reading the results of the data compared at the individual level, that is, the matched data between each aphasic participant–proxy pair.

individuals and family members and friends say at an individual level and at a group level.

Results – comparisons at the individual level

Table 6.2 illustrates that proxy respondents' matched views accounted for between 20 and 34% of what aphasic participants said about the quality of their lives. It must be understood that proxy respondents said a lot more than what is portrayed in the second column, which represents only those numbers from the matched group.

An analysis of matched units of data by category in Appendix 6.A makes it easier to identify whether there was a trend in terms of what type of content participants and proxies matched on. The data shows that the most matches occurred on the People, Activities, and Verbal communication categories, and some key points can be drawn out from the data as follows:

1. A proportion of matched proxies recognized that having people in one's life contributed to their aphasic partners' quality of lives, and losing people would worsen their future life quality.
2. A proportion of matched proxies recognized that doing activities and having activities contributed quality in life, and not being able to do activities or being limited detracted from current life quality. Proxies did not realize that doing activities would improve their partners' future life quality, and do not refer to activities that people can no longer do when asked about the impact of communication on life quality.
3. A proportion of matched proxies were aware of verbal communication difficulties having an impact on their aphasic partners' life quality, but were more likely to say this in response to a specific question about the

Table 6.2 Client–proxy matched views

Structured interview question	Number of units of data that matched between proxy and participant data	Total number of units of data coded in aphasic participants' data to the question	Percentage matched as a proportion of aphasic data (%)
1a	10	30	33.33
1b	16	68	23.53
2	24	93	25.8
3	15	62	24.19
4	11	54	20.37
5	12	43	27.9
6b	16	47	34.04

impact of communication, and not in a general question about what takes quality away from their partners' current life. A proportion realized that improved verbal communication would improve future life quality. Proxies did not recognize that communication (positive examples) gave quality to their partners' current lives, and did not raise any positive examples of communication at all (in contrast to the aphasic sample who reported remaining communication strengths in Question 6).

Thus, the message from this comparison at the individual aphasic participant–proxy level is that, approximately, only one-third of family members or friends (based on coded units of meaning) raised the same or similar issues around People, Activities and Verbal communication as aphasic individuals. Furthermore, many categories raised by aphasic participants were not identified by their proxy partner. It implies that each family member or friend was a relatively poor informant for their aphasic partner, and that asking relatives and others is not a reasonable substitute for the aphasic person's views.

Results – comparisons at the group level

Comparing and contrasting the 30 aphasic participants' data as a group and the 30 family members' and friends' data as a group reveals a completely different picture in this study. The following results are presented in terms of what categories are shared between both groups, that is, both data sets include, for example, 'being mobile' as contributing to quality of life now, even though there may be no exact matches between an aphasic individual and their proxy partner. This is followed by the categories specifically reported in the aphasic data, and then the categories specific to family member and friend data. Categories are presented in order of decreasing priority as they appeared in the data. Quotes (i.e. units of data) from interviews are included in Appendix 6.B.

Shared perspectives of quality of life with aphasia

Aphasic persons and family members and friends both mentioned the following eight categories when describing what gave people quality in life now (Question 2):

- having people in one's life;
- having activities one can do and/or doing activities;
- having a positive outlook;
- socializing and/or being with others;
- having a choice;
- perceiving improvement in one's state

- being mobile; and
- being happy in one's home or community area.

They both mentioned the following eight categories when describing what currently took quality away from people's lives (Question 3):

- limited ability and/or being unable to do activities and things;
- impaired functioning;
- difficulties in speaking;
- poor mobility or loss of mobility;
- having had the stroke;
- difficulties in reading and writing;
- dependence; and
- poor health.

Both mentioned the following four categories in response to what would improve quality of life (Question 4):

- being able to speak better;
- being able to do activities;
- having better body functioning; and
- being more independent.

Finally, both mentioned the following three categories in response to what would make life quality worse (Question 5):

- having another stroke;
- loss (of people, existing speech, ability to do activities and/or things, and mobility); and
- becoming poorer in health.

Different perspectives of quality of life with aphasia

The magnitude of the different perspectives between aphasic individuals and family members and friends was small. The concepts or categories described below (highlighted in the text by bold font) were not largely represented across all respondents. Nonetheless, their presence in one group (e.g. aphasic data) and absence in the other group (e.g. family and friend data) is worth noting.

Categories specific to people with aphasia

Three individuals mentioned **communication** when asked about what gave their life quality, for example, 'speaking to my son' and 'talking to people, I delight in talking'. Two individuals described **support from others** in response to this same question: 'that lady has given me a new lease of life' (referring to a new manager for the caravan park, easing the stress he and his wife were having) and 'I think it's wonderful because if it's not so well, we can tell you' (referring to a call bell in her unit that she can use to alert staff in emergencies). Four individuals were worried about **losing functioning of hand and leg body parts** impacting on future life quality, for example, 'if I couldn't use my right hand' and 'had a broken leg'. In response to the final interview question, five individuals described a **negative impact of communication on their activities**, for example, '[I used to travel about Queensland] and talk to people [about religion] and now I couldn't tell you how to' and 'stops me going out' (referring to going shopping on his own).

Categories specific to family members and friends

Family members and friends talked more about the **emotional consequences** of the communication difficulties now experienced by their aphasic partners, for example, 'finds it embarrassing communicating with other people', 'upset because of difficulties understanding' (said by one daughter in reference to her mother not being able to follow the new computer course she was attending), and 'insecure and the feeling she can't cope unless there's someone around to support her'. Some family members even went as far as describing the **impact on self**, for example, 'feels like a burden and that he's not contributing' and 'feels useless'.

Family members and friends talked both positively and negatively about **socializing** (whereas aphasic persons tended to focus more on specific social activities), for example, 'he loves people, seeing people and having a cup of tea. Likes to come to the hairdresser with me, likes all the girls' and 'he's a people person who likes to talk to them. It doesn't matter whether they are friends or strangers'. There were many negative statements about the impact of aphasia and other consequences on the **ability to socialize and participate**: 'at picnics, R is an observer, before he was always a participator' and 'there's times where she'd like to communicate with other people aside from me'. Family members and friends also tended to talk more comprehensively about the **changes in communication**, for example, 'the fact that he can't have a lengthy conversation with anyone', 'usually the conversation moves too quickly' and 'a lot of the time he can't understand, the main thing, he can't understand what I'm saying'.

Family members spoke more about the **financial situation** than did the aphasic individuals on the whole.[3] Being secure contributed to quality in life, for example, 'has a new bank account', 'not terribly well off but we're comfortable' and 'no financial worries', and more money would

[3] Finance was a designated category three times in the family member and friend data, whereas a few aphasic persons raised it during interviews, but it was coded as 'other'.

improve future quality of life. Family members also discussed the **need for purpose or activity** in life quality, for example, 'keeping himself busy' and 'to be of help to somebody'. Finally, family members spoke more about **good health and health concerns**, than had been mentioned by isolated aphasic individuals, for example, 'his health is pretty good', 'the three disabilities (means diseases) that he has', 'if she lost her sight' and 'probably better health, the number one priority'.

In summary, both people with aphasia and family members and friends valued the following in quality of life with aphasia: (1) other people, activities, speech, mobility, body functioning and health as foremost important; and (2) mental outlook, choice, independence, improvement, living environment, and residual speech, activities and mobility as secondarily important. Prevention of further strokes was an obvious factor in achieving life quality. The small differences that arose between the two groups related to the different emphases placed on: (1) the consequences of aphasia and stroke on communication and activities; and (2) the emotional, social, psychological and financial aspects of life.

Discussion

The content-related findings of the current study, that is, focus on activities, relationships with others and so on, are confirmed by other quality of life research in aphasia, stroke and healthy ageing. These are discussed in the following paragraphs. However, the finding that is perhaps the most striking from this study is the impact of individual versus group analysis on the overall outcome from the study. By analysing at an individual level, the matched pairs data reveals that the majority of family members and friends are exceedingly poor at accurately guessing what quality of life means for their aphasic partners. On the face of it, no one would ever consult family members again; however, leaping to this conclusion is too hasty and requires a little further deliberation. It may well be that family members provide reasonable and appropriate information about their partner's communication styles and preferences, and provide insight into how communication may be affected within the home or when out socially or for business. However, it seems that quality of life is an entirely different consideration, and a complex one too. There are many questions that remain unanswered in this field: has the aphasic person truly understood the question? Does he or she have sufficient language for inner or private speech to support thinking and reasoning (see Varley, Chapter 2 this volume), which is needed when reflecting on one's life? How is the aphasic person making judgements about their life – on the basis of their current state now compared with earlier states, or pre-morbid state or with others in the same situation? Has the family member thought about his or her partner's priorities? Has the family member reflected on the same events as the aphasic person when answering the questions?

By matching the proxy data onto the aphasic partner, we are effectively considering the aphasic person's views to be the 'right' or 'accurate' views (this is the traditional assumption in the general quality of life field). However, in speech and language therapy, we are more aware of differing perspectives from differing information sources, and thus are more inclined to consider both views as useful and valid. Questioning this assumption leads us to re-evaluate how we compare data and undertake group level analysis, yielding different findings. These are more positive in the sense that the data shows that both aphasic individuals and family members and friends have similar ideas about the important issues in quality of life. For example, even though Wendy's responses did not often match with her husband John's data, what she said was still of relevance to other aphasic individuals in the sample. Building consensus by combining both views in this manner is a more credible method than accepting either view in isolation, and leads to a more complete understanding of quality of life with aphasia after stroke.

The current study confirms that *having and being with others*, *having and doing activities*, and *having choice and/or independence*, which have previously been identified as altered with aphasia after stroke (Le Dorze and Brassard, 1995; Zemva, 1999), specifically contribute to quality in life for older men and women with chronic aphasia. Altered communication with aphasia (Le Dorze and Brassard, 1995; Zemva, 1999) was also identified as influencing quality of life; however, respondents in the current study focused almost exclusively on *expressive speech* when discussing their quality of life, unlike the variety of changes in communication situations that Le Dorze and Brassard (1995) had found. Three explanations for this finding are proposed. It is possible that expressive speech was the most powerful aspect of communication in determining quality of life (ahead of reading, writing and comprehension), perhaps because of the greater self-awareness of one's expressive difficulties. Alternatively, expression could have been more of a problem than comprehension for individuals, given that minimum comprehension ability was required to participate in the study. Furthermore, it is equally likely that respondents needed prompts to reflect on *all aspects* of communication in terms of how they influence quality of life and were limited in doing so because the administration procedure did not support them in this way.

Comparisons and contrasts can be made between non-aphasic and aphasic stroke individuals' quality of life. A review of 39 stroke quality of life studies conclusively established that depression, physical and functional disablement, and impaired social functioning constituted quality of life after stroke (Bays, 2001). There is some overlap between Bays' finding and the current study; however, there are also differences. In the current study, no respondent actually explicitly referred to *depression* or *emotional health*. However, family members and friends did refer to embarrassment, frustration, insecurity, being a burden and lack of self worth, and two aphasic individuals were tearful during the interview, resulting in minimal contributions and discontinuation of their interview. It is likely that: (1) aphasic individuals do not have the vocabulary to express the impact of depression on their life quality; (2) aphasic respondents do not consciously make the link between the two; or (3) emotional issues are better revealed on questionnaires that specifically target changes in emotional status and limitations on daily activities. Body functioning and mobility (current study) is a similar concept to *physical and functional disablement* (Bays, 2001), and respondents were specific at mentioning right arm, hand and leg functioning (as well as sensory and cognitive functioning). *Impaired social functioning* was alluded to in the current study, with respondents reporting the importance of doing activities with others, being with others, having others in one's life and the negative impact of aphasia on the individual's ability to communicate and participate in activities and social situations. It is interesting to note that fatigue and energy, which are frequently reported in stroke quality of life (Bays, 2001), were not reported by respondents in the current study.

Finally, respondents in the current study raised *health*, *finances* and *living conditions or community* as quality of life issues. These are infrequently reported in stroke literature but frequently reported by healthy ageing individuals without neurological problems (see Farquhar, 1995; Fry, 2000[4]). It is not uncommon within the field of disability for general areas such as health to be passed over in favour of the dominant emphasis on the person's disability. Furthermore, areas such as finance and living conditions, which are considered not related to health and therefore not targeted by the health care service provision, are also neglected in comprehensive quality of life evaluation.

Clinical implications

This study has implications for our initial and ongoing information gathering practices with clients in order to make intervention more personally relevant to their needs and future goals. This could be achieved by using the six quality of life questions as they are or by generating an interview topic guide[5] to ensure that all possible issues are covered. Both represent a step towards understanding more about our client's *life* perspective and not just their opinion of their communication difficulties. Furthermore, the study demonstrates that a more comprehensive understanding of quality of life is gained by soliciting views from both parties. Gathering information from the aphasic person alone may mean that we omit discussing the health, emotional, psychological, social and financial quality of life concerns that may be present. Conversely, gathering information

---

[4] These studies also support *activities* and *relationships with others* as important contributors to quality of life.

[5] This would include all categories raised by aphasic individuals and family members and friends.

from the family member alone may mean we miss out on hearing about communication strengths, support from others, concerns about losing residual body functioning and the specific negative impact of communication difficulties on people's life activities. The findings also imply that family members and friends are poor *individual* informants about their aphasic partner's life quality, with only one-third of the sample providing some of the same information as their partner about people, activities and verbal communication. Substituting their views for the aphasic person's is not recommended.

The findings of this study also have implications for intervention with people with chronic aphasia. Within the speech and language therapy profession, the findings suggest that improving someone's ability to speak and reducing the difficulties they experience in speaking will influence the client's quality of life. How we go about this though is still to be explored. For example, the clinician and client may choose to work directly on conversation, or indirectly on compensatory strategies and the communication partner's skills. What is implied by the findings though is therapy or intervention that is based on meaningful life activities, delivered in a group format, with a social frame of reference, is more likely to address a broader range of quality of life issues than one-to-one therapy sessions with a therapist (see Marshall (Chapter 3 this volume), however, for a useful illustration of meaningful one-to-one therapy around note-writing skills for work). It would follow that outcome measures of someone's daily and social activities, social network and conversation would be helpful in demonstrating changes in the person's life.

The philosophy or principles behind how such intervention is delivered is equally important. That is, it needs to minimize the embarrassment and frustration that can be potentially experienced, it needs to prevent situations where people feel they cannot cope, it needs to provide the person with an authentic opportunity to contribute to other's lives and thus gain self-worth, it needs to minimize the limitations caused by impaired hand and arm functioning and impaired mobility, and so on. Ultimately though, the study suggests that intervening to change someone's quality of life is going to require going beyond the professional boundary, and looking beyond communication. It suggests that a team perspective is necessary, with professionals working jointly for the client's achievement of life activities. As a final point, the study also highlights the need to prevent further strokes and ill health; therefore, accurate and accessible health information and services is required.

Looking forward

This research has shown that people with aphasia can reflect on their quality of life in a structured interview situation facilitated by a speech and language therapist. Further research is needed to address the main limitation of this study, which is the question of whether or not the respondents said all they wanted to in responding to the interview questions. No further probing of the respondents' answers was requested, and there was no checking with the respondents afterwards to ensure that their data had been coded and interpreted as they had intended it to mean. More specific questioning and probing will yield greater detail and insights into the quality of people's lives, and is worthy of carrying out to identify *how* people with aphasia reflect on their life quality. Making the invisible cognitive and linguistic processes explicit may be undertaken using think-aloud procedures or retrospective cognitive interviews, and as such will make the 'language to support thinking and reasoning' argument available to clinicians and researchers (see Varley, Chapter 2 this volume), so that we may better understand how to facilitate aphasic clients in achieving life quality.

It is important to understand not only the unique processes in reflecting on life quality in older age, but also to understand the impact of aphasia and stroke on younger men and women of working age, whose employment, life relationships with family members and friends, and personal development are interrupted at a much earlier stage in life. Similarly, we need to explore quality of life for persons with more impaired comprehension and physical functioning, as we cannot assume that severe impairments predict severely poor quality of life. Previously published research (e.g. Cruice et al., 2003) shows the dissociation of impairment from social/quality of life functioning, reminding us to *consider*, but not *predict*, a pattern of association. Making an interview procedure accessible and meaningful for persons with substantial comprehension deficits remains a challenge for clinicians and researchers.

Finally, there is no reason why discussions about quality of life cannot be had with children and teenagers with language difficulties, their immediate family and their friends. Although the concepts need to be made more concrete for the younger children, it is thought that children as young as 4 years can comment on their health, family, friends, kindergarten or nursery, and how happy they feel about life and themselves (see KINDL-R, http://www.kindl.org/daten/pdf/englisch/ec_kiddy.pdf). We need to think less about measuring quality of life *per se*, and more about facilitating clients and their families to *improve* their quality of life or achieve quality *in* life.

Concluding remarks

In 1988, Salomon and colleagues wrote, 'life quality for most people is dependent upon the ability and the opportunity to communicate' (p. 164). Whilst this study shows that this statement is certainly true for people with aphasia, it also sounds a warning to clinicians and researchers not to restrict quality of life to communication. It demonstrates that doing activities and having and being with others in life gives people quality in life; it demonstrates that limited ability or being unable to do activities and things, followed by impaired functioning, difficulties speaking and poor mobility take quality away from life. The entire allied health team are needed in addressing the quality of life issues of men and women with chronic aphasia after stroke. Finally, we realize that we build consensus in understanding what quality of life after stroke with aphasia is by combining the views of clients and their family members and friends, suggesting we need to involve others much more in daily clinical practice.

Acknowledgements

The primary author wishes to acknowledge the financial support received via the City University Research Development Fund in 2006, as well as that from the departmental Disability and Society Research Group. This enabled Ruth Hill to work as a research assistant on the data analysis (descriptive coding and thematic definitions) for this research.

References

Addington-Hall J, Kalra L (2001) Measuring quality of life: who should measure quality of life? BMJ 322: 1417–20.

Bays C (2001) Quality of life of stroke survivors: a research synthesis. Journal of Neuroscience Nursing 33(6): 310–16.

Cruice M (2002) Communication and quality of life in older people with aphasia and healthy older people. Unpublished doctoral dissertation, University of Queensland, St Lucia, Australia.

Cruice M, Worrall L, Hickson L (2000) Quality-of-life measurement in speech pathology and audiology. Asia Pacific Journal of Speech, Language, and Hearing 5(1): 1–20.

Cruice M, Worrall L, Hickson L et al. (2003) Finding a focus for quality of life with aphasia: social and emotional health, and psychological well-being. Aphasiology 17(4): 333–53.

Cruice M, Worrall L, Hickson L et al. (2005) Measuring quality of life: comparing family members' and friends' ratings with those of their aphasic partners. Aphasiology 19(2): 111–29.

De Haan R, Limburg M, Van der Meulen J, Jacobs M, Aaronson N (1995) Quality of life after stroke: impact of stroke type and lesion location. Stroke 26: 402–8.

Farquhar M (1995) Elderly people's definitions of quality of life. Social Science and Medicine 41(10): 1439–46.

Fry P (2000) Whose quality of life is it anyway? Why not ask seniors to tell us about it? International Journal of Aging and Human Development 50(4): 361–83.

Hilari K, Wiggins R, Roy P et al. (2003) Predictors of health-related quality of life (HRQL) in people with chronic aphasia. Aphasiology 17(4): 365–81.

Hilari K, Owen S, Farrelly S (2007) Proxy and self report agreement on the stroke and aphasia quality of life scale – 39 (SAQOL-39). Journal of Neurology,

Neurosurgery and Psychiatry. Published Online First: 26 January 2007. DOI:10.1136/jnnp.2006.111476.

Kertesz A (1982) The Western Aphasia Battery. New York: Grune & Stratton.

LaPointe L (1999) Quality of life with aphasia. Seminars in Speech and Language 20(1): 93–4.

Le Dorze G, Brassard C (1995) A description of the consequences of aphasia on aphasic persons and their relatives and friends based on the WHO model of chronic diseases. Aphasiology 9(3): 239–55.

Markham C, Dean T (2006) Parents' and professionals' perceptions of quality of life in children with speech and language difficulty. International Journal of Language and Communication Disorders 41(2): 189–212.

Oxenham D, Sheard C, Adams R (1995) Comparison of clinician and spouse perceptions of the handicap of aphasia: everybody understands 'understanding'. Aphasiology 9(5): 477–93.

Pal D (1996) Quality of life assessment in children: a review of conceptual and methodological issues in multidimensional health status measures. Journal of Epidemiology and Community Health 50: 391–6.

Patton M (1990) Qualitative evaluation and research methods 2nd edn. Newbury Park, CA: Sage.

Rosenbaum P, Saigal S (1996) Chapter 82. Measuring health-related quality of life in pediatric populations: conceptual issues. In: B Spilker (ed.), Quality of Life and Pharmacoeconomics in Clinical Trials, 2nd edn. Philadelphia, PA: Lippincott-Raven Publishers, pp. 785–92.

Ross K, Wertz R (2003) Quality of life with and without aphasia. Aphasiology 17(4): 355–64.

Salomon G, Vesterager V, Jagd M (1988) Age-related hearing difficulties: (I) hearing impairment, disability, and handicap – a controlled study. Audiology 27: 164–78.

Segal M, Schall R (1994) Determining functional/health status and its relation to disability in stroke survivors. Stroke 25(12): 2391–97.

Taylor Sarno M (1997) Quality of life in aphasia in the first post-stroke year. Aphasiology 11(7): 665–79.

Zemva N (1999) Aphasic patients and their families: wishes and limits. Aphasiology 13(3): 219–34.

Appendix 6.A Matched units of data per category per question

The reader will note that the categories that generally have longer names have been reduced to keywords for ease of presentation. Categories in which there are no matches between participant and proxy table have not been included in the appendix. When reading this table, it is important to view the final percentage carefully, in the context of the third column that suggests how important the category was to the aphasic participants.

Category by question	Number of units of data that matched between proxy and participant	Number of units of data coded in this category in the aphasic participants' data	Percentage matched as a proportion of aphasic data (%)
Question 1a			
Quite good	5	9	55.55
Average/okay	2	9	22.22
Not good	3	4	75
Question 1b			
People	3	11	27.27
Socializing	2	5	40
Choice	1	2	50
Personal change	1	2	50
Impairments	1	7	14.28
Personal outlook	3	10	30
Other negatives	2	5	40
Limited in ability to do things	3	14	21.42
Question 2			
Activities	9	27	33.33
People	13	40	32.5
Mobility	1	6	16.66
Home	1	4	25
Question 3			
Activities	7	23	30.43
Verbal communication	4	15	26.66
Impairments	2	9	22.22
Dependence	1	4	25
Other	1	2	50
Question 4			
Better verbal communication	4	12	33.33
Ability to/ activities	2	18	11.11
Full/better use of body parts	2	12	16.66
More independence	1	3	33.33
No stroke	1	2	50
Other	1	2	50
Question 5			
Another stroke	4	8	50
Losing people	3	8	37.5
Losing speech	2	4	50
Inability to do things	2	4	50
Losing mobility	1	5	20

Category by question	Number of units of data that matched between proxy and participant	Number of units of data coded in this category in the aphasic participants' data	Percentage matched as a proportion of aphasic data (%)
Question 6			
Verbal communication difficulties	10	13	76.92
Other (general)	3	5	60
Other mediums (negative)	1	6	16.66
General difficulties	1	4	25
Other people (positive)	1	7	14.28

Appendix 6.B Examples of units of data from respondents' accounts of quality of life

AI = aphasic individual
FF = family member or friend

What gives quality in life:

Having people in one's life: 'my husband, he makes it good' AI; 'my family, my two girls' AI; 'enjoying the company of other people ... having other people around us' AI; 'friends, she enjoys that' FF; 'she likes having the grandchildren around' FF; 'me and the kids and the family' FF; 'me, she always says I'm the most important thing' FF; 'her friends and her family' FF; 'relationship, stable marriage' FF

Having activities one can do and/or doing activities: 'picture framing, my professional training' AI; 'I go to the pictures' AI; 'she loves her drawing' FF; 'she loves going out ... theatre, meals' FF; 'goes and watches a game of bowls' FF

Having a positive outlook: 'life's worth living' AI; 'I delight in my life' AI; 'the only way to get better was to have confidence in herself and get on with it' FF; '[it] hasn't stopped her' FF

Socializing and/or being with others: 'when I go out with the girls' AI; 'seeing people and having a cup of tea' FF; 'loves going to the uni things where people are involved' FF

Having a choice: 'I love everything I want to do' AI; 'well I do what I want' AI; 'capable of doing anything he wants' FF; 'does what she wants to do' FF

Perceiving improvement in one's state: 'my speech priority some getting better' AI; 'I was sick and now I'm so much better' AI

Being mobile: 'being able to get out of bed in the morning' AI; gesture being able to walk about home and garden, AI; 'her scooter, she gets out on that' FF; 'being able to move around' FF

Being happy in one's home or community area: 'moving, moving' AI (refers to an imminent move to a new home, closer to his daughter); 'have my house' AI; 'lovely place to live in X' AI; 'she loves the house' FF; 'being in her own home' FF; 'being in secure, happy environment' FF

What takes quality away from life:

Limited ability and/or being unable to do things: 'I can't swim yet' AI; 'can't play the piano' AI; 'being able to play table-tennis meant a lot to me' AI; 'not being able to contribute to household things' FF (referring to washing up, ironing); 'he can't play golf anymore' FF; 'the Indonesian language she was learning, she can't do that' FF; 'not being able to go in the pool' FF

Impaired functioning: 'not being able to think properly' AI; 'I don't taste as well' AI; 'not being able to move the hand' AI; 'her hand in her problem' FF; 'she hasn't got the use of her hands' FF

Difficulties speaking: 'this is bad' (pointing to mouth) AI; 'I spose not as speak fluently as I used' AI; 'can't talk to family' AI; 'I can't do these sort of things' (brings hand to mouth) AI; 'not being able to get out what she wants to say' FF; 'not being able to have a phonecall' FF; 'lack of communication' FF; 'not being able to speak properly' FF; 'The things that affect him most is that he can't express himself' FF

Poor mobility or loss of mobility: 'I can't walk so good yet' AI; 'It's hard to physically move' AI; 'she hates the wheelchair, getting out of cars' FF; 'not being able to walk properly' FF

Having had the stroke: 'just the stroke' AI; 'nothing took my life away as much as died' AI; 'having the stroke' FF

Difficulties in reading and writing: 'reading' FF; 'not being able to write' FF

Dependence: 'the feeling of helplessness, the little things you can't do for yourself' AI; 'you've always got to have someone else there' AI; 'he's got to rely on people to take him' FF; 'he can't do things on his own' FF; 'not being able to go out on her own' FF

Poor health: 'diabetes' AI; 'lymphoma' AI

What would make quality of life better:

Being able to speak better: 'I like to speech clearly' AI; 'if he (the words) would come back out I'd be great' AI; 'get your voice back' AI; 'being able to speak better' AI; 'for his speech to get better' FF; 'to be able to talk to people' FF

Being able to do activities: 'could get away a lot more' AI; 'I'd like to go on trips again' AI; 'fishing' AI; 'washing up' AI; 'travel like he used to' FF; 'to go to concerts again' FF; 'if she could go to exhibitions' FF

Having better body functioning: 'the arm and the leg' AI; 'get your arm back' AI; 'if the knee leg was better' AI; 'B would have pointed to her right arm' FF; 'if she could use the right hand more' FF; 'if her eyes stayed the same' FF

Being more independent: 'would like to move into a little house, maybe I'll cope by myself' AI; 'have a car' AI; 'drive a car' FF; 'being able to please herself and go out without having to have someone with her' FF

What would make quality of life worse:

Having another stroke: 'another stroke' AI; 'if he had another stroke' FF

Losing people, losing existing speech, losing ability to do activities and/or things, and losing mobility: 'I wouldn't like to lose my husband' AI; 'if I couldn't speak at all' AI; 'if I couldn't even do the little bit now' AI; 'unhappy if I couldn't get moving' AI; 'if something happened to me' FF; 'if her good neighbour was no longer living over the road' FF; 'worsening aphasia' FF; 'if she couldn't get out of the house and go shopping' FF; 'to be totally bedridden' FF; 'if he couldn't go fishing' FF

Becoming poorer in health: 'if your breathing wasn't good' AI; 'if his health deteriorated' FF

CHAPTER 7
Autism and specific language impairment: a tantalizing dance

MICHAEL RUTTER

SGDP Centre, Institute of Psychiatry, De Crespigny Park, Denmark Hill, London, UK

Introduction

During the 1970s, the prevailing concept was that autism and developmental language disorders (now more usually termed specific language impairment – SLI) were quite separate and distinct. SLI was thought of as a pure language disorder and autism was conceptualized as a psychotic disorder with an unusually early onset. Nevertheless, from the very first descriptions of autism (Kanner, 1943), it had been obvious that language and communication deficits were more or less universal. The language features associated with autism involved both a serious deficit in language skills, and especially in the social communicative use of language but, in addition, there are various qualitative language abnormalities (Kanner, 1946; Rutter, 1966, 1968; Rutter and Lockyer, 1967; Rutter et al., 1967, 1971). Despite the fact that there were striking differences between autism and SLI as usually described, it might be that an unusually severe language deficit could be the basic cause of autism (Rutter, 1968).

In this chapter, the findings of a multiphase long-term follow-up study of a small sample extending from early childhood to the late 30s are summarized. The initial focus was on a comparison between autism spectrum disorders, ASD (arising in males with a normal non-verbal intelligence) and severe SLI involving a marked impairment of receptive language (also in males with a normal non-verbal IQ). The initial comparison showed the very marked differences between the two and rather minor

Language Disorders in Children and Adults: New Issues in Research and Practice. Victoria Joffe, Madeline Cruice, Shula Chiat.
© 2008 John Wiley & Sons, Ltd. ISBN 978-0-470-51839-7

overlap. As the young people grew older, similarities increased and, in particular, it became apparent that marked social impairment was a feature of about half the SLI sample. The final follow-up when the participants were about 36 years of age switched from a comparison of ASD and SLI to a more intensive focus on the SLI group, which was compared with their siblings, with an IQ-stratified control group and with a much larger general population sample. The findings are briefly compared with other research, and the overall pattern is used to draw conclusions on the meaning of commonalities and differences between ASD and SLI.

It was decided to test the hypothesis that ASD is due to a language deficit by means of a comparative study of 19 boys of normal intelligence who had autism and 23 boys of normal intelligence who had SLI involving a serious deficit in language comprehension (Bartak et al., 1975; Cox et al., 1975). Both groups were first given a research assessment at the age of about 7–8 years. Their mean non-verbal IQ was 92–93, the great majority had failed to gain phrase speech by 13 months (83–89% of cases) and the mean Reynell (Reynell, 1969) language comprehension age was 56 months in the SLI group and 46 months in the autism group. The language deficit in the autism group was associated with language abnormalities that were uncommon in the SLI group. Also, the social and behavioural features were hugely different in the two groups. Accordingly, the first answer to the question that had been posed was that autism and SLI were very different in spite of the fact that both involved serious language impairment (Bartak et al., 1977). It was concluded that a severe language deficit was *not* the cause of autism and that most boys with even a severe impairment in receptive language showed very few autistic features.

Follow-up into middle childhood

From the outset, it had been appreciated that adequate tests of the differences and similarities between autism and SLI had to involve what happened over the course of development. Accordingly a follow-up after 2 years was undertaken of 15 boys with autism and 14 with SLI, when the children were aged between 9 and 10 years (Cantwell et al., 1989). The findings were striking in two main respects. First, although the SLI and ASD groups were very comparable at the outset with respect to both showing a severe impairment in language functioning, there were substantial differences in language development between early and middle childhood. In the autism group, there was very high stability, with almost all continuing to show poor language functioning. By contrast, nearly half of the SLI group showed marked improvement, such that their overall language functioning at follow-up was generally good. Second, the changes in the quality in peer relationships went in the opposite direction. Although there was major stability in social functioning in the autism group, there were a few who, by middle childhood, showed fairly good peer relationships. In the SLI group, on the other hand, there was an overall minor deterioration in peer relationships. Accordingly, the second answer to the original question raised the possibility that ASD and SLI might be connected to some degree in view of the fact that peer relationships are problematic for some children with SLI, despite their improvement in language in middle childhood.

Follow-up in mid-/late 20s

It seemed important to follow through on this possibility and, as a result, a follow-up with the same groups (19 with ASD and 20 with SLI) was undertaken when they were aged 23–27 years (Howlin et al., 2000; Mawhood et al., 2000). As before, there was systematic cognitive and language testing of the subjects and standardized interviews with parents. In addition, there was a standardized interview and observations of the subjects themselves. By the time of this follow-up in the mid-20s, it had become evident that there were three boys in the SLI group who, when assessed clinically at the time the sample was selected, had been thought to have normal hearing but who were now known to have a substantial hearing deficit and therefore were omitted from the follow-up assessment.

In middle childhood, the vocabulary scores of the SLI group were considerably higher than those in the autism group. The difference between the groups narrowed somewhat by the mid- to late 20s as a result of a relative fall in vocabulary scores in the SLI group and a marginal improvement in the autism group. Both groups showed a drop in performance IQ on both the Raven's Matrices and the Wechsler scales (Mawhood et al., 2000; Figure 7.1). Two-thirds of the autism group showed definitely poor

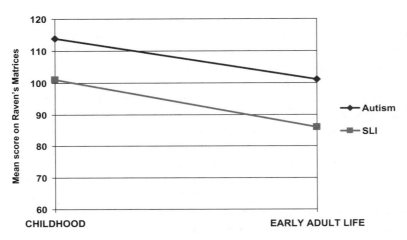

Figure 7.1 Autism spectrum disorders and specific language disorder (SLI): changes in performance IQ between 7–8 and 23–27 years. (Based on Mawhood et al., 2000.)

conversational skills, whereas that applied to very few individuals in the SLI group (Figure 7.2). Over half the SLI group had adequate conversational skills, as compared with less than one in six in the autism group. Nevertheless, just over two-fifths of the SLI group had only marginal conversational skills despite having acquired reasonable language as assessed psychometrically.

Poor social responsiveness was evident in most of the individuals who had ASD but in no one in the SLI group (Figure 7.3). By contrast, adequate social responsiveness was evident in about two-fifths of the SLI group but applied to no one in the autism group. Nevertheless, despite the generally better social functioning in the SLI group, the majority were assessed as showing only marginal social responsiveness (Howlin et al., 2000). Only

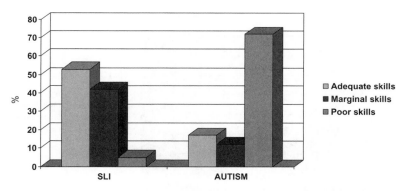

Figure 7.2 Autism spectrum disorders and specific language impairment (SLI): conversational skills in the mid-20s as observed. (Based on Mawhood et al., 2000.)

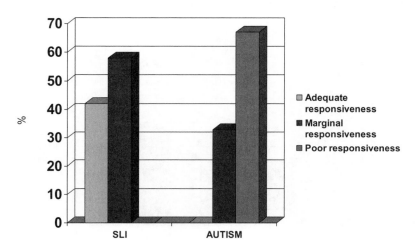

Figure 7.3 Autism spectrum disorders and specific language impairment (SLI): social responsiveness in the mid-20s as observed. (Based on Howlin et al., 2000.)

about 10% of the individuals with ASD were in regular employment compared with about a third of the SLI group (Figure 7.4). A third of the SLI
group had never had paid employment. This was a much lower proportion
than the 80% in the ASD group, but it represented a surprisingly high level
of social impairment, given that all individuals in both groups were initially
of normal non-verbal intelligence. Although the two groups had come
closer together with respect to poor social functioning, they remained
substantially different with respect to the stereotyped and repetitive behaviours that are characteristic of autism (Figure 7.5). They were found, to a
definite degree, in only 1 in 10 of the SLI group, and nearly two-thirds
had no behaviours of that kind. By contrast, that was so for only a quarter
of the autism group.

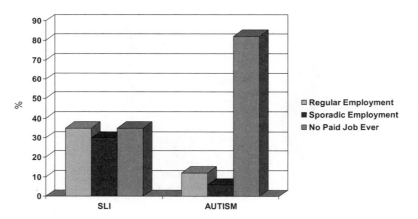

Figure 7.4 Autism spectrum disorders and specific language impairment (SLI):
employment in the mid-20s. (Based on Howlin et al., 2000.)

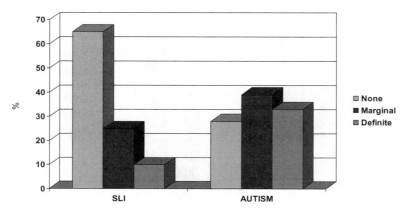

Figure 7.5 Autism spectrum disorders and specific language impairment (SLI): com-
pulsions and rituals in the mid-20s. (Based on Howlin et al., 2000.)

Returning to the starting point of the extent to which ASD and SLI are similar or different, both concepts apply. That is, by the time that they reached adulthood, individuals with a severe SLI showed even more social impairment than they did in middle childhood; also, their language skills and cognitive performance showed some increasing relative deficit. On the other hand, SLI and ASD remained different to an important extent. The inference is that it has to be accepted that SLI that involves severe receptive difficulties and pragmatic impairments is a much broader disorder than had been traditionally conceptualized.

Given the provocative nature of these findings, it was crucial to undertake a further follow-up when the groups were in their mid-30s (Clegg et al., 2005). Because there had been other follow-up studies of individuals with ASD, it was decided, for this final follow-up, to shift to an exclusive focus on SLI. In order to understand better how the group was functioning, the scope of assessment was broadened and comparisons for the 17 men with SLI were made with the 16 siblings and 17 age- and performance IQ-matched men without SLI siblings and a general population sample of 1384. The point of studying siblings was to check whether the deficits found in the SLI group might be a function of disadvantaging family features rather than the language impairment as such. Because it was anticipated that the siblings were likely to have a somewhat higher IQ level (as, indeed, turned out to be the case), a general population control group was selected, with matching of IQ with the SLI sample. The performance IQ of the SLI group was 92, the IQ-matched controls 90 and the siblings 108. The much larger general population sample, derived from the National Child Development Study, was mainly used to assess employment status.

All the findings showed that there was no systematic difference between the siblings and the IQ-matched controls, but the SLI group were hugely impaired in almost all respects (Clegg et al., 2005). This was so, for example, with respect to their receptive language as assessed by the British Picture Vocabulary Scales (Dunn et al., 1982; Figure 7.6), their phonological processing as assessed by an adult test of non-word repetition (Gathercole and Baddeley, 1993) and their reading as assessed by the Wechsler (1993) WORD composite score (Figure 7.7). The same pattern applied to their social functioning. Thus, almost none of the siblings had had no continuous regular employment, whereas that applied to two-thirds of the SLI group (Figure 7.8). Only about 1 in 10 of the siblings had not had any cohabitation relationship, whereas that was so for some two-thirds of the SLI group (Figure 7.9). Because of the consistent evidence that theory of mind deficits are found in the great majority of individuals with autism (Frith, 2003), and the evidence from our own follow-up study that social deficits were frequent in individuals with SLI, it had been decided to undertake a systematic assessment of theory of mind functioning at the mid-30s follow-up. The composite score (combining different tests of theory of mind) showed that the SLI group had a mean score that

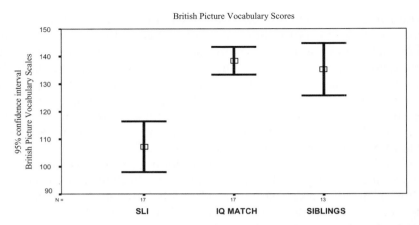

Figure 7.6 Language levels in the mid-30s of males with specific language impairment (SLI) compared with their siblings and IQ-matched controls. (Based on Clegg et al., 2005.)

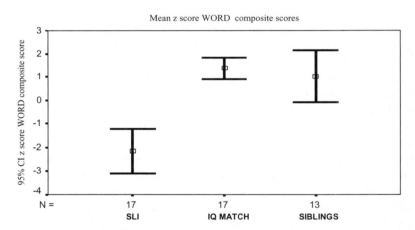

Figure 7.7 Reading in the mid-30s of specific language impairment (SLI) men. (Based on Clegg et al., 2005.)

was nearly two standard deviations below normal (Figure 7.10). By contrast, both the siblings and the IQ-matched controls had a normal mean score.

This follow-up study extending over a period of 28 years gave rise to 12 main conclusions:

1. All the children with a severe SLI that involved impairments in receptive language gained language. By their early 20s, their language levels had risen to about 11 years, but there was little change over the next decade.

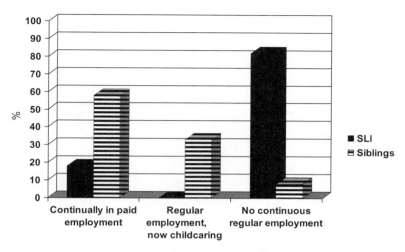

Figure 7.8 Employment history of specific language impairment (SLI) men up to mid-30s. (Based on Clegg et al., 2005.)

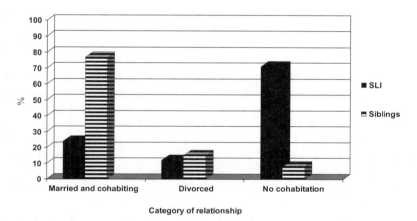

Figure 7.9 Marital relationships of specific language impairment (SLI) men up to mid-30s. (Based on Clegg et al., 2005.)

2. Nevertheless, half continued to show important deficits in conversational skills even in mid-adult life.
3. The mean score on receptive vocabulary at a mean age of 36 years was still only at the 12-year level, some 5 years below that of their siblings and of age-matched controls.
4. As social demands increased with age, social deficits in people with SLI become more apparent.
5. Surprisingly, there was little association, within the SLI group, between the severity of the language deficit in early childhood and the level of social functioning in adult life.

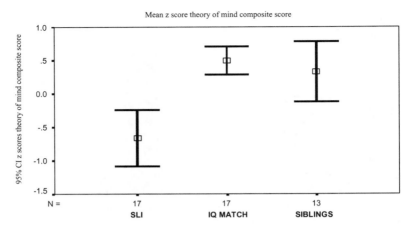

Figure 7.10 Theory of mind in the mid-30s of specific language impairment (SLI) men. (Based on Clegg et al., 2005.)

6. Despite their having attended, at primary school level, the best special schools in the country for children with developmental language disorders, the educational attainments of the SLI group in adult life were poor. On the other hand, education provision for the secondary level had not been satisfactory for most boys. It had not been recognized at the time that the fact that they had gained spoken language did not mean that they no longer required special educational help.

7. At the 36-year follow-up, the average reading level of the SLI individuals was only about 9 years and, in sharp contrast to the scholastic success of their siblings, none had received any education after the age of 16 years.

8. Although most of the men with SLI continued to show IQs in the normal range, cognitive performance on non-verbal tests was not quite as good in adult life as it had been in childhood. However, in so far as there had been a drop in performance, it occurred in childhood/adolescence rather than during the adult years.

9. When seen in their early 20s, the SLI men and the men with autism, although still rather dissimilar, were more alike than they had been in childhood.

10. The greater similarity with increasing age between SLI and autism mainly arose because the social and communicative deficits associated with SLI became more manifest. Some abnormal language features and some repetitive, stereotyped behaviour occurred with SLI, but these abnormalities were much less striking than the social and communicative deficits.

11. In their mid 30s, most of the men with SLI showed marked (albeit sometimes subtle) social deficits. Very few had developed a love relationship.

12. The SLI group showed 'theory of mind' deficits that were similar to those seen in individuals of normal IQ with autism, although the average deficits were not quite as marked as those typical of individuals with autism.

Evidence from other studies

The findings from this very extensive long-term follow-up study are striking and compelling, but it was an investigation of a small group of individuals with an SLI of unusual severity that involved impairments in receptive, as well as expressive, language. Moreover, the study began during the early 1970s, when SLI was less well understood, when the main educational focus was on the primary school years and when specialist support services at the secondary level were very limited. Accordingly, it is necessary as well to turn to the findings from other follow-up studies and from other research strategies. The follow-up study by Dorothy Bishop and her colleagues provides the most appropriate comparison with respect to follow-up evidence. Stothard et al. (1998) followed up to age 15–16 years a group of 71 children first studied by Bishop and Edmundson (1987) at age 4 years, having been referred to clinics for a heterogeneous mixture of speech and language problems. Children with SLI were compared with those whose non-verbal IQ was below 70 and therefore showed a general cognitive delay. By the age of 5½ years, about 44% appeared to have largely resolved their speech/language problems, with the remainder showing a persistent disorder. At age 15, the 'persistent' group fell even further behind with respect to language skills and, in addition, had a level of reading that was equivalent to the 'general delay' group. It is very evident that children who show substantial SLI do not 'grow out' of their problems; on the contrary, they are likely to show continuing pervasive problems. The 'resolved' group fared distinctly better with respect to spoken language, but their reading and spelling skills were below age norms (albeit not in the diagnosis of dyslexia range). SLI constitutes a disorder that often persists.

The second study, also undertaken by Bishop and her colleagues (Bishop et al., 1995), was a twin study of young people with SLI. The concordance for SLI in monozygotic (MZ) pairs was much greater than that in dizygotic (DZ) pairs, pointing to a substantial heritability for the liability to show a developmental language disorder. What is even more striking, however, is that, within MZ pairs, the co-twins who did not have an SLI as determined by standard diagnostic criteria usually did have language problems of some kind or low IQ. This was much less the case within DZ pairs. The implication is that SLI involves a genetic liability that extends well beyond the usually accepted diagnostic boundaries. That does not necessarily mean that SLI constitutes just the extreme of normal variation. A general population twin study (Bishop et al., 2003) showed that genetic influences tended to be rather stronger in the case of persisting language problems that led to professional involvement.

The third study, also from Dorothy Bishop's group, concerned a comparison with children with pragmatic language disorders and high-functioning children with autism (Bishop and Norbury, 2002). In brief, the findings showed both similarities and differences between these two groups. Bishop and Norbury (2002) compared groups of children with pragmatic language impairment (PLI), typical SLI, high-functioning autism and normal development. Their findings showed that PLI was often, but by no means always, accompanied by autistic features. Interestingly, the PLI group's receptive and language skills were slightly better than those of the typical SLI group. Pragmatic problems are a distinctive feature, but they do not necessarily index the severity of the language deficit as assessed in other ways. Botting and Conti-Ramsden (2003), in a separate study, drew very similar conclusions.

Conti-Ramsden et al. (2001) followed up to age 11 years a large cohort (242) of children who were attending infant language units at 7 years of age. Nearly two-thirds still had widespread difficulties in some aspect of language, and over a quarter were scoring less well on performance IQ tests than at age 7. Only 16 children seemed to have entirely resolved their language difficulties. Social and behavioural difficulties were also evident in a substantial minority, this being most often in those with pragmatic problems (Conti-Ramsden and Botting, 2004). The children with pragmatic impairment included some with autistic features and some without. It was notable that the pragmatic group with autism were not the most impaired on other language and cognitive features (Botting and Conti-Ramsden, 2003). A further follow-up at the end of compulsory schooling at age 16 years (Conti-Ramsden, in press) showed that just over a fifth of those with SLI had only minimal qualifications, as compared with none of the children without SLI. On the other hand, 44% achieved age-appropriate scholastic levels (compared with 88% of controls). About one in six of those with SLI achieved good academic achievement. Non-verbal IQ was the strongest predictor of academic achievement, but language skills were also of some predictive value. The most striking difference from the earlier studies is the rather better educational achievement of the individuals with SLI, albeit well below that of those without SLI.

Studies of ASD

At this point, there needs to be a return to studies of ASD, focusing on research strategies similar to those employed with SLI. Over the last 40 years or so, there has been a plethora of studies examining cognitive features in autism (Happé, 1994; Hermelin and O'Connor, 1970; Frith, 2003; Rutter and Bailey, 1993). The evidence is strongest with respect to 'theory of mind' deficits, which are found in the great majority of individuals with ASD. These provide a reasonable possible basis for the social/communicative deficits in autism, but they are less obviously relevant for the repetitive/stereotyped behaviours. A lack of central coherence (meaning an excessive focus on details and the lack of attention to the overall gestalt of perceptions) might provide a better explanation for the basis of stereotyped/repetitive behaviours. There is also good evidence for the importance of pragmatic language deficits as part of the overall pattern of findings for ASD (Landa et al., 1992). In addition, in infancy and early childhood, joint attention deficits are prominent (Sigman and Ruskin, 1999), and there are executive planning impairments (Ozonoff et al., 1991). Although these are more frequent in individuals with ASD than in the general population, they show a less specific association and they cover a rather heterogeneous range of cognitive functions. In addition, although the main attention has been on deficits in cognitive functioning, there is also good evidence that autistic individuals have an unusual tendency to show 'splinter' or 'savant' skills (Hermelin, 2001). It is by no means clear how these various, somewhat disparate, cognitive features come together (Happé, 2003), but what is clear is that social cognitive deficits are an intrinsic and all-pervasive feature of ASD, and it is highly likely that they underlie many, if not most, of the social, communicative and behavioural features of autism. It is these findings, more than any others, that focus attention on the possible connections between ASD and SLI.

Follow-up studies into adult life of individuals with autism, but an initial IQ within the normal range, show parallels with SLI but, to a much greater extent, emphasize the differences (Howlin et al., 2004). It might be expected that individuals with autism who have a normal non-verbal IQ (with all the positive prognostic factors that are likely to go along with that) have a good social outcome in adult life. The findings show that, indeed, they do have a better outcome than those with major cognitive impairment, but the overall outcome is nevertheless far from satisfactory. Howlin et al. (2004) found that less than a fifth of their sample had a very good outcome as indicated by living independently, holding a job and having some friendships. A similar proportion had a fairly good outcome in that they were living with parents or in some kind of sheltered provision, holding a job and had some friendships. On the other hand, well over two-fifths had a poor or very poor outcome in terms of being substantially impaired in all respects. Those are very much worse outcomes than for SLI. It remains quite unclear what, within this good prognosis group, made the difference between good and poor social functioning in middle adulthood.

As with SLI, quantitative genetic findings are also informative (Bailey et al., 1995; Rutter, 2005). A huge disparity with concordance rates between MZ and DZ pairs points to a heritability of above 90%. On the other hand, the findings have also shown that the concordance concerns a much broader phenotype than implied by the traditional diagnosis of a seriously

handicapping disorder of autism. Thus, Le Couteur et al. (1996) found
that, within pairs that were discordant for autism and ASD, the concordance was very high for a broader phenotype within MZ pairs but quite low
within DZ pairs. The implication, as with SLI, is that the genetic liability
extends much more broadly than the traditional diagnostic boundaries.
The family data give rise to the same conclusion (Bolton et al., 1994), that
is, the rate of autism in the siblings of probands with autism was much
higher than that in a comparison group of siblings of a proband for Down
syndrome. However, the rate of a combination of cognitive and social difficulties that fell short of the diagnostic criteria of autism showed a similar
disparity with the Down syndrome group. About one in five of the siblings
of a proband with autism showed some kind of mixture of cognitive and
social abnormalities, whereas that was true for only some 2–3% of siblings
in Down syndrome families.

Putting these findings together with those of other studies, it may be
concluded that autism includes a major impairment in communicative
language (as well as other deficits and abnormalities); it also involves a
broader phenotype that extends far beyond the handicapping condition
as traditionally diagnosed, and that there is a major overlap between
autism and semantic/pragmatic language disorders, but nevertheless, the
two are not synonymous.

Conclusions

Coming back to the tantalizing dance between ASD and SLI, it is evident
that the research findings force both a coming together and a separation.
The two disorders are both heterogeneous, and involve important similarities with respect to social functioning; but the abnormal language features (such as delayed echolalia and pronominal reversal) are much more
characteristic of ASD than SLI. Also, although repetitive/stereotyped behaviours and 'splinter' or 'savant' skills can and do occur with a few cases of
SLI, they are much more characteristic of ASD. From a research perspective,
it is obvious that there is a need for further research into both the social
deficits and pragmatic features of some cases of SLI. Molecular genetic
research into SLI needs to incorporate dimensional phenotypes and needs
to consider the overlap among SLI, ASD and dyslexia. The changing picture
of SLI that we found over this 28-year follow-up emphasizes both the great
value of well-planned longitudinal studies, even when the sample studied
is small, and the need for a lifespan perspective. The advantage of systematic detailed individual assessments is that they are in a good position to
note the unexpected (a key need across the whole of science). Of course,
in order to gain a broader perspective, there is also a need for longitudinal
studies of much larger samples, carrying the advantage that they are in a
much better position to examine heterogeneity in life trajectories and the
possible influences that shape such heterogeneity.

One policy and practice implication is that interventions with SLI need to include considerations of communication, pragmatics, social reciprocity and scholastic performance, as well as spoken language *per se*. A further implication that derives out of the overall body of research into SLI is that dimensional approaches, as well as categories, are essential. Clearly, there is value in categorical diagnoses if only because decision making is essentially categorical in nature. On the other hand, the diagnostic boundaries are nothing like as clear-cut as implied by the official classifications. Moreover, for many purposes, dimensional measurement of key language, cognitive and social features is a necessary part of any adequate assessment. Clinical practice needs to take that on board.

The findings of this long-term follow-up might seem to provide a rather pessimistic picture of the outcome of SLI. Two points need to be made in that connection. First, the SLI groups that we studied all showed a very marked impairment in receptive language. Accordingly, they represented a particularly severe variety of SLI. It would be unwarranted to extend the findings to all SLI. Moreover, even with this extreme group, there was marked heterogeneity in outcome. Second, especially with respect to educational outcome, it is important to bear in mind that the findings concern what happened a generation ago when services were less well developed than today. Much more recent follow-up studies (of less severe groups) provide a somewhat more encouraging picture. Nevertheless, it would be a mistake to assume that all is now well. It is not. The extent and severity of the social impairments that we found emphasize that there are considerable challenges to be met.

As yet, we lack an adequate understanding of the neural basis of autism and of SLI, but the key point is that practitioners concerned primarily with SLI need to be alert to the research and clinical developments in relation to autism and, conversely, practitioners primarily concerned with autism need to be much more aware of research into SLI than they are at the moment.

References

Bailey A, Le Couteur A, Gottesman I et al. (1995) Autism as a strongly genetic disorder: evidence from a British twin study. Psychological Medicine 25: 63–77.

Bartak L, Rutter M, Cox A (1975) A comparative study of infantile autism and specific developmental receptive language disorder. I. The children. British Journal of Psychiatry 126: 127–45.

Bartak L, Rutter M, Cox A (1977) A comparative study of infantile autism and specific developmental receptive language disorders. III. Discriminant function analysis. Journal of Autism and Childhood Schizophrenia 7: 383–96.

Bishop D, Edmundson A (1987) Language-impaired 4-year olds: distinguishing transient from persistent impairment. Journal of Speech and Hearing Disorders 52: 156–73.

Bishop D, Norbury C (2002) Exploring the borderland of autistic disorder and specific language impairment: a study using standardized diagnostic instruments. Journal of Child Psychology and Psychiatry 43: 917–29.

Bishop D, North T, Donlan C (1995) Genetic basis of specific language impairment: evidence from a twin study. Developmental Medicine and Child Neurology 37: 56–71.

Bishop D, Price T, Dale P et al. (2003) Outcomes of early language delay: II. Etiology of transient and persistent language difficulties. Journal of Speech, Language, and Hearing Research 46: 561–75.

Bolton P, Macdonald H, Pickles A et al. (1994) A case-control family history study of autism. Journal of Child Psychology and Psychiatry 35: 877–900.

Botting N, Conti-Ramsden G (2003) Autism, primary pragmatic difficulties, and specific language impairment: can we distinguish them using psycholinguistic markers? Developmental Medicine and Child Neurology 45: 515–24.

Cantwell DP, Baker L, Rutter M et al. (1989) Infantile autism and developmental receptive dysphasia: a comparative follow-up into middle childhood. Journal of Autism and Developmental Disorders 19: 19–32.

Clegg J, Hollis C, Mawhood L et al. (2005) Developmental language disorders: a follow-up in later adult life. Journal of Child Psychology and Psychiatry 46: 128–49.

Conti-Ramsden G (in press) Heterogeneity of specific language impairment (SLI): outcomes in adolescence. In: C Norbury (ed.), Understanding Developmental Language Disorders: From Theory to Practice. London: Psychology Press.

Conti-Ramsden G, Botting N (2004) Social difficulties and victimisation in children with SLI at 11 years of age. Journal of Speech, Language, and Hearing Research 47: 145–61.

Conti-Ramsden G, Botting N, Simkin Z et al. (2001) Follow-up of children attending infant language units: outcomes at 11 years of age. International Journal of Language and Communication Disorders 36: 207–19.

Cox A, Rutter M, Bartak L (1975) A comparative study of infantile autism and specific developmental receptive language disorder. II. The families. British Journal of Psychiatry 126: 146–59.

Dunn LM, Dunn LM, Whetton C et al. (1982) British Picture Vocabulary Scale. Windsor, England: NFER – Nelson.

Frith U (2003) Autism – Explaining the Enigma, 2nd edn. Oxford: Blackwell Publishing.

Gathercole SE, Baddeley AD (1993) Phonological working memory: a critical building block for reading development and vocabulary acquisition? European Journal of Psychology of Education 8: 259–72.

Happé F (1994) Autism – An Introduction to Psychological Theory. London: UCL Press.

Happé F (2003) Cognition in autism: one deficit or many? In: G Bock, J Goode (eds), Autism: Neural Basis and Treatment Possibilities. Chichester: John Wiley & Sons, Ltd, pp. 198–212.

Hermelin B (2001) Bright Splinters of the Mind: A personal Story of Research with Autistics Savant. London: Jessica Kingsley.

Hermelin B, O'Connor N (1970) Psychological Experiments with Autistic Children. London: Pergamon.

Howlin P, Mawhood L, Rutter M (2000) Autism and developmental receptive language disorder – a follow-up comparison in early adult life. II: social, behavioural, and psychiatric outcomes. Journal of Child Psychology and Psychiatry 41: 561–78.

Howlin P, Goode S, Hutton J et al. (2004) Adult outcome for children with autism. Journal of Child Psychology and Psychiatry 45: 212–29.

Landa R, Piven J, Wzorek M et al. (1992) Social language use in parents of autistic individuals. Psychological Medicine 22: 245–54.

Kanner L (1943) Autistic disturbances of affective contact. Nervous Child 2: 217.

Kanner L (1946) Irrelevant and metaphorical language in early infantile autism. American Journal of Psychiatry 103: 242.

Le Couteur A, Bailey AJ, Goode S et al. (1996) A broader phenotype of autism: the clinical spectrum in twins. Journal of Child Psychology and Psychiatry 37: 785–801.

Mawhood L, Howlin P, Rutter M (2000) Autism and developmental receptive language disorder – a comparative follow-up in early adult life. I: cognitive and language outcomes. Journal of Child Psychology and Psychiatry 41: 547–59.

Ozonoff S, Pennington B, Rogers S (1991) Executive function deficits in high functioning autistic children: relationship to theory of mind. Journal of Child Psychology and Psychiatry 32: 1081–106.

Reynell J (1969) Reynell Developmental Language Scales. Slough: Bucks.

Rutter M (1966) Behavioural and cognitive characteristics. In: JK Wing (ed.), Early Childhood Autism. Oxford: Pergamon, pp. 51–81.

Rutter M (1968) Concepts of autism: a review of research. Journal of Child Psychology and Psychiatry 9: 1–25.

Rutter M (2005) Genetic influences and autism. In: F Volkmar, R Paul, A Klin et al. (eds), Handbook of Autism and Pervasive Developmental Disorders, 3rd edn. New York: John Wiley & Sons, Inc., pp. 425–52.

Rutter M, Lockyer L (1967) A five to fifteen year follow-up study of infantile psychosis. I. Description of sample. British Journal of Psychiatry 113: 1169–82.

Rutter M, Bailey A (1993) Thinking and relationships: mind and brain. In: S Baron-Cohen, H Tager-Flusberg, D Cohen (eds), Understanding Other Minds: Perspectives from Autism. Oxford: Oxford University Press, pp. 481–505.

Rutter M, Greenfeld D, Lockyer L (1967) A five to fifteen year follow-up study of infantile psychosis. II. Social and behavioural outcome. British Journal of Psychiatry 113: 1183–99.

Rutter M, Bartak L, Newman S (1971) Autism – a central disorder of cognition and language? In: M Rutter (ed.), Infantile Autism: Concepts, Characteristics and Treatment. Edinburgh: Churchill Livingstone, pp. 148–71.

Sigman M, Ruskin E (1999) Continuity and change in the social competence of children with autism, Down syndrome, and developmental delays. Monographs of the Society for Research in Child Development (64). Malden, MA: Blackwell Publishing.

Stothard S, Snowling M, Bishop D et al. (1998) Language-impaired preschoolers: a follow-up into adolescence. Journal of Speech, Language, and Hearing Research 41: 407–18.

Wechsler D (1993) The Wechsler Objective Reading Dimensions. New York: Psychological Corporation.

CHAPTER 8

Outcomes for young people with a history of specific language impairment at 16–17 years: a more positive picture?

GEOFF LINDSAY[1] and JULIE DOCKRELL[2]

[1]Centre for Educational Development, Appraisal and Research (CEDAR), University of Warwick, Coventry
[2]Faculty of Children and Health, Department of Psychology and Human Development, Institute of Education, University of London

Introduction

Parents of children with special educational needs (SEN) typically have concerns both for the present and the future. Practitioners are well used to being asked to predict how the child will develop later during their school careers and also as an adult. In the past, there was a higher level of certainty expressed by professionals, particularly when the child had severe SEN. For example, general cognitive ability as measured by IQ was considered to be stable and hence a good predictor. Over recent decades, this view has altered as evidence for variation in assessed intelligence and developmental changes has been gathered (Hindley and Owen, 1978). It is now clear that children with apparently similar types of difficulties may differ in their developmental trajectories (Leonard, 1998). To provide parents, young people and practitioners with the ability to consider learning needs and developmental trajectories, it is important to gather information from a range of sources. Longitudinal data provide information to address these issues.

The prognosis for children with developmental language difficulties has previously been shown to be a cause for serious concern. A longitudinal study in England of a group of children with receptive language difficulties followed up from age 7–8 years through to their mid-20s and their mid-30s suggested a poor prognosis (Mawhood et al., 2000; Clegg et al., 2005; see Rutter, Chapter 7 this volume). Longitudinal studies by Beitchman and

Language Disorders in Children and Adults: New Issues in Research and Practice. Victoria Joffe, Madeline Cruice, Shula Chiat.
© 2008 John Wiley & Sons, Ltd. ISBN 978-0-470-51839-7

colleagues and by Conti-Ramsden and colleagues, to be discussed below, which have followed young people through to adolescence have provided a more mixed picture, but continued to raise concerns about long-term outcomes. Our own longitudinal study, which has followed a group of young people with specific language impairment (SLI)[1] from 8 to 17 years, has revealed some more positive findings.

This chapter presents data from our longitudinal study, with a focus on the young people's status at ages 16 and 17 years. We explore a range of developmental strands, including language, educational attainment and socio-behavioural development. We also draw on the views of the young people themselves, their parents and their tutors. By triangulating different informants and different sources of evidence, we consider the implications of these findings for the general prognosis of children with SLI. By making connections across these different sources of data, it is possible to consider both within-child factors and contextual factors that support development for children with SLI.

The study

A group of children with SLI were identified at the beginning of Key Stage 2 (Year 3, age 8). To ensure that the range of provision available was not constrained by local policies or geographical factors, children were identified in two local authorities (LAs): one urban, the other mainly rural. In order to control for selective access to services, children were identified by a range of professionals working in different settings in the LAs, namely speech and language therapists (SLTs), SEN coordinators and educational psychologists (EPs). This allowed for a broader range of children to be identified than if selection had been constrained by, for example, clinic attendance or being educated within special provision such as a language unit.

During the identification phase, children were excluded if they had any other additional difficulty that might question the specific or primary nature of their language difficulty. Fifty-nine children were identified (0.75% of the Year 3 population across the two LAs); in addition, 10 children from two national special language schools were added to the sample to include children attending special schools who might be expected to have more severe SLI ($N = 69$; 52 boys, 17 girls). There were no significant differences between the two populations on any language or cognitive measure at this point in time (see Dockrell and Lindsay, 2007).

Criteria for the identification of SLI vary across and within research and clinical settings. One of the major difficulties relating to the study of SLI is how it is precisely defined (Bishop, 1997), and there are important differences between clinic, special education and population samples. There is,

---

[1] Also referred to as specific speech and language difficulties (SSLD) in the United Kingdom (Dockrell et al., 2006).

however, a general consensus that SLI represents an impairment in one or more of the language domains that is disproportionately greater than the impairments in other non-linguistic areas. However, the extent of the language difficulty (−1 standard deviation (SD), −1.25 SD or larger) is a matter of significant debate, and criteria vary greatly across research studies and clinical diagnosis. Our first criterion for inclusion in the study was that professionals identified a specific language problem and that there were no other identified contributing factors. Our second criterion was that the children scored more than 1 SD outwith the norm on measures of receptive or expressive language. In addition to at least one depressed language score, for inclusion in the sample, participants had a significant discrepancy between the measure of non-verbal ability and the depressed language score. Given the heterogeneity of children with SLI, we expected different profiles within the cohort that would parallel what is found in practice.

Assessment at 8 years confirmed that the sample met the criteria for SLI: scores on language tests were more than 1 SD below the mean, but non-verbal ability was within the normal range (Dockrell and Lindsay, 1998). Sixty-seven percent of the sample had scores below 1 SD on two or more measures of expressive and receptive vocabulary. Of those with only one score below 1 SD (N = 22), 10 children were in special schools for children with language impairments. The majority (N = 14) of participants with only one depressed language score experienced difficulty with phonological processing, as indicated by scores on the phonological assessment battery (<1 SD). To facilitate comparisons between tests, all scores have been translated into Z scores, where the mean is 0 and an SD is 1. At age 8, the sample scored at mean −1.03 for expressive vocabulary (British Ability Scales (BAS) naming; Elliott et al., 1997) and −1.12 for receptive vocabulary (British Picture Vocabulary Scale (BPVS); Dunn et al., 1997). Level of understanding of grammar (Test of Reception of Grammar (TROG); Bishop, 1989) was even lower – mean = −1.45, with narrative production (Bus Story – Information Scale; Renfrew, 1997) lower still, mean = −1.55. Non-verbal ability (BAS Matrices) was within the average range, mean = −0.77 (Table 8.1).

To validate the identification of these children as those with SLI, a series of repeated-measures t tests confirmed that vocabulary scores, grammar scores, narrative production and phonology scores were all significantly below measures of non-verbal ability (BAS naming vocabulary: $t = -2.06$, $p = 0.04$, $d = 0.29$; BPVS: $t = -3.91$, $p < 0.0005$, $d = 0.47$; Understanding grammar TROG: $t = -6.22$, $p < 0.0005$, $d = 0.42$; Narrative Bus Story information: $t = -5.74$, $p < 0.0005$, $d = 0.75$; and phonological awareness: $t = -2.08$, $p = 0.04$, $d = 0.27$).

Further assessments have been carried out on a range of language, literacy and cognitive measures when the children were in Years 6, 7, 9, 10, 11, up to the end of compulsory education, and again during their first year of post-16 education, training and work (Dockrell et al., 2007). The focus of this chapter is primarily on the young people's status at their

Table 8.1 Z scores on language and non-verbal ability at 8 years

Assessment	N	Mean	Standard deviation
Vocabulary: receptive	68	−1.12	0.62
Vocabulary: expressive	68	−1.03	0.93
Understanding: grammar	68	−1.45	0.94
Narrative production	68	−1.55	1.16
Non-verbal ability	68	−0.77	0.87

transition from school to post-16, but reference will also be made to results of the earlier assessments in order to examine the trends. In addition, we shall draw upon interviews with 54 of the young people in their final year of post-16 education, and with 50 of their tutors and 50 of the parents – full details are provided in Dockrell et al. (2007). It is important to note that in the later years of secondary school, pupils were still exhibiting difficulties with aspects of oral language. *All* pupils scored below 1 *SD* on the recalling sentences measure of the Clinical Evaluation of Language Fundamentals (CELF): Recalling Sentences (Semel et al., 1987), with all except two pupils scoring below −2 *SD*. Vocabulary scores showed greater variation; nonetheless, 72% of the pupils tested (*N* = 44) continued to have depressed scores, with 50% of the sample scoring below −1.25 *SD*.

The young people at 16–17 years

Data were collected on 64 of the original 69 young people, and interviews were held with 54. Comparison of the interview sample and the missing participants indicated that the two groups were comparable on both a language measure (CELF: Recalling Sentences (Semel et al., 1987): *t*(67) = 0.34, *ns*) and reading (BAS Word Reading Scale: *t*(69) = −0.91, *ns*) assessed in Year 9. The large majority of the young people (80%) were continuing in full-time education, most attending colleges of further education (FE) (*n* = 37), with seven attending residential colleges for students with speech and language difficulties, four attending school sixth forms within mainstream schools and three still in Year 11.

This high level of young people continuing their education is a positive indication of outcomes at the end of compulsory education, and may be compared with, for example, the sample originally studied by Bartak et al. (1975). Howlin et al. (2000) report that none of their language group obtained any formal qualifications, and about 70% had no FE.

Examination of the level of attainment at the end of compulsory schooling indicated that the young people in our sample were achieving at a level below the average, but there were also signs of positive achievement. Pupils in English schools typically take the General Certificate of Secondary Education (GCSE) in a number of subjects, each of which may be passed at grade A*–G, the target level (Level 2) being A*–C. In addition, 'entry level' qualifications, which are the first level in the national qualifications framework, are available to pupils who are expected to perform below foundation or Level 1, that is, below grade G, GCSE. The young people in our sample, two-thirds of whom had statements of SEN at that time, took an average of seven formal qualifications (range 0–14), with a mean of five GCSEs, and a smaller but substantial proportion taking lower-level qualifications. On average, the young people passed five GCSEs. The majority achieved qualifications at Level 1 (grades D–G); however, one in eight (12.5%) achieved five GCSEs at Level 2.

The level of achievement does not match the norm for young people without SEN. For example, nationally, 63.4% of young people with no identified SEN achieved five A*–C grades in the year in question (2005); the comparable outcomes for the two LAs in this study were 55.7% for the urban LA and 62.5% for the rural LA. On the other hand, the percentage of our participants with SLI achieving this level at this time (12.5%) is almost double the national percentage of young people with statements of SEN (7.1%) who achieve it. Furthermore, 73% of the young people achieved a GCSE in Maths ($n = 47$), but in contrast, only 42% achieved a GCSE in English. Taking the new national standard of five GCSEs A*–C, including English and Maths, the proportion achieving the target dropped from 12.5 to just 2.8% – compare this with the reduction in the national non-SEN group from 63.4 to 49.9%. This indicates that our young people had difficulties in the core subjects of Maths and, in particular, English.

These results represent some positive outcomes, but the young people's difficulties with English GCSE suggest a continuing impact of the oral language difficulties the young people had at 8 years and which persisted to the age of 16 years for the group as a whole (Table 8.2). The mean Z scores of two language competencies were more than 1 SD below the mean compared with the standardization norm: language understanding $Z = -1.16$; vocabulary comprehension $Z = -1.2$. Only the test of grammatical understanding (TROG) was within normal limits ($Z = -0.23$), and this result appears to reflect a ceiling in the test rather than a relative improvement of the cohort.[2] Table 8.2 also shows that there were significant and large differences between the scores of the SLI cohort and the published test norms for young people at this age. This was true for all measures except for grammatical comprehension (TROG). Indeed, when the literacy measures (reading and writing) were considered alone, the two populations overlap for only 20% of the distributions.

Table 8.2 also indicates the substantial and indeed greater levels of relative disadvantage the young people had on the basic skills of reading, spelling, writing and numeracy. These ranged from $Z = -1.60$ for reading

---

[2] Our data suggest that the TROG is not sensitive for the 16-year-olds since they show a ceiling effect. It is the only language measure for which the cohort score within the average range. In previous phases of the study, they were significantly impaired on this test.

Table 8.2 Differences between children with a history of specific language impairment and the norm at 16 years of age

Competency assessed	Mean Z	Standard deviation	t	Effect size d
Language understanding	−1.16	0.66	−13.80***	1.75
Language grammatical comprehension	−0.23	1.03	−1.79	0.23
Vocabulary comprehension	−1.28	1.11	−9.01***	1.15
Single-word reading	−1.82	0.95	−14.97***	1.95
Reading comprehension	−1.60	0.71	−17.77***	2.26
Spelling	−1.68	1.01	−13.06***	1.65
Writing	−2.20	1.10	−15.71***	2.14
Numeracy	−1.55	1.12	−10.82***	1.24

*** $p < 0.001$.

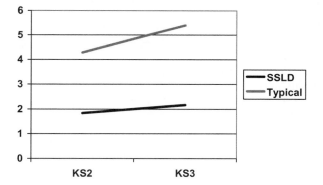

Figure 8.1 Changes in mean scaled scores for English SATs KS2–KS3. *Note*: KS2, Key Stage 2; KS3, Key Stage 3; SSLD, specific speech and language difficulties.

comprehension to −2.30 for writing (using the Wechsler Objective Language Dimension).

The impact of these basic skills deficits may be seen in the GCSE results for English, and to a lesser extent Maths as discussed above, and also on the pattern of development at an earlier stage. Between the end of Key Stage 2 (at 11 years) and Key Stage 3 (14 years), national Standard Assessment Tests (SATs) indicate an almost flat trajectory for the SLI group for English (Figure 8.1). Whereas a typically developing comparison group improved from a mean level of about 4 to over 5 during this period, the SLI group barely improved, hovering just above Level 2. The differences between the attainments of the SLI and typically developing cohorts in later Maths scores at GCSE are also indicated in the earlier trajectories between Key Stages 2 and 3 (Figure 8.2). However, although the SLI group was achieving at a much lower level than the typically developing group,

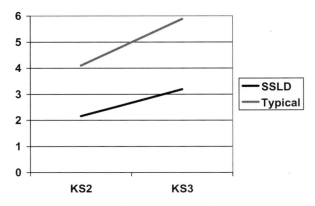

Figure 8.2 Changes in mean scaled scores for Maths SATs KS2–KS3. *Note*: KS2, Key Stage 2; KS3, Key Stage 3; SSLD, specific speech and language difficulties.

Table 8.3 Relationships between standardized measures at age 16 and total points achieved in national tests controlled for non-verbal ability

Competency assessed	Age 16 points
Language understanding	0.48**
Language grammatical comprehension	0.21
Vocabulary comprehension	0.44**
Single-word reading	0.46**
Reading comprehension	0.48**
Spelling	0.40**
Writing	0.57**
Numeracy	0.57**

** $p < 0.01$.

there are clear signs of progress over the period from about 11–14 years of age. Age trends were statistically significant for both English and Maths, but in each case, there was an interaction by cohort effect, reflecting the increase in attainment of the typically developing cohort. The pupils in the SLI cohort showed no significant change in their English SAT levels between age 11 and 14 ($t = -1.296$, df 50, *ns*), whereas there was a significant improvement in Maths ($t = -6.205$, df 55, $p < 0.005$, $d = 0.62$).

Further evidence of the impact of basic skills difficulties on later GCSE outcomes is available from examination of the correlation between the language and attainment measures at 16 years and the total points score at GCSE (Table 8.3). Apart from grammatical understanding (TROG), all measures show moderate correlation, ranging from 0.40 for spelling to 0.57 for writing and numeracy. Furthermore, similar patterns were found when the correlations between assessment at 14 years and GCSE total points score at 16 years were examined, and examination of correlations of earlier assessments indicated that at both 8 and 11 years oral language and literacy abilities were significantly associated with GCSE total points score at 16 years. These results indicate the substantial and persistent influences of oral language and literacy difficulties on attainment during and at the end of secondary education (Key Stages 3 and 4).

Socio-emotional development

Earlier studies have indicated that children with language difficulties are at increased risk of socio-behavioural difficulties (Howlin et al., 2000; Beitchman et al., 2001; Clegg et al., 2005). For example, Beitchman's study indicates that at 19 years, there were higher rates of anxiety disorder among the sample of young people identified with language difficulties at 5 years of age, and that males had higher levels of antisocial personality disorder.

Earlier stages of the present study found higher rates of socio-behavioural difficulties than the norm (Lindsay and Dockrell, 2000; Lindsay et al., 2007b). One measure used to explore this domain was the Strengths and Difficulties Questionnaire (SDQ; Goodman, 1997), which has four problem scales (emotional symptoms, hyperactivity, conduct problems and peer problems) that can be summed to produce a total difficulties score. The SDQ also has a measure of positive behaviour, the prosocial scale. Both teachers and parents completed the SDQ when the cohort was 8, 10 and 12 years, but only teachers completed it at 16 years. At 8 years, almost half of the children's teachers rated them as having significant hyperactivity problems, and about a third rated them as having peer problems, compared with the 10% expected. However, over time, the percentage judged to have hyperactivity problems decreased steadily until by 16 years, this was just 3% of the cohort. Peer problems, however, continued to be apparent, as judged by the teachers at 16 years, and the percentage rated as having significant problems increased from 27% at 8 years to 51% at 16 years. This is a particularly substantial increase that mainly occurred between 12 and 16 years, indicating the cohort's difficulties in developing peer relationships during adolescence as perceived by teachers in the secondary school setting.

Parents' ratings, however, did not match well with those made by teachers (Lindsay et al., 2007b). For example, parents consistently produced higher rates of significant conduct problems and emotional symptoms between ages 8 and 12 years (no parent ratings were collected at 16) as shown in Figures 8.3 and 8.4.

The SDQ total difficulties score provides a general measure of behavioural, emotional and social difficulties (BESD). This indicates high levels of BESD over the period 8–16 years with between a quarter and third of teachers rating the young people with significant problems, a level significantly different from the expected 10% ($p < 0.0005$).

Again, these findings present a mixed picture. There is clear evidence of increased levels of BESD concerning this sample of young people with SLI. However, it is also important to note that the patterns differ between

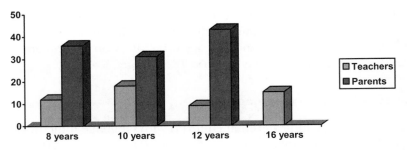

Figure 8.3 Teachers' and parents' ratings of conduct problems at 8–16 years (%).

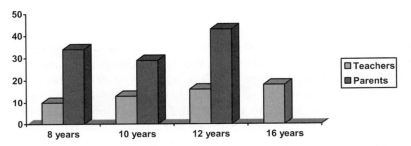

Figure 8.4 Teachers' and parents' ratings of emotional problems at 8–16 years (%).

types of difficulty and the person rating the young person: teacher and parent. The latter may represent a context rather than rater variation as teacher's judge behaviour in school and parent's judge behaviour at home. In a previous phase of the study, there was evidence that teachers' judgements of the pupils' behaviour were influenced by their language skills, while this was not the case with the parents (Lindsay et al., 2007b). Thus, the importance of identifying strengths and patterns of difficulties across situations is important in understanding the children's needs.

The young people's views

The findings presented so far have come from standardized measures, designed to examine different aspects of the young people's development. Our study also explored the young people's own perspectives using some standardized measures, for example, of self esteem. In addition, we conducted semi-structured interviews to capture the young people's own views. We were interested in how they thought about their own difficulties, the schooling they had experienced and their hopes for the future.

All except one of those interviewed acknowledged they had had SEN while at school, and three-quarters of these were either accepting or actively seeking to overcome their problems. For example, one stated:

I tried not to focus so much on my special needs but to do my best in order to overcome these difficulties. I tried to improve my skills as much as I could.'

(P16)

Not all were so positive; a quarter reported feeling upset, frustrated, worried or ashamed by their difficulties:

I felt, like, ashamed, I felt ashamed especially when people were asking about my handwriting and when I had to ask people all the time about spelling or can you read this for me.

(P25)

However, even here, the young person went on to show a more positive attitude, continuing:

I think now I'm getting on with it. I'm not bothered any more.

As shown above, these young people had a history of persistent speech and language difficulties, and most (43/54) described the problems they had experienced in these terms. However, the prevalence of difficulties with literacy, confirmed by the individual assessments, was also recognized: 39 referred to difficulties with reading, 35 with writing and 26 with spelling.

One of the changes in educational provision or pupils with SEN over recent years has been the development of inclusion. The sample of young people with language difficulties followed up by Rutter and colleagues were attending either special schools or hospital provision when identified at 7–8 years. Contrast this with our sample. At 8 years, 47 of the 59 LA sample were in mainstream; 10 children from special language schools were added in order to boost the number with this experience. Over the rest of their schooling, a substantial minority of the total sample of 69 moved type of educational provision (Figure 8.5). Nevertheless, by 16 years, only 18 of the remaining 65 in the sample were attending special schools: nine in specialist language schools and nine in schools for pupils with moderate learning difficulties (MLD). While 47/69 had originally attended mainstream schools, 47/65 were in mainstream at 16 years: nine were attending mainstream schools that had designated special provision (integrated resources), which provided additional specialist support, whereas 38 were attending mainstream schools without such specialist provision.

The nature of support within schools has changed considerably over the past 20–30 years. Nowadays, schools have considerable numbers of non-teaching staff to offer additional support, including teaching assistants (TAs) and learning mentors. The effectiveness of these new professionals has not yet been clearly demonstrated by research (see Lindsay, 2007 for a review), but there are a number of positive indications (Riggs and Mueller, 2001; Blatchford et al., 2004). Our study provides substantial evidence that the young people with SLI valued the support of TAs (often

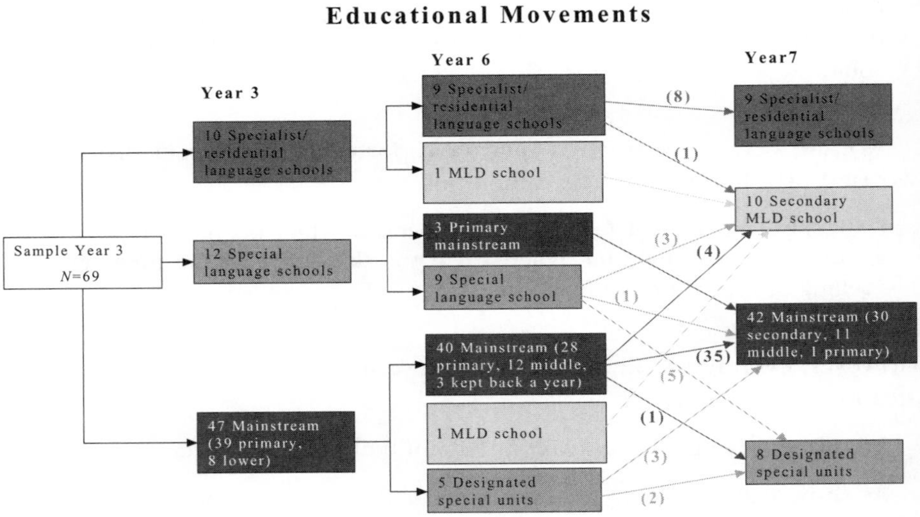

Educational Movements

Figure 8.5 Educational movements of children with specific language impairment between ages 8 and 11 years. *Note*: MLD, moderate learning difficulties.

called learning support assistants or a variety of other names) as well as teaching support. For example, when asked about the types of support that had most helped them, 15 of the 54 interviewees specified a personal tutor (secondary school), 14 a TA at primary school and 10 a TA at secondary school. Some participants reported more than one type of support. These responses may be compared with the number specifying speech and language therapy – just five. This may, of course, reflect limited speech and language therapist (SLT) provision. SLTs may not work directly with young people regularly during Key Stages 3 and 4, which would influence their recollections. Indeed, the young people reported that speech and language therapy, unlike TA support, tended not to be available at secondary school: only 9/54 reported receiving SLT support at secondary school compared with 25 at primary school, whereas TA support increased (25 primary and 31 secondary pupils). This relative lack of SLT provision has been confirmed in our study of educational provision for children with SLI in England and Wales (Lindsay et al., 2005a).

The in-school support was valued, as exemplified by these two young people:

I'm very grateful for the support I received, especially in primary school. I wouldn't have been at college if it wasn't for this support.

(P15)

The support) was good. I thank them for that. I've done well. It helped me a lot.

(P13)

Although there were positive views overall regarding support, it is clear that there is still a long way to go in order to meet young people's needs adequately. Compare these comments from young people in mainstream with those of a young person in a residential special school for pupils with SLI:

> I used to have a teacher by my side all the time . . . It was [helpful]. She used to sign to me, to lip read. This was helpful because I understood more. [In the residential school] there would be my teacher, my speech therapist and a support assistant and if I needed help, one of them would come to help me.
>
> (P138)

This young person gained eight GCSEs (one at A*–C).

The size of classes and other challenges presented by peers must be considered, as well as the positive contribution of teachers, TAs and others indicated above. For example, interviews with teachers of the children when they were 8 years old highlighted that they considered they did not have adequate skills to meet the children's educational needs (Dockrell and Lindsay, 2001), and secondary school teachers reported the need to make high levels of curriculum differentiation across all the core subjects (Dockrell and Lindsay, in press). Similar concerns are indicated by the young people when 16 years old: 'There were many times when I didn't know what to do in class and when I asked some of the teachers to help me out, they just didn't know what to do' (P37). Concerns were also expressed about class size.

> I don't really think I did that well at school. I didn't know. No, [nothing helped me the most] because the classes were so big and you only had one teacher and they couldn't – it would be so hectic in the class, they couldn't get round to everybody.
>
> (P51)

Post-16

Fifty-one of the 64 young people followed up after compulsory schooling were in some form of education post-16, with 37 attending a college of FE. Most were studying at Level 1. This reflects their attainment in Year 11, but importantly, they were continuing in education, so providing the opportunity for further qualifications at higher levels. A minority were studying at Level 2, and four of those who had remained at school were working towards Level 3 (AS level).

Whereas the school curriculum, particularly since the introduction of the National Curriculum, has been characterized by a high level of uniformity, post-16 education provides a much wider choice. This was seized upon by our sample. Most (41/54) stated that their choice for post-16 had been determined by their interests and enjoyment, with 25 relating choice to hopes for subsequent employment. Whereas there had been little evidence of vocational courses being undertaken at school, the practical side of learning was often mentioned as a rationale for post-16 courses:

> [I enjoy] doing the practical side of this course. . . I just enjoy it generally.
>
> (P13)

A greater sense of freedom was noted:

> You get more freedom, not so much in what we do but you're treated better. I mean, like an adult.
>
> (P138)

The work could be challenging, especially where they had entered a higher-level course:

> I had some problems with coursework. It's harder than GCSE. [For GCSE] the work you had to produce was much shorter. It's longer here. The questions are harder and more research has to be done.
>
> (P71)

However, this concern is no different from that likely to be expressed by many young people entering the next level of education.

The importance of support was evident at post-16, as it had been at school. Literacy support was less frequently mentioned but was still seen as necessary and welcomed by some young people, but increasingly, the focus was on the subject-related challenges.

> [College staff] go through it with you. They read, they sit beside you and go through [the work]. If you don't get it, they'll say it over and over again until you eventually get it.
>
> (P16)

These young people also reported social networks and support from friends. All but one reported that friendships were important to them, and most reported they got on well with peers at college or other post-16 destinations. Indeed, only one reported that he had not made new friends post-16. Interestingly, most also reported that they had some long-term friendships from secondary and even, for a quarter, from primary school. These views present a more positive picture than indicated by the teachers' ratings at 16 years, when peer problems were judged to be significant for half of the group. Evidence that these were valid judgements by the young people was obtained from the interviews with their tutors and parents. Nine out of 10 tutors interviewed reported that the young person's academic progress was at least 'ok', with over half reporting it to be quite or very good. Tutors interviewed considered that about three-quarters of the young people had a positive or very positive perception of themselves as learners and deemed this unrealistic in only six cases. The tutors generally saw the young people as having positive personal qualities and people skills, and a third of the tutors interviewed also judged them to have strengths in communication skills. About 9 out of 10 (41/47) tutors judged the young people to get on quite well (12), and even very well (29), with peers.

Interviews with the parents also presented a positive picture post-16. Over two-thirds were pleased or very pleased with the young person's progress post-16, and three-quarters of the young people were stated to have good or very good relationships with their peers. On the other hand, five young people were described by their parents as isolated outside the classroom, and a third were reported to fight or quarrel with their peers. Many different strengths were identified by parents, for example:

> Good confidence in herself. Speaks up for herself. Works hard.
>
> (Parent 39)

> Generous and kind. Good sense of humour. Good natured.
>
> (Parent 19)

These positive views by tutors and parents were reflected in the improvement in the young people's self-perceptions. For example, statistically significant improvements in self-perception were found for scholastic competence ($t(43) = 3.39$, $p = 0.002$) and global self-worth ($t(58) = 3.02$, $p = 0.004$) between Year 11 and post-16.

Why are these outcomes better than in earlier studies?

The evidence summarized here, and presented in more detail in Dockrell et al. (2007), suggests a more positive status at 16 and 17 years than might have been predicted for a group of young people identified as having SLI at 8 years of age, given previous reports – see Rutter (Chapter 7 this volume). In this final section, we explore the possible reasons for this, but first, it is important to acknowledge and re-emphasize that not all was positive. Academic outcomes at 16 years across the group were well below the norm; above expected numbers of young people were judged by their teachers at 16 years to have problems with peers; and a small minority of young people were having substantial problems post-16. This latter group includes some young people we were unable to interview but where information was available from other sources. Nevertheless, it is reasonable to conclude that the overall picture is relatively positive when compared with earlier studies.

Methodological factors

The first, obvious issue is comparability of samples. The study by Rutter and colleagues sampled exclusively 7- to 8-year-olds from six special units attached to hospitals and from six special schools specializing in teaching pupils with severe language difficulties and/or autism – only the language difficulties group are considered in this discussion. Two other studies to consider, from Canada and England respectively, had different samples again. The study by Beitchman and colleagues (e.g. Beitchman et al., 2001) used a sample of one in three of all children in Ottawa, Canada, from which, by process of a three-stage screening procedure, a sample of children with speech and/or language impairment was identified. The study by Conti-Ramsden and colleagues used a sample of children attending language units in England at age 7 (e.g. Botting et al., 2004). However, all except the Beitchman study specifically focused on children with *specific* or *primary* language difficulties, with non-verbal ability in the normal range and significantly lower levels of language functioning. In addition, the present study and those of Rutter and Conti-Ramsden excluded children who had additional difficulties that would preclude a designation of SLI, including significant hearing loss and autism. Other possible factors include severity of difficulties. However, receptive language ability at age 7–8 years in the Rutter study was similar to that of the present sample at mean age 8.3, (see Chapter 7 this volume), and comparison with the Conti-Ramsden study has also shown levels of language difficulties similar to those shown by the present sample. This does not, however, rule out more subtle differences between samples.

The second issue concerns changes in diagnosis. There are two subsidiary issues here. First, the diagnosis applied to individual children may vary as they mature, and different profiles of impairments and needs become apparent. We have evidence of this in the present study, with the changes in the designation of the young people's SEN as they reached Key Stage 4, to include autistic spectrum disorders (ASD) and MLD (Dockrell et al., 2007). The second issue concerns differences in professional practice regarding diagnosis and also differences over time. For example, we have found substantial variation among speech and language therapy services in the use and nature of diagnostic criteria for SLI (Dockrell et al., 2006). The reasons for the growth in the prevalence of children with autism and ASD is unclear, but two factors that are proposed concern the broadening of diagnostic criteria and variation in severity thresholds when judging comparable qualitative domains of impairment (Baird et al., 2007), a possibility supported by our own study of practitioners' reports (Lindsay et al., 2005a).

The third major issue concerns the time frame of the studies. The children in the Rutter study were born around the late 1960s, those in Beitchman's study in the mid-1970s, while those in both Conti-Ramsden's and our study were born around the late 1980s. This variation raises the main issue on which we will focus, changes in the education system (see below).

The final methodological factor to be noted is that of the measures used. For example, across the studies discussed here, there were differences in measures of language and indeed of the different aspects of language measured; different measures of non-verbal ability and differences in whether the measure changed within a study as the sample became older; and different measures of behavioural, emotional and social functioning and indeed of the domains addressed. To some extent, it is necessary to change the tools used to assess competence: children get older and their skills develop and vary, and the psychometric tests must respond to these changes. However, there are also differences in terms of evidence collected. There is an important difference between assessing for competence (e.g. measures of self-esteem and emotional intelligence) compared with impairment (e.g. depression and anxiety). The measures used reflect not only the theoretical perspective of the researchers, but also influence the way results are presented. For example, results may focus on percentage with psychiatric problems or focus on the percentage reporting good adjustment. Furthermore, the present study has investigated non-child factors, and has accessed the views of the young people themselves as well as the views of their parents, teachers/tutors and other professionals. This is unusual, if not unique, in the study of SLI.

Changes in the education system

The investigation of within-child factors provides crucial information on the abilities of children with SLI – (see also Rutter, Chapter 7 this volume). However, it is also necessary to explore relevant non-child factors if a systemic perspective is to be achieved. In this case, the focus is not only on the child but rather on the child in a context, and the interaction between within-child factors and context, and how this may change over time. An important dimension to be considered here concerns changes to the education system over the period of the study. The educational experience of children with SEN educated in England over the past 10–15 years will have substantial differences from that available during the 1970s–1980s. With respect to SEN, the 1981 Education Act, which fundamentally changed the system of provision for children with SEN, was only enacted in 1983. This brought in a legally based system that required and gradually promoted annual reviews of need, parental involvement and a gradual move away from special schools to increased provision in mainstream settings.

The mainstream education system also changed over this period, driven in particular by the Education Reform Act 1988, which brought in the National Curriculum and, importantly, the philosophy that all children had an entitlement to access the National Curriculum. The focus on improving standards across the education system, including the SEN system, gathered pace (Department for Education and Employment, 1997a, 1997b). Ofsted was set up and charged with inspecting schools, including special schools, and reporting on the education of children with SEN in mainstream.

Schools themselves have changed, with a political philosophy promoting choice and diversity (Department for Education and Employment, 2001). New types of schools have been introduced, including grant-maintained and, later, foundation schools and academies, that have different funding and governance systems. Competition between schools (e.g. in terms of increasing standards to attract more pupils) has been joined by, and is in tension with, the development of collaborative partnerships between schools. For example, federations of schools allow the possibility for a radical improvement to optimize provision for pupils with SEN by sharing resources and playing to individual schools' strengths (Lindsay et al., 2007c).

Support for young people with SEN has improved. Every school now has an SEN coordinator, who must be a qualified teacher, and a number of TAs. Other professionals, including learning mentors and, more recently, parent support advisers (Lindsay et al., 2007a) have been introduced. The Connexions service system of personal advisors has been introduced and was found by many of the young people in our study to be of great assistance (Cullen et al., in preparation). LAs have increased their links with speech and language therapy services, including the employment of SLTs jointly with LAs (Law et al., 2000), and professional practice has changed to welcome greater levels of collaboration between services such as SLTs, EPs and education staff (Lindsay et al., 2005b; Palikara et al., 2007). Although the system of support for children with SLI provided by the education and health services is far from perfect, we would argue that it is far better than in the past.

Conclusions

The young people in our study had substantial difficulties associated with their SLI. Unlike the 'resolved' group in the study by Snowling and colleagues (2001, 2006), these youngsters had not overcome their language problems as they entered Key Stage 2 at 8 years. Rather, as a group, they continued to have substantial language problems. Furthermore, these were associated with even greater levels of difficulties with literacy, with a consequent negative impact on curriculum access especially during Key Stages 3 and 4. The young people over the period 8–16 years were also characterized by an increased risk of a range of BESD.

Nevertheless, by the end of compulsory education at 16 years, the cohort were securing a range of passes at GCSE, albeit mainly Level 1. Their outcomes at this stage were substantially more positive than as suggested by earlier research. Of even more significance, the large majority of the cohort chose to continue in education, and their transition to post-16 provision, most commonly FE college. This was proving successful in a number of ways and more so than these young people's school experience. Although they had received support over their schooling, whether in mainstream or special provision, which they valued, this had been limited in extent and, in mainstream schools, limited also in expertise. Support post-16 was also valued, but now it was related to curricula that were often more practically oriented and which the young people had chosen to take.

As the young people enter the end of adolescence, they still face many challenges. Their relatively low level of achievement is a risk factor, for example. However, there are positive signs for the young people for the future, and certainly, both they and their parents had positive perspectives. Over half the young people planned to undertake further training or study when their current course ended, and the others intended to get a job – this was a very different profile compared with a comparison group of young people with non-language-based SEN in our study, of whom only 1 in 10 planned to continue their education/training (Dockrell et al., 2007). Four out of five expected to be living independently in 5 years' time, and 52/54 expected to have a job.

This study has indicated that young people with significant specific language difficulties in primary school can achieve positive outcomes by 16–17 years, and that this could be interpreted as the norm for this sample. This is not to say that they were very successful, but overall, they had the basis for effective social adjustment and integration into the adult world. The study also gives some indication of the factors that have supported these developments, and how further action could prove even more beneficial for young people in the future. For example, inclusion may have brought many benefits in terms of expectations and availability of in-school support, but there remain major challenges to developing *effective* inclusive education (Lindsay, 2007). The development of new systems of education such as federations of schools may render obsolete the special–mainstream dichotomy; they have the potential for supporting even greater improvements in provision for children and young people with SEN (Lindsay et al., 2007).

Finally, it is important to acknowledge the role of these young people's parents. Parents were sensitive to their children's needs from the earliest phases of the study (Lindsay and Dockrell, 2004). Throughout the pupils' school careers, parents provided reliable descriptions of progress and the barriers they were encountering. They also provided different insights into the pupils' behavioural, emotional and social development compared with those of the teachers (Lindsay et al., 2007). We had many examples of how parents added value to the school's actions not only by helping with schoolwork, but also by easing transitions, forward planning and providing emotional support, even in difficult circumstances.

In conclusion, we return to the starting point for this chapter, namely the previous evidence that presented a generally negative and worrying prognosis for children with SLI. Our study has provided a more positive picture. This is important news, especially for the young people and their parents. It also has implications for professional practice of SLTs and education professionals for the planning of provision to meet the SEN of children and young people with SLI. The future task is to provide increasingly improved services to these youngsters and help them optimize their potential.

Acknowledgements

We are grateful to all the pupils, parents and professionals who have supported the project, to the Department for Children, Schools and Families for funding this phase of the project, to Gail Treml and Klaus Wedell for critical guidance, and to the research officers, Mairi-Ann Cullen and Olympia Palikara.

References

Baird G, Siminoff E, Pickles A et al. (2007) Prevalence of disorders of the autism spectrum in a population cohort of children in South Thames: the Special Needs and Autism Project (SNAP). Lancet 368: 210–15.

Bartak L, Rutter M, Cox A (1975) A comparative study of infantile autism and specific developmental receptive language disorders. I. The children. British Journal of Psychiatry 126: 127–45.

Beitchman JH, Wilson B, Johnson CJ et al. (2001) Fourteen-year follow-up of speech/language-impaired and control children: psychiatric outcome. Journal of the American Academy of Child and Adolescent Psychiatry 40: 75–82.

Bishop DVM (1989) Test of Reception of Grammar, 2nd edn. Manchester: The Author and the University of Manchester Age and Cognitive Performance Research Centre.

Bishop DVM (1997) Uncommon Understanding: Development and Disorders of Language Comprehension in Children. Hove: Psychology Press.

Blatchford P, Russell A, Bassett P et al. (2004) The Effects and Role of Teaching Assistants in English Primary Schools (Years 4 to 6) 2000–2003. Results from the Class Size and Pupil-Adult Ratios (CSPAR) Project. Research Report 605. London: DfES.

Botting N, Crutchley A, Conti-Ramsden G (2004) Educational transitions of 7-year-old children with SLI in language units: a longitudinal study. International Journal of language and Communication Difficulties 33: 177–97.

Clegg J, Hollis C, Mawhood L et al. (2005) Developmental language disorders – a follow-up in later adult life. Cognitive language and psychosocial outcomes. Journal of Child Psychology and Psychiatry 46: 128–49.

Cullen MA, Lindsay G, Dockrell JE (in preparation). The role of the Connexions service in supporting the transition from school to post-16 provision for young people with a history of specific speech and language difficulties.

Department for Education and Employment (1997a) Excellence for All Children. London: The Stationery Office.

Department for Education and Employment (1997b) Excellence in Schools. London: The Stationery Office.

Department for Education and Employment (2001) Schools Building on Success. London: DfEE.

Dockrell JE, Lindsay G (2001) Children with specific speech and language difficulties: the teachers' perspectives. Oxford Review of Education 27(3): 369–94.

Dockrell JE, Lindsay G (2007) Identifying the educational and social needs of children with specific speech and language difficulties on entry to secondary school. Educational and Child Psychology 24: 101–15.

Dockrell JE, Lindsay G, Letchford C et al. (2006) Educational provision for children with specific speech and language difficulties: perspectives of speech and language therapy managers. International Journal of Language and Communication Disorders 41: 423–40.

Dockrell J, Lindsay G, Palikara O et al. (2007) Raising the Achievements of Children and Young People with Specific Language and Communication Needs and Other Special Educational Needs through School, to Work and College. RR837. Nottingham: Department for Education and Skills.

Dunn LM, Dunn LM, Whetton C et al. (1997) The British Picture Vocabulary Scale, 2nd edn. Windsor: NFER-Nelson.

Elliott CD, Smith P, McCulloch K (1997) The British Ability Scales II. Windsor: NFER-Nelson.

Goodman R (1994) A modified version of the Rutter parent questionnaire including items on children's strengths. Journal of Child Psychology and Psychiatry 35: 1483–94.

Goodman R (1997) The strengths and difficulties questionnaire: a research note. Journal of Child Psychology and Psychiatry 38: 581–6.

Hindley CB, Owen CF (1978) The extent of individual changes in I.Q. for ages between 6 months and 17 years, in a British longitudinal sample. Journal of Child Psychology and Psychiatry 19: 329–50.

Howlin P, Mawhood L, Rutter M (2000) Autism and developmental receptive language disorder – a follow-up comparison in early adult life, II: social behavioural and psychiatric outcomes. Journal of Child Psychology and Psychiatry 41: 561–78.

Law J, Lindsay G, Peacey N et al. (2000) Provision for Children with Speech and Language Needs in England and Wales: Facilitating Communication Between Education and Health Services. London: DfEE.

Leonard L (1998) Children with Specific Language Impairments. Cambridge, MA: MIT Press.

Lindsay G (2007) Educational psychology and the effectiveness of inclusive education/mainstreaming. British Journal of Educational Psychology 77: 1–24.

Lindsay G, Dockrell JE (2000) The behaviour and self-esteem of children with specific speech and language difficulties. British Journal of Educational Psychology 70: 583–601.

Lindsay, G, Dockrell, JE (2004) Whose job is it? Parents' concerns about the needs of their children with language problems. Journal of Special Education 37: 225–36.

Lindsay G, Dockrell JE, Mackie et al. (2005a) Local education authorities' approaches to provision for children with specific speech and language difficulties in England and Wales. European Journal of Special Needs Education 20: 329–45.

Lindsay G, Dockrell JE, Mackie et al. (2005b) The role of specialist provision for children with specific speech and language difficulties in England and Wales: a model for inclusion? Journal of Research in Special Educational Needs 5: 88–96.

Lindsay G, Band S, Culllen MA et al. (2007a) The Parent Support Adviser Pilot: The First Interim Report from the Evaluation DCSF-RR020. Nottingham: Department for Children, Schools and Families.

Lindsay G, Dockrell J, Strand S (2007b) Longitudinal patterns of behaviour problems in children with specific speech and language difficulties: child and contextual factors. British Journal of Educational Psychology 77: 811–28.

Lindsay G, Muijs D, Harris A et al. (2007c) A Study of Federations of Schools 2003–2007. Nottingham: Department for Children, Schools and Families RR759.

Lindsay G, Dockrell J, Mackie C (2008) Vulnerability to bullying and impaired social relationships in children with specific speech and language difficulties. European Journal of Special Needs Education 23: 1–16.

Mawhood L, Howlin P, Rutter M (2000). Autism and developmental receptive language disorder a comparative follow-up in early adult life, 1: cognitive and language outcomes. Journal of Child Psychology and Psychiatry 41: 547–59.

Palikara O, Lindsay G, Cullen M et al. (2007) Working together? The practice of educational psychologists and speech and language therapists with children with specific speech and language difficulties. Educational and Child Psychology, 24: 77–88.

Renfrew K (1997) The Bus Story. Bicester: Winslow.

Riggs CG, Mueller PH (2001) Employment and utilization of paraeducators in inclusive settings. Journal of Special Education 35: 54–62.

Semel E, Wiig EH, Secord W (1987) Clinical Evaluation of Language Fundamentals – Revised. London: The Psychological Corporation, Harcourt Brace Jovanovich.

Snowling M, Adams JW, Bishop DVM et al. (2001) Educational attainment of school leavers with a preschool history of speech-language impairment. International Journal of Language and Communication Disorders 36: 173–83.

Snowling M, Bishop DVM, Stothard SE et al. (2006) Psychosocial outcomes at 15 years of children with a preschool history of speech-language impairment. Journal of Child Psychology and Psychiatry 47: 759–65.

CHAPTER 9

Making new connections – where to next?

JAMES LAW

Centre for Integrated Healthcare Research, Queen Margaret University, Edinburgh

Introduction

This final chapter picks up on a number of issues emerging from the Making New Connections 2 (MNC2) conference. The first concerns the original conceptualization of the connections between adult- and child-focused models of language processing that we were looking for in the initial meeting in 1996 and what we are able to conclude now, 10 years later. The second relates to the idea of continuities and the measurement of those continuities across the lifespan, and the third picks up on the concerns expressed about the central issue of evidence-based practice (EBP) and the direction it is taking in speech and language therapy. The chapter concludes by drawing out a number of further connections that would have the potential to take the field further forward.

The modelling connection?

The first Making New Connections (MNC1) conference was designed to explicitly examine the link between language disorders in children and adults. This was not exactly a *new* connection, in that many of the early practitioner researchers in the field of speech and language therapy had started by drawing connections between the presenting symptomatology in adults and that in children. For example, by the time she was writing

Language Disorders in Children and Adults: New Issues in Research and Practice.   Victoria Joffe,
Madeline Cruice, Shula Chiat.
© 2008 John Wiley & Sons, Ltd. ISBN 978-0-470-51839-7

in the 1960s and 1970s, Morley clearly linked the term 'dyspraxia', which had until that point been most commonly used in adult diagnostics, to 'developmental dyspraxia or apraxia of speech' in order to capture a set of behaviours that mirrored those experienced by a subgroup of people with acquired speech disorders (Morley, 1972).

MNC1 was an attempt to re-examine this link at a time when increasing specialization had led to an apparent adult/child split in the speech and language therapy profession and in the contribution made by supporting disciplines such as linguistics and psychology. The key issue in the 1980s was the increasing role that cognitive neuropsychology was starting to play in relation to adult disorders, and the contribution that psycholinguistics was making to the study of disorders in children. Both had begun to make claims about the explanatory, as well as the descriptive, power of their models.

It was interesting that, not long after MNC1, attempts were being made to address explicitly the same issue in empirical terms. The Thomas and Karmiloff-Smith (2002) paper that is cited by Joffe et al. in the introduction to this volume addresses this issue directly. The authors argue that, whereas in adult models it is possible to find domain-specific brain damage, it is much less easy to postulate the existence of highly specific deficits in children because of the diffuse effects of development in terms of down-stream behaviours. They suggest that residual normality, which is taken as a *sine qua non* of cognitive neuropsychological models of performance in adulthood, makes much less sense in childhood. As if in anticipation of the reaction of those who have a special interest in this area, they maintain that:

> Researchers have been too prone to assume that superficially normal behaviour (as determined on standardised tests) corresponds to normal underlying process, irrespective of the developmental plausibility of RN (residual normality) in each cognitive domain.
>
> Thomas and Karmiloff-Smith, 2002, p. 54

And they go on:

> We believe that this tendency (to assume RN exists) has also impeded the discipline (unspecified) in building links to developmental cognitive neuro-science and developmental neurobiology, since the use of RN with static models stipulates rather than explores the developmental origins of deficits.
>
> Thomas and Karmiloff-Smith, 2002, p. 54

Thomas and Karmiloff-Smith (2002) are not saying that disorders based on specific patterns of strengths and difficulties cannot exist, just that 'compensation and plasticity mitigate against it on a fine-scale decomposition of cognitive domains' (p. 54). In other words, these specific profiles may work more effectively in terms of broader functional distinctions in the brain (anterior/posterior, cortical versus subcortical, etc.) than they do in terms of performance on specific psychometric measures.

Others have been rather more tolerant of the possibility of dissociations. For example, Temple has suggested that

> downstream effects do not preclude a modular organisation to the merging language system, but they may reduce the potential for neat double dissociations to be evident within the specific language deficits.
>
> Temple, 1997, p. 39

In the end, the key issue may be one of the distinctions that can be drawn between *description* and *explanation*, and indeed the nature of knowledge itself in this area. Temple goes on that '(children with language disorders) could create problems for (developmental cognitive neuropsychological) models . . . since the model either predicts downstream effects in all cases or in none, but this does not permit a differential influence without some degree of further partitioning or fractionation of its components' (Temple, 1997, p. 39). It is also relevant to consider what might be considered 'normal variability' between elements of the subsystems. For example, it may well be possible to identify statistically significant discrepancies between aspects of verbal comprehension and grammar formulation in an individual child and then make great claims for the specific nature of the disorder in that child, but this assumes that the child or adult with 'normal' language cannot have a similar level of dissociation. Indeed, work carried out in the early 1990s suggested that the whole idea of discrepancy with regard to children was one that needed to be treated with considerable care (Cole et al., 1992), and this in turn has led to a re-conceptualization by many therapists away from a static diagnostic model of the interaction of a specific set of skills towards a more dynamic model of assessing an individual's capacity to learn, or what has come to be known in the United States particularly as the 'responsiveness to intervention' (Ehren and Nelson, 2005; Justice, 2006; Dodd, Chapter 4 this volume; Joffe, Chapter 5 this volume).

The principal focus of MNC1 was the elucidation of psycholinguistic models that could explain aetiology and inform intervention (Black, 1997). If one theme crosses the chapters in this volume, based on the papers in MNC2, it is that the nature of the person, their experience, their behaviour and the way that they see the world is critical to understanding both the condition and the way that they respond to intervention. It is not that the models discussed in MNC1 are necessarily wrong in a sense that the boxes and arrows referred to by Marshall (Chapter 3 this volume) need to be modified, only that they are insufficient in terms of what they can tell us about intervention for adults and children with language disorders. One solution is to include pragmatics in such models. But is it really feasible to include even pragmatics in a psycholinguistic model? What would it look like? I recall that we struggled with this issue when we set up the first conference and included a section of pragmatic interventions in adults and children but never really managed to reconcile where it sat from a theoretical point of view. Of course, this becomes even harder when the notion of pragmatics transcends its historical linguistic origins to include non-verbal behaviours and social cognition. Another solution might be to revise what are essentially 'cold' models of cognition, that is, cognition disembodied, in the truly Cartesian sense, from the emotional development of the individual. This idea of a more sophisticated 'hot' model of cognition that includes, rather than disregards, affect, is not a new idea (Greenberg and Safran, 1984) and would appear to have some biological support (Schaeffer et al., 2003; David and Szentagotai, 2006), but such models have generally not made it to second base in speech and language therapy. One exception to this can be found in Roy and Chiat (Chapter 1 this volume), who propose that social cognition should be seen as a developmental precursor to the development of language, and they illustrate this with their very early processing skills measures. Beyond this, there is a wider context that goes beyond social cognition associated with constructs such as quality of life, emotional well-being, social skills and aspects of behaviour. This shift is reflected in much of the content of this volume, and this differs markedly from that of the earlier MNC1 conference.

Trajectories and change across time

In order to understand diagnosis, it is essential to see it in the context of developmental and social change experienced by the individual. Trajectories, pathways and long-term outcomes are clearly critical to our understanding of language disorders (Roy and Chiat, Chapter 1 this volume; Rutter, Chapter 7 this volume; Lindsay and Dockrell, Chapter 8 this volume). Indeed, much of the argument is based upon the premise that there is 'child' and 'adult' language, a developing system and a static system and that the two merge into one another at some unspecified point. Although it is now clear that poor language skills at school entry represent a risk for later difficulties in terms of language, literacy, and emotional and behavioural development, it is equally clear that the outcomes are not certain and children move in and out of different groups across time (Stothard et al., 1998; Conti-Ramsden and Botting, 1999; Johnson et al., 1999). Indeed, it may be that trajectories are best determined by the initial level of language difficulty rather than anything about the quality of that difficulty (Dollaghan, 2004; Law et al., forthcoming). This rather suggests that diagnostic groupings, so apparently useful at a single time point, do not, in the main, stand the test of time. Despite this, we still know relatively little about the extent to which poor language learning skills in childhood translate into adulthood. Data from extreme clinical cases would suggest that the implications are considerable (Clegg et al., 2005; Rutter, Chapter 7 this volume), but it is less clear if this is true of all those children presenting with difficulties in childhood, especially once social and demographic risk is taken into consideration.

Another factor that is relevant to the consideration of longitudinal data is the role played by intervention in affecting the course of that trajectory. To date, we can demonstrate short-term intervention effects, but it has proved much more difficult to demonstrate that developmental trajectories can be altered over the longer term. This can be very difficult to do from a methodological point of view. It is easier to demonstrate association than it is to show causation. Lindsay and Dockrell (Chapter 8 this volume) demonstrate that, despite persistent problems, the children in their cohort were doing better as teenagers than had been anticipated. However, as they say themselves, the higher level of achievement in national qualifications may well be a function of improved services to children when they leave school rather than within-child change.

However, all such discussions are prefaced upon an acceptance of the use of psychometric measures with all that this entails. We almost certainly need to be cleverer about assessment, as both Joffe (Chapter 5) and Marshall (Chapter 3) maintain in this volume. Some aspects of communication do not translate very easily into psychometric assessments and certainly do not function like the concept of 'g' believed by many to underpin IQ tests. The interaction between verbal and non-verbal skills is also of direct concern. As Varley (Chapter 2 this volume) has pointed out, language has a bearing on all reasoning skills because it influences the way in which we think about what we are doing and inevitably impacts on all cognitive performance, and the higher the function the less likely it is that we can truly separate out language and thinking, particularly when it comes to learning and contextualized assessment. She highlights the specific example of navigation as a test for whether language and visual spatial thinking can truly be separated. She concludes that while separation between language and thought can be demonstrated in some domains – for example, mathematics – this does not detract from the basic assumption that thinking about cognition and language as discrete entities is probably not very helpful in practical terms. 'Even if natural language words and sentences are not the substance of thoughts, they might be very useful in scaffolding our thinking' (Varley, Chapter 2 this volume).

The limitations of available measures are probably particularly apparent when we consider relatively loose constructs such as mental health or well-being, to which reference is made in a number of chapters in this volume (e.g. Cruice et al., Chapter 6; Lindsay and Dockrell, Chapter 8). Another problem for existing models of measurement, which represents a particular challenge to the notion of change across time, is the increasing recognition of the need to take into consideration the role of the interlocutor. Take for example the concept of 'communication support needs', a term introduced over the past 15 years to capture the extent to which a communication difficulty had an impact on the person with whom the person with communication needs is speaking, whether that be a parent, a teacher, a spouse or the person who works behind the till in Tesco. In other words, the impairment does not reside within the individual but is reflected in the behaviour of those around them (Law et al., 2007). Of course, *need* may mirror the severity of the symptoms. Someone with more severe difficulties is likely to have greater need in the sense that the person with whom they are talking is likely to have to do more to construct the intended meaning during communication, but this is not necessarily the case. Two people with the same level of difficulty on a standardized assessment may respond differently to that difficulty, expressing more frustration for example, and thus placing higher demands on their conversation partner. The level of need in this case is therefore constructed by both parties – the person with the communication support need and the person with whom they are speaking. To a certain extent, this variability is reflected in the findings of Lindsay and Dockrell (Chapter 8) in this volume, who demonstrated that teachers and parents can have very different perceptions of a child's behaviour, with parents expressing much higher levels of concern than teachers. Of course, the use of the Strengths and Difficulties Questionnaire (SDQ), which specifically taps the views of both parties, allows for this. We have less sense whether you would obtain the same variability in ratings of communication support needs. Cruice et al. (Chapter 6 this volume) make the same point about quality of life measures, which inevitably reflect different ideas of what quality of life means. They conclude that

> By analysing at an individual level, the matched pairs data reveals that the majority of family members and friends are exceedingly poor at accurately guessing what quality of life means for their aphasic partners. On the face of it, no one would ever consult family members again,

although they continue 'however leaping to this conclusion is too hasty and requires a little further deliberation', and then proceed to unpick what it is that these differences mean.

Significantly, and this is where the idea of *needs* meshes with the measurement of *trajectories*, needs may increase and decrease across the lifespan according to all sorts of external factors, such as available support in the family and in school or employment, and for specific circumstances, such as completing exam papers or travelling on a bus. Likewise, needs may be a function of the specificity of the problem, with specific impairments having more circumscribed needs, but the reality is that how an individual experiences those needs across time is as likely to reflect what they want to talk about and their expectations for their own communication. And in this context, the specificity of the impairment becomes far less significant than the specificity of the need. Great strides have been made in recent years in the assessment of this level of need and we know much more about quality of life and emotional health as is witnessed in some of the papers (Cruice et al.) in this volume. But we still know relatively little about the way that those needs change across the lifespan. One of the most obvious gaps in our knowledge is our understanding of the transition between childhood and adolescence. We still know relatively little about what happens once children with such difficulties leave school. There are a variety of reasons for this but, essentially, no services are available for them or such services as are available remain erratically distributed. As a result, they start dropping off the radar once they enter secondary school services (Joffe, Chapter 5 this volume), and this gets worse as they move across into the world of employment. Although we commonly discuss adolescence as a key life transition, it is not as if we stop making transitions across adulthood. In fact, once we take a 'person-centred' perspective, our lives are characterized by an endless succession of transitions of one sort or another – having children, getting married, experiencing bereavement, going into hospital and so on. Successful transitions invariably rely heavily on verbal mediation with those managing the transition (i.e. teachers and employers) and those with whom the transition is shared (i.e. peers). Of course, the strength of this concept of need is potentially also a limitation when it comes to researching trajectories. It is difficult enough to measure cohorts of sufficient size at different time points to establish long-term outcomes using well-designed psychometric measures. Introduce a person-centred relativistic notion of need and the problems are multiplied.

Longitudinal considerations are also important because they help us come to understand 'natural history' – what happens to people who are identified as cases in need of intervention but who are not then in receipt of services. Natural history has a direct effect on our understanding of intervention. If we are not able to estimate the rate at which people would change normally without intervention, effectively the noise of development, it is difficult to be clear what it is that we are measuring in an intervention. Our lack of precision in this area probably goes some way to explaining the difficulty we have had in interpreting the results of those intervention studies that have proved inconclusive. In fact, the performance of the comparison or control groups is often as interesting as that of the intervention group. There is often so much movement among those who do not receive the intervention that it can be difficult to detect change in groups that have received it. Of course, we are probably not talking about true *natural history* in the sense that the individual receives no input at all. Any level of stimulation may contribute to an outcome, irrespective of whether that intervention is delivered by a speech and language therapist. Environments commonly adjust to contribute to the needs of specific individuals. How effectively they do so is, of course, another matter. The same is not the case if an individual does not receive a prosthetic device or a medicine. In short, we need more information about change across the lifespan, but recent shifts in the direction of person-centred care pose real challenges to understanding that change.

Motherhood, apple pie and EBP

It is difficult to say that you are not interested in EBP when it comes to health care. This is the same in the field of speech and language therapy as it is in other more obviously 'medicalized' aspects of health care delivery. But EBP can become a little like motherhood and apple pie; being against it automatically places you in the flat earth society. There is a consensus that EBP is a good thing, but this same consensus can rather stifle debate about what 'evidence' actually entails and who it is designed to benefit. And this is where we are prone to venturing into a type of methodological warfare, with different sides taking up positions and digging in, comparable to the sort of sterile debates that have sometimes characterized the separation between qualitative and quantitative research. The problem is that it can often be very difficult to translate EBP into the way that practitioners provide and patients receive services (see Marshall, Chapter 3 this volume; Dodd, Chapter 4 this volume; Joffe, Chapter 5 this volume). There are numbers of issues that affect the translation of evidence into practice. The first of these is the availability of materials, the second is the type of evidence that is commonly reported in the literature and the third to be addressed here is the interpretation of available data.

The move towards EBP is prefaced on it being available in the first place and whether practitioners have access to it. Journal articles can be inaccessible to all but the most tenacious or to those working in universities who have the time and the facilities at their disposal. Of course, the choice of the articles themselves can be a problem for those who are not familiar with searching databases or in critiquing literature. But help is at hand. In fact, there is a range of sources that are readily available to those who are interested. For example, we now have a series of EBP texts in health care (Greenhalgh, 1997), in education (McEwan and McEwan, 2003), in speech pathology specifically (Reilly et al., 2003; Dollaghan, 2007) and most recently Dollaghan (2007). Similarly, there is a wealth of developing systematic reviews in the Cochrane (http://www.cochrane.org) and Campbell Collaboration databases (http://www.campbellcollaboration.org), the Evidence for Policy and Practice Information and Co-ordinating Centre (http://eppi.ioe.ac.uk/cms), the What Works Clearing House (http://www.w-w-c.org/) and the Centre for Reviews and Dissemination (http://www.york.ac.uk/inst/crd/), and the Canadian Centre for Knowledge Mobilisation has a section devoted to speech and language pathology (http://www.cckm.ca/index2.htm).The great advantage of these databases is that the best-quality literature is drawn together and they provide a condensed version of what is available. In many cases, these reviews are regularly updated, and effectively, they are living documents. And within these databases, there is a variety of reviews of speech and language therapy practice, the most substantive being those on speech and language disorder in children and in language disorders following stroke. But even access to these databases may be providing information at the wrong level for practitioners, who often want short précis of key research in a more readily digestible format than a systematic review or even full journal articles. To this end, we have seen the introduction of a new journal in the field of speech and language pathology – *Evidence Based Communication Assessment and Intervention* – that provides summaries of reviews as they are published across the field. Indeed, there is plenty of material here and many groups of practitioners make use of it in journal clubs and the like.

Of course, availability in itself is not enough. Practitioners need to have the time and the support available for this sort of activity, and there is always a question as to who owns, that is, who funds, a clinician's continuing professional development. They also need to have access to help in interpreting the available literature. An assumption is commonly made that the introductory education that speech and language therapists receive is sufficient for them to be research literate, able to interpret data within journal articles and form their own conclusions about the implications. Although training in research design and statistics and EBP are now common features of courses for speech and language therapists, passing an exam does not necessarily equip someone sufficiently to take this activity forward themselves. But, of course, these skills, like clinical skills, develop with practice and active engagement with the evidence base. This is a process that needs to be fostered very early on in a practitioner's development and not only when they have developed clinically and a specific technical question arises. Of course, the potential obstacles facing the speech and language therapist are multiplied for professional groups that have no such training but provide services to people with communication disabilities.

There is also an issue about the expectations of research and what it can contribute to clinical practice. Many health professions take a view that their own specific domain of expertise is too complex to be subject to standard intervention designs. Take for example the following statement about the application of EBP:

> (Practice) is highly conditional. It depends on a range of physical, . . . personal, individual and circumstantial factors which are complex, often unique, and sometimes inter-twined. Practice may also be affected by chance or accidental events and it may therefore be conceptualised as 'contingent'. Practitioners appear to draw on tacit and instinctive knowledge to respond to this contingency. This knowledge is likely to be experiential rather than evidence based. Critics of the application of evidence based practice to this field contend that there are fundamental differences between its knowledge base and the types of knowledge required for clinical practice. Practitioners in particular have been quick to articulate their fears about EBP and the threat to their art.
>
> Pope, 2001, Abstract No. 196

Sounds familiar? This could easily have been a statement related to speech and language therapy but in fact it refers to surgery, an area in which one might assume that the criteria for EBP might be more readily met (Solomon and McLeod, 1998).

At the heart of this concern about applicability is the tension identified by Joffe between efficacy and effectiveness studies. The former are more controlled and delivered under optimum conditions. The latter are based on what happens in practice and are therefore more readily interpreted by practitioners. The medical parallels are between lab and field studies of a given intervention, and although this distinction does not translate directly to speech and language therapy, it is easy to see the problem from the practitioner's perspective. Effectiveness trials are probably more meaningful to practice, but they can only be carried out once efficacy studies have demonstrated that the intervention *can* work. But the need to separate these two types of study in itself highlights the need to collect the right sort of information at the right time and to know where a study fits into the sequence of evidence articulated so clearly in the Medical Research Council (MRC) guidelines on the development of complex interventions (MRC, 2000). We need to recognize this developmental progression and ensure that we interpret different levels of evidence correctly. If we do not do this, as Dodd (Chapter 4) observes in this volume, there is a very real danger of running a complex clinical field trial and obtaining negative results but then not being able to interpret the result.

However, it is not just a matter of understanding the implications of specific research methodologies. The fact is that researchers and clinicians have different jobs and different priorities, and they are never likely to be completely at one with each other, even if they did all read the same literature or understood research design and statistics to the same degree. Many clinical questions are of the 'does it work' variety, which will require the close definition of what 'it' is, and often the manualization of the therapy, so that the therapy can be carried out by any therapist and not just the person who originally designed it. Practitioners often have questions about the value of the way that services are delivered, what is sometimes known as 'health services research'. Such research has the potential to feed directly into policy at both a local and a national level, but to date, relatively little of this type of research has been carried out in speech and language therapy. By contrast, researchers often focus on theoretical concerns, which, while undoubtedly interesting, are often quite removed from practice. Their work is also partially driven by the priorities of funders and funding councils, and these do not necessarily prioritize the types of research that would be most useful from the practitioners' perspective. Roy and Chiat's (Chapter 1) exploration of the interaction between social cognition and early language development in this volume is an interesting example of the fusion of theory and practice, and this undoubtedly renders the research more relevant for practitioners. In part, this has resulted from an awareness of the need for clinical accessibility that has permeated this particular research from its inception. In summary, there are inevitable differences in perspective between practitioners and researchers and, in the main, this is, as Joffe (Chapter 5) observes in this volume, the result of differences in the nature of their respective enterprises. Greater linkage between the academic and clinical domains should be encouraged at every opportunity. Hopefully, in the United Kingdom at least, this will be facilitated by the forthcoming development of clinical research posts for nurses and the allied health professions (UK Clinical Research Collaboration, 2007). Similarly, PhD and master's programmes help facilitate this sort of linkage, allowing practitioners and academics to engage in a dialogue about the nature of evidence that is required to understand the effectiveness of interventions.

One of the touchstones of EBP is the systematic review of the literature. Such reviews are intended as a mechanism for providing replicable syntheses, usually, of intervention of data. But encountering them can be a frustrating experience for clinicians. Although reviews draw on the best available evidence, they do not always provide answers to clinical questions. Obviously, they can only review what is available in the literature. But this can lead to a frustration with this interpretation. For example, in a recent commentary on our own systematic review (Law et al., 2003), we were criticized for only reporting data about young children and for not paying enough attention to practice (see Johnston, 2005 and our response (Law et al., 2005)). In fact, as was clearly stated in the review, we did search for papers across childhood but there were few, if any, that met our quality criteria. Similarly, we would have taken any good-quality evidence that related to 'practice', but there was none that met our criteria. The point is that such criticisms are often a little like Vlad the Impaler nailing the turbans onto the heads of messengers sent from his Ottoman enemies. Practitioners, and indeed researchers, may be looking for answers that the review was never intended to address.

Having said this, there is a real issue with producing EBP that is readily accessible for clinicians. Some of the authors in this volume express concerns about what they see as a division between clinicians and researchers (Dodd, Chapter 4 this volume; Joffe, Chapter 5 this volume). The key here is the need for translational research, where the goals of both parties are clearly articulated and brought together and the outputs from a given piece of work are tailored to the needs of the target consumer. As indicated above, availability of information is less of an issue nowadays than the time needed to access that information. But more work is needed on what is sometimes referred to as the co-construction of knowledge in this area, with practitioners working closely with researchers in taking the field forward. Many researchers have started developing ways of doing this, exemplified by a review of the literature completed with colleagues for the City of Edinburgh and relating to the provision of services for speech and language therapists and occupational therapists (Forsyth et al., 2007). In this case, the funders wanted a wide-ranging review to demonstrate where knowledge was strongest and where they could have greatest confidence in the intervention being offered. Although a systematic review was completed, this was carried out in close collaboration with the therapists themselves and mapped onto what they considered their priorities. Rather than reporting the data in terms of forest plots and standardized mean differences – the common metrics of meta-analyses – the data are displayed so that they are readily accessible to practitioners, with a traffic light system indicating how the evidence stacked up in a given area. This has been accompanied by a programme of engagement with practitioners supported by the funders, and this in turn is now leading to a set of practice statements, which are specifically designed to allow practitioners in health and education to develop a shared understanding of what it is that can be achieved.

One direction that this approach lends itself to is the manualization of therapy, in which the details of the therapy that has been found to have an evidence base indicating potentially positive outcomes are fixed so that a therapist can replicate that therapy with comparable client groups and, presumably, with the same effects. This issue is covered by Marshall (Chapter 3) in this volume and is beginning to come into some aspects of practice, much as 'care pathways' have come to accepted practice in many health care interventions. It is unclear how such applications of evidence-based care are being interpreted by therapists who have, for a long-term time, fiercely guarded their right to autonomy in treating individuals. The researchers would almost certainly argue that if protocols are not followed, results will not be replicated, but whether it is possible to be this prescriptive remains to be seen. Key here is the fact that the manualization process adds clarity by being very specific about what it is that the therapist does with the client.

New connections?

In summary, the chapters in this volume based on the MNC2 conference provide a rich source of information about the current state of knowledge in speech and language therapy, with the connections that have been explored in this volume going far beyond those discussed in the original volume. Despite the complexity alluded to by most of the authors in this volume, there are a number of directions arising out of the foregoing discussion, which can be highlighted as potentially fruitful future connections.

The first of these is the connection between researcher and practitioner, specifically with relevance to the application of EBP and how evidence is generated and translated for practitioners. This is a corporate endeavour, with input and commitment needed from all parties whether they be the providers of health care, education or social services who employ speech and language therapists and the specialist teachers, teaching assistants and carers who support people with communication support needs, whether they be those who provide education for the different professional groups or whether they are those who carry out the research. There is clearly a need to ensure that those that are going to use the evidence understand the process by which it is obtained. Although a small proportion of practitioners will go on to complete master's courses and PhD programmes, the emphasis for this basic level of understanding of the research process falls fair and square on the establishments that provide the basic education for speech and language therapists and other practitioners. But it is not simply a matter of providing people with basic skills and expecting them to get on with it. EBP needs to be supported in practice with reading groups, practice development web sites and all the other mechanisms that have been developed over the past decade and more. This, of course, requires the support of managers in releasing staff to support this type of continuing professional development. But it also needs a commitment from academics and their managers to facilitate their involvement in the process. It also calls for more work on the part of researchers to make the literature more accessible. Such translational work, or 'knowledge transfer' as it is currently termed, needs a higher priority in academic circles.

Related to this is the nature of the evidence required. Undoubtedly, speech and language therapy represents a complex set of interventions that require a great deal of careful description if they are to be adequately captured. We need more work evaluating different aspects of intervention using high-quality design methodologies. But as we have seen in relation to surgery, most disciplines have concerns about the application of evidence-based principles to their specific domains. However, the great virtue of adhering to such principles is that adherence allows others to understand what it is that is being achieved. In effect, EBP represents a solution to the problem of communicating about communication disabilities to those outside the immediate field of the speech and language therapy profession. The challenge for clinicians and researchers alike is the application of those principles so that the research remains true to the practice on the one hand and readily translatable on the other.

My conclusion would be that we need to avoid special pleading that speech and language therapy is inherently different from other disciplines at the level at which evidence is gained. There is not one sort of EBP for speech and language therapists and another for everyone else. This is not to say that we necessarily have to carry on doing the same sort of research. New developments need to be taken up and explored in speech and language therapy, as they would be in other fields. For example, we have yet to see the application of 'realist synthesis' as an alternative to existing models of systematic review (Pawson et al., 2004). This may be more applicable to the needs of some aspects of practice than traditional methods of research synthesis. Similarly, there has, to date, been very little in the way of economic analysis of provision for people with communication support needs. This will be critical in terms of our future understanding of policy and practice in this area and will be of direct relevance to those planning services. More importantly for the purposes of the present argument is that such analyses will provide another opportunity for practitioners to feed into the evaluation process what it is that they are aiming to achieve with people with communication disabilities and how they believe outcomes can best be measured.

A second connection is the link between externally and internally defined need. The psychometric measures upon which so much research, and indeed practice, is based have proved problematic in terms of the consistency of the constructs that they measure, and as practice has shifted to focus on what might best be described as functional communication and a more 'person-centred' model of care, they may not be measuring the target construct at all. One alternative would be the development of more sensitive measures to tap the views of the individual as has been used – a more appropriate wording here might be 'as has happened' – with quality of life measures. Another might be the use of triangulation of the same measure but reported for different people in the environment of the person with communication needs, as we have seen in the use of the SDQ with parents, teachers and, potentially, the young people themselves (see Lindsay and Dockrell, Chapter 8 this volume). The problem has been that need is a relative construct, interpreted differently by different people. This represents on the one hand a very real challenge for researchers and clinicians alike, but on the other hand a very real opportunity for the different parties to get together to discuss how this particular circle can be squared.

The third connection, which needs further elucidation, is the link between cross-sectional assessment and change across time. Inevitably, this links in closely to what we know about EBP and how we approach measurement. We need to better understand how people with communication difficulties perform across time and what it is that improves their chances of doing well and, by the same token, what it is that increases the chance of their having poor outcomes. Closely related to this issue of communication performance across time is the relationship between communication and other demographic factors such as social class, parental education, housing and so on. In other words, communication need is only ever one element of a complex pattern of risk across the lifespan. It is only when we become clear about continuities and discontinuities that we can interpret cross-sectional data meaningfully. For example, an assumption has developed that early language difficulties necessarily translate into adult difficulties. But we know too little about this process, and this makes it difficult to establish how important it is to identify and treat children with early difficulties. If we found that only a relatively small proportion of those with difficulties at school entry were at risk of meaningful differences throughout their schooling and into employment, would it make a difference as to who we targeted? If we target all children with potential difficulties irrespective of their potential outcomes, there is a risk of raising undue anxiety and perhaps lowering expectations at the start of a child's schooling.

Of course, it is a difficult and expensive operation setting up long-term studies, and there is a danger – and experience commonly suggests – that the measures do not link very easily across time, with different measures for the same construct at different points. This is commonly done because the age ceilings of the measures are reached. But to then link different measures at different time points, especially given the variability of performance across measures, requires an understanding of a unified latent construct of language development, which has only very rarely been discussed in the literature. To avoid this, it might be appropriate to focus on the measurement of change across specific transitions, points which we know cause concern for any vulnerable groups, such as moving between primary and secondary school and between acute hospital and community setting. Once we have a sense of what to expect in terms of development without intervention, we are better placed to ascertain what is the added value of intervention.

Finally then, it is important to see these developments in a historical context. As Dodd (Chapter 4) points out in this volume, speech and language therapy is still relatively young in terms of its research base. Given this, it is hardly surprising that there often seem to be more gaps than there is evidence. As the authors of the chapters in this volume have clearly demonstrated, there is a wealth of research activity in this field that was simply not there 20 years ago. We still have a long way to go before we can plan services based on the evidence, but we need to recognize that the same is true in many other related disciplines. Communication disability is a complex area and one in need of a great deal of critical thought. It is also one in which practitioners and researchers need to take the research agenda forward together, and it is this common enterprise that will lead to the new connections of the future.

References

Black M (1997) Making new connections: are patterns emerging? In: S Chiat, J Law, J Marshall (eds), Language Disorders in Children and Adults. London: Whurr Publishers, pp. 241–9.

Clegg J, Hollis C, Mawhood L et al. (2005) Developmental language disorders – a follow-up in later adult life. Cognitive, language and psychosocial outcomes. Journal of Child Psychology and Psychiatry 46(2): 128–49.

Cole KN, Dale PS, Mills PE (1992) Stability of the intelligence quotient relation: is discrepancy modelling based on a myth? American Journal on Mental Retardation 97: 131–45.

Conti-Ramsden G, Botting N (1999) Classification of children with specific language impairment: longitudinal considerations. Journal of Speech, Language, and Hearing Research 42: 1195–204.

David D, Szentagotai A (2006) Cognitions in cognitive-behavioral psychotherapies; toward an integrative model. Clinical Psychology Review 26: 284–98.

Dollaghan CA (2004) Taxometric analyses of specific language impairment in 3- and 4-year-old children. Journal of Speech, Language, and Hearing Research 47: 464–75.

Dollaghan CA (2007) The Handbook for Evidence Based Practice in Communication Disorders. Baltimore, MD: Paul Brookes.

Ehren BJ, Nelson NW (2005) The responsiveness to intervention approach and language impairment. Topics in Language Disorders 25: 120–31.

Forsyth K, Law J, MacIver D et al. (2007) A Systematic Review of the Evidence for the Effectiveness of Occupational Therapy and Speech and Language Therapy Interventions for Children in Primary School. Edinburgh: Edinburgh City Council.

Greenberg LS, Safran JD (1984) Hot cognition – emotion coming in from the cold: a reply to Rachman and Mahoney. Cognitive Therapy and Research 8: 559–665.

Greenhalgh T (1997) How to Read a Paper. London: BMJ Publications.

Johnson CJ, Beitchman JH, Young A et al. (1999) Fourteen-year follow-up of children with and without speech/language impairments: speech/language stability and outcomes. Journal of Speech, Language, and Hearing Research 42(3): 744–60.

Johnston JR (2005) Re: Law, Garrett and Nye (2004a). The efficacy of treatment for children with developmental speech and language delay/disorder: a meta-analysis. Journal of Speech, Language, and Hearing Research 48: 1114–17.

Justice L (2006) Evidence based practice, response to reading intervention and the prevention of reading disabilities. Journal of Speech, Language, and Hearing Research 42: 284–97.

Law J, Garrett Z, Nye C (2003) Speech and language therapy interventions for children with primary speech and language delay or disorder. Cochrane Database of Systematic Reviews, Issue 3. Art. No.: CD004110. DOI: 10.1002/14651858. CD004110.

Law J, Garrett Z, Nye C (2005) The specificity of a systematic review is the key to its value: a response to Johnston. Journal of Speech, Language, and Hearing Research 48: 1118–20.

Law J, Van der Gaag A, Hardcastle B et al. (2007) Communication Support Need: A Review of the Literature: Project Report. Edinburgh: Scottish Executive.

Law J, Tomblin JB, Zhang X (forthcoming) Characterising the growth trajectories of language impaired children between seven and eleven years. Journal of Speech, Language, and Hearing Research.

McEwan EK, McEwan PJ (2003) Making Sense of Research: What's Good, What's Not, and How to Tell the Difference. Thousand Oaks, CA: Corwin Press.

Medical Research Council (MRC) (2000) A Framework for Development and Evaluation of RCTs for Complex Interventions to Improve Health. London: Medical Research Council.

Morley M (1972) The Development and Disorders of Speech in Childhood. Edinburgh: Churchill Livingstone.

Pawson R, Greenhalgh T, Harvey G et al. (2004) Realist Synthesis: An Introduction: RMP Methods Paper 2/2004. Manchester: Centre for Census and Survey Research, University of Manchester.

Pope C (2001) Can the art of surgery and evidence based medicine be reconciled? Annual Meeting of the International Society for Technology Assessing Health Care. International Society for Technology Assessing Health Care Meeting, 2001, 17, (Abstract No. 196), http://gateway.nlm.nih.gov/MeetingAbstracts/102274528.html (accessed 10 October 2007).

Reilly S, Douglas J, Oates J (2003) Evidence Based Practice in Speech Pathology. London: Whurr Publications.

Schaeffer A, Collete F, Phillippot P et al. (2003) Neural correlates of 'hot' and 'cold' models of emotional processing: a multi level approach to the functional anatomy of emotion. Neuro Image 18: 938–9.

Solomon MJ, McLeod RS (1998) Surgery and the randomised controlled trial: past, present and future. Medical Journal of Australia 169: 380–3.

Stothard SE, Snowling MJ, Bishop DVM et al. (1998) Language-impaired pre-schoolers: a follow-up into adolescence. Journal of Speech, Language, and Hearing Research 41: 407–18.

Temple C (1997) Developmental Cognitive Neuropsychology. Chichester: Psychology Press.

Thomas M, Karmiloff-Smith A (2002) Are developmental disorders like cases of adult brain damage? Behavioural and Brain Sciences 25(6): 727–50.

UK Clinical Research Collaboration (2007) Developing the Best Research Professionals: Qualified Graduate Nurses Recommendations for Preparing and Supporting Clinical Academic Nurses of the Future. Report of the UKCRC Subcommittee for Nurses in Clinical Research. London: UKCRC.

Index

Language Disorders in Children and Adults: New Issues in Research and Practice.   Victoria Joffe,
Madeline Cruice, Shula Chiat.
© 2008 John Wiley & Sons, Ltd. ISBN 978-0-470-51839-7